# Tampa Review 57/58

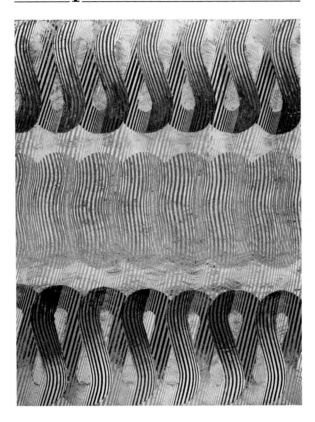

❖ A GALLERY OF LITERARY AND VISUAL ART IN PRINT FOR 55 YEARS ❖

*Tampa Review* is published twice each year by the University of Tampa Press. Founded in 1964 as *UT Poetry Review*, *Tampa Review* is the oldest continuously published literary journal in Florida. Subscriptions in the United States are $25 per year; basic subscription is the same outside the U.S., but write for mailing cost by surface mail. Payment should be made by money order or check payable in U.S. funds. International airmail rates are available and vary; write for specific information. Subscription copies not received will be replaced without charge only if notice of nonreceipt is given by subscribers within six months following publication.

Editorial and business correspondence should be addressed to *Tampa Review*, The University of Tampa, 401 West Kennedy Boulevard, Tampa, Florida 33606-1490. Manuscripts are read only during September, October, November, and December. and must be submitted online through Submission Manager. See guidelines at http://tampareview.ut.edu.

*Tampa Review* is indexed by *Index of American Periodical Verse* (Metuchen, N.J.: Scarecrow Press), *Annual Bibliography of English Language and Literature* (Cambridge, England: Modern Humanities Research Association), *POEMFINDER* (CD-ROM Poetry Index), *The American Humanities Index* (Albany, N.Y.: Whitston Publishing), and the *MLA International Bibliography*. Member of the Council of Literary Magazines and Presses (CLMP), Council of Editors of Learned Journals (CELJ), and the Florida Literary Arts Coalition (FLAC).

The editors gratefully acknowledge the generous and substantial assistance of Robin Perry Dana, Curator, and Leslie Curran, Owner, of ARTicles Art Gallery, St. Petersburg, Florida. We also appreciate the kind help of Nathan Beard, Shiv Dutta, and J. Malcolm Garcia, who provided high-resolution digital images for some of the visual art for this issue.

Typography and design by Richard Mathews

Printed on acid free paper ∞

Manufactured in the United States of America

**For additional information visit *Tampa Review* at tampareview.ut.edu or tampareview.org**

*Editor*

**Richard Mathews**

*Fiction Editors*

**Shane Hinton**
**Yuly Restrepo**

*Nonfiction Editor*

**Daniel Dooghan**

*Poetry Editors*

**Geoffrey Bouvier**
**Elizabeth Winston**

*Editorial Assistants*

**Sean Donnelly**
**Joshua Steward**

*Staff Assistant*

**Laura Stewart**

*Contributing & Consulting Editors*

**Kendra Frorup**
**James Michael Lennon**

*Published by the*

**University of Tampa Press**

# Tampa Review 57/58

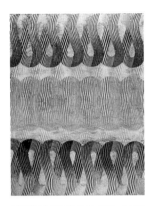

ON THE COVER: *Exit Music #58 (The Effects of Passing through One Another)* by Nathan Beard. Panel 4 of 5. Acrylic on panel. 48 x 36 inches. Private Collection. Photo by Scuderi Studios.

Artist Nathan Beard explains that "exit music is played at the end of a performance or movie while the audience is departing, signaling both the end of the imaginary world they were privy to and their sobering reemergence into daily life." This is exit music, surely, but we all experience it in other contexts, too—to move presenters offstage at the Academy Awards, to send a congregation home with a recessional hymn in church, to signal the departure of bride and groom from their wedding ceremony, or to sound as requiem and funeral march for a departed soul.

Beard's artist's statement for a 2017 show at the Highlands Museum of the Arts in Sebring, Florida, referred to these pieces as "personal meditations upon interconnectedness, the power derived through transformation and the nature of consciousness." Over the past four years, in more than seventy numbered pieces, Beard has shared his meditations in a remarkable series of interconnected works evoking vibrancy, motion, flexibility, variety, rhythm, pattern, harmony, dissonance, and beauty.

| | | |
|---|---|---|
| Cover | **Nathan Beard** | *Exit Music #58* |
| 5 | **Nathan Beard** | *Pond's Edge #33* |
| 6 | **Nathan Beard** | *Exit Music #60 (Lost in Translation)* |
| 7 | **Hannah Weyer** | *Sanctuary City* |
| 13 | **Mark Rubin** | *Coloring the Pigeons* |
| 14 | **John Sibley Williams** | *Small Treasons* |
| 15 | **Calvin Olsen** | *Overgrown* |
| 17 | **J. Malcolm Garcia** | *These Are the Stories I've Grown up with All My Life: The Rohingya Refugees of Bangladesh* |
| 33 | **Michele Wolf** | *Postcards at the Museum* |
| 34 | **Randall Watson** | *Ghost Month* |
| 36 | **Nathan Beard** | *New Mexico Memory* |
| 37 | **Liana Jahan Imam** | *Tore a Hole in the World* |
| | | *What Did You Expect* |
| 41 | **Marsha Truman Cooper** | *Tendencies to Nest* |
| 42 | **Dorothy Chan** | *Ode to Andrew McCarthy and Your Hand on My Thigh* |
| 45 | **Jennifer Key** | *The Horizon Has a Way of Disappearing* |
| 51 | **Jan C. Grossman** | *The Pope's Chair* |
| 52 | **Marianne Chan** | *Viewing Service* |
| 53 | **Virginia Konchan** | *Investment Circle* |
| 54 | **Stephen Brook** | *Food to Go* |
| 55 | **Taylor Bostick** | *Girl, Freckles* |
| 60 | **Michael Lavers** | *A Portfolio of Poems from* After Earth |
| 66 | **Robert Ross** | *Pause* |
| 67 | **Molly Rideout** | *The Metairie Loop* |
| 75 | **J. Malcolm Garcia** | *El Basurero (The Dump)* |
| 89 | **Carolyn Guinzio** | *Is This about Absence?* |
| 90 | **Carolyn Guinzio** | *Ravines* |
| 92 | **Robin Perry Dana** | *Soliloquy* |
| 93 | **Nadia Villafuerte** | *The Salt Frontier* |
| 98 | **Heike Mueller** | *Lady 3* |
| 99 | **Paul Lindholdt** | *Swaddled in Rose Silk* |
| 105 | **Shiv Dutta** | *Home* |
| 112 | **Marc Frazier** | *All about Us* |
| 113 | **Eleanore Lee** | *Maintenance* |
| 114 | **Lisa Hatcher** | *The Promise (Detail)* |
| 115 | **Halvor Aakhus** | *Two Women, One Gay Viking* |
| 121 | **Levi Andalou** | *Untitled Poem from State of the Wards* |
| 122 | **Jaclyn Dwyer** | *Job's wife brings store-bought cookies* |
| 123 | **Carol Guess** | *First a Decision, Not a Feeling* |

# Tampa Review 55/56

## Contents (continued)

| | | |
|---|---|---|
| 124 | Liza Flum | *Emarginate (adj.)* |
| 125 | Bipin Aurora | *The YMCA* |
| 131 | A. Loudermilk | *Could Be Worse* |
| 135 | Gordon Thompson | *Greasy Spoon* |
| 139 | Sabatino Smith | *Tunnel of Cheap Breakfast (or Love)* |
| 140 | Rob Stephens | *After Hearing the News* |
| 141 | Zack Strait | *Television* |
| 142 | John Davis Jr. | *Statue Boys* |
| 143 | Adam Tavel | *My Father's Truck* |
| 144 | Jack Barrett | *Cascading Figures* |
| 145 | Christopher Heffernan | *My Only Hunting Story* |
| 147 | Kostas Anagnopoulos | *Highlight* |
| 148 | Peter Schireson | *Weeding* |
| 149 | John Schneider | *Bottomless Water* |
| 150 | Tom Paine | *Noah Gave Us the Ark* |
| 151 | Christine Poreba | *Gaps in the Sky* |
| 153 | Dan Lundin | *A Narcissist's Guide to Catalina* |
| 160 | Joshua Eversfield Jenkins | *Pit* |
| 161 | Cammy Thomas | *A Constant* |
| 162 | Jane Medved | *Measures of* |
| 163 | Michael Malan | *Despite What They Say* |
| 164 | Robin Perry Dana | *Why I Wake Early*, from the *Watershed* series |
| 165 | Priscilla Long | *Seeing Green* |
| 168 | Zachary Lundgren | *Lithia Springs, Three Times* |
| 169 | Alex Quinlan | *Near Mint* |
| 172 | Gabrielle Frahm Claffey | *Grade-B* |
| 173 | Gabrielle Frahm Claffey | *The Impression Room* |
| 174 | Chris Green | *Reading for Ms. Doyle's First Grade Class* |
| 175 | Bonnie Naradzay | *They Workshop My Poem* |
| 176 | Gustave Doré | *It Was Wondrous Cold* |
| 177 | William Walker | *FedEx* |
| 181 | Notes on Contributors | |

Nathan Beard. *Pond's Edge #33*. Charcoal, graphite, and pastel on paper. 30 x 22 inches. Private Collection.

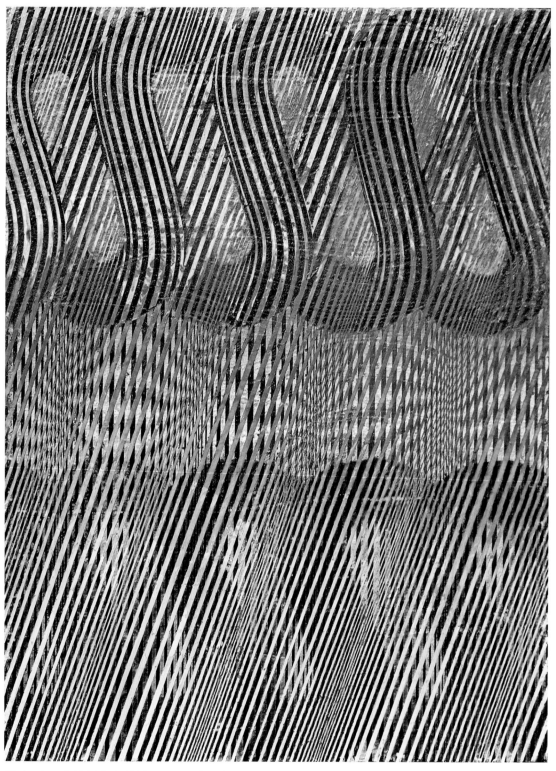

Nathan Beard. *Exit Music #60 (Lost in Translation).* Acrylic on canvas. 24 x 18 inches.

# Sanctuary City

Esme thought she'd been lucky, racing down the stairs against the first outpouring of commuters and making it onto the train. The car was crowded, but she wedged her way along the aisle, past the bulk of winter coats and handbags, into a pocket of space near a center pole. At rush hour, even this was something to be grateful for.

She stood expectant, anticipating the ding and the doors to close. But the seconds stretched on and she felt her palms moisten inside her gloves. A bitter wind had swept through the city, bringing snow, then a hard pelting of sleet, but here, underground, the train car was warm and airless. Esme pulled off her gloves, then unzipped her jacket.

More riders slipped on. There was a slight shuffling and the space around Esme disappeared. On all sides, she was hemmed in. She shifted her weight, and the motion sent a shooting pain into her lower back. *Ay, ya . . .* She wished she were home already, but then there'd be Junior, who was probably stretched out on the couch right now, and the excuses he'd make, or worse yet, his phony acquiescence. Someone's sour breath caught in her nose and she swallowed, lifting her chin. The doors shuddered closed.

Then, with a lurch, they were moving. Esme clung to the pole as riders swayed, bumping each other like fish on a string. The shoulder of a tall blanquita just inches from her face, Esme turned, looking up at the advertisements that lined the car. A subway advisory caught her eye. *"It's nothing, you think. But can you be sure?"* In the photograph, a backpack was framed beneath a row of empty subway seats.

Esme glanced around the car. She saw only body parts defined in relief: an arm extended, the sweep of dark hair, a tired face whose eyelids hung low and flickered in sleep.

Someone was playing a game with the volume up, *ping, blip, bleep.* No one told the rider to turn it down. No one said anything. She didn't see any backpacks, except one, on the car floor, sandwiched between a pair of trouser legs. A hand went into the pack and pulled something out. Esme couldn't see what it was, but a crumpled brown bag dropped to the floor next to the man's feet. Esme tsked, *Pendejo.*

She spent eight hours a day cleaning up after people. Pulling hair out of drains in the girls' and boys' locker rooms, reaching her hand into tepid, grey water to unclog sinks, scraping wads of paper towel from the ceiling. The mopping, the wiping, the emptying of things into other things.

She thought of Miss Perrell sitting behind the security desk in the school lobby, her portable TV on CNN, murmuring to herself: *Mm-mm-mm, can you believe it? It's a sickness, it is. These days. Can't go anywhere.* Miss Perrell liked to keep up with the news, her West Indian accent clipping pieces of her thoughts into the world. *All those innocent, blood spilt, a travesty, it is.* Travesty, tragedy. Esme never fully understood what she meant, her own English still imperfect after all these years in the United States. She'd shoulder the Hoover to her back and plug in. Miss Perrell glancing from the bank of monitors to images, terrible images, on the TV, as the vacuum whined and Esme worked the corners of the room.

Sometimes Esme took her breaks with Miss Perrell, but lately she'd been working steadily through her shift, a distraction from her own troubles. Three weeks ago, word spread that Mr. Duke, the manager of Building G where Esme lived, had been fired, replaced by a stranger whose name no one could pronounce. All her neighbors were whispering, *Watch out, cuidado, they're checking leases, paperwork de todos.* Already, the Guerreros from upstairs had been given notice, and Esme didn't know if they were going floor by floor or alphabetical, or whether she needed to worry at all, the whole situation a slow-burning fuse in the pit of her stomach.

And before that, on a rainy December night, Esme came home to find her daughter, Yesenia, unrecognizable, her lip split down the middle, one side of her face a swollen, bruised mess, and Junior on the couch, reeking of mota, playing a game on his phone. "She was jumped at school," he said without looking up, as if it was no big thing, an aside in life's grand scheme. "Cállate pendejo," Yesenia screamed, slamming the bathroom door.

A woman's handbag nudged against her arm. Esme looked up. They'd pulled into a station. Passengers exited. More riders stepped on, shaking the chill from their shoulders. The train doors closed and they were in motion again, the car rocking gently from side to side as they picked up speed. Esme found her balance, then searched her purse for her phone. She knew there'd be nothing new, but dug it out anyway. She pressed the message icon, scrolling to find the text from her son.

It read: *I be there.*

But he hadn't come during her lunch break as he promised. She'd stood outside the back entrance of the school, waiting in the cold, watching the town cars come and go along East 63rd, but no Junior.

Four times she called, texted, no response. She tried Yesenia.

*tu hermano alli*

*He went out.*

*donde*

*No se*

*digale llamame*

*Mama, he ain't here.*

Carlos had teased her. *Maybe he's got a girl, Esme.* Esme was too furious to answer. She'd parked her cleaning cart next to the floor waxer, smoothed her hair into a ponytail, and stepped into the open doorway of the director's office.

"Excuse me, Mr. Denworth, my son, I'm sorry, he called me sick, I bring him to clean on Monday, it's okay?"

The school director was seated behind his large wooden desk. He glanced up from his computer and looked out at Esme.

"It's only a temporary position, Esmeralda. I need that mold gone now. What did Carlos say?"

He was a friendly enough man, but Esme did her best to avoid him—something in their exchanges left her anxious and cross, feelings which then shadowed her throughout the day.

But now hearing mention of Carlos, the crew foreman, Esme felt emboldened and stepped further into the office.

"Carlos, he say it's okay. My son come on Monday."

Mr. Denworth stood, moving around the desk with one arm lifted, reaching toward Esme, who pivoted to let him pass. But his hand landed on her shoulder, and he left it there as he led her out of his office and down the hall.

"We have a ticking clock here, Esmeralda. No mucho tiempo. We need those rooms mold-free ahora."

"Ahorita?" he added, looking at her for approval.

"Si, ahorita, you correct."

He nodded, patting her shoulder. "Ahorita, yes. Otherwise, I'm going to have a lot of angry parents on my hands." He chuckled. "And they form committees. *Comisiones!* Esmeralda, if anything goes wrong."

In the hallway, Mr. Denworth stared at the floor waxer, then looked around. "Now where did Carlos go?"

That evening, as she was about to clock out, she heard Carlos call to her from down the hall. "You want me to drop by, take a belt to him?"

Even though his voice was playful and they were alone in the basement, Esme turned sharply, "No, shhh, Carlos." She stepped into the closet where the cleaning supplies were kept and searched for her time card in the metal rack. She found it and punched out. Carlos leaned against the door frame, watching her put on her scarf, then gloves.

"¿Pero qué te dijo Mr. Denworth?" she whispered, looking up at him with worry. "It's okay to bring him Monday?"

He was smiling, unaffected by her mood, and reached to touch her face. She flinched, stepping back, and he raised his hands.

"You have something," he said, pointing to his cheek. She brushed at her face and a piece of lint came away.

They stood for a moment without speaking, then he said, "you know I got you, Esme, just bring that malcriado on Monday." He had nice eyes, good teeth, nice hands, she noticed his hands, but she would never. No matter how much she wanted him, no matter how often she thought about the way he looked at her. To feel his hands on her body, to slide onto him, the sudden thrust of his hips against hers . . .

She felt a throb of longing and gave a quick glance around the subway car. No one was paying attention. Esme tucked a strand of hair behind her ear. She hadn't been able to look at him as she brushed past, saying only, "Gracias Carlos, ya me voy."

At the next station, the woman and her large handbag departed. Esme straightened, stretching her back. She felt the same stab of pain in her lower muscles. She hated the Hoover. Barely thirty-eight, and already she felt old, like a bruised piece of fruit. She rolled her neck, working at the knot, and she noticed him then, the boy seated in front of her. His legs spread wide, an elbow jutting into the empty seat next to him. A knit ski cap covered a long kinky afro which had been pulled back into a loose ponytail.

She pictured Junior, slumped that morning in a sleepy daze, his face puffy with sleep. She'd almost reached over and hugged him. Instead, she slid three dollars across the table, saying, "Don't be late." Someone guffawed loudly and ski cap boy turned, tilting his chin toward a stream of *nigga this,* and *nigga that.* Esme glanced over and was surprised to see it was a Chinese boy talking. Leaning one foot up against the subway door, a smattering of coarse hair on his upper lip. Another boy wedged himself in front of her, forming a triangle with the others. Esme stared at his narrow back. His striped cotton underwear pooching out, *SU-PREME* written across the waistband.

*. . . always instigating some shit*
*can't stand that nigga*
*saying soft*
*who soft, Farragut nigga got capped.*

The word punched the air. *Capped.* These hard boys, someone shot, what story do they tell? Her eyes swept the car. Was anyone else listening? She wanted to move, stand somewhere else, but the train was accelerating through the tunnel, racing down beneath the river, and Esme was forced to hold on. The boys' talk grew louder.

*Nigga came at me . . .*
*I said . . .*
*But then . . . leathe stra—*
*pulled it out . . .*
*Went to cut me here and here.*

Esme glanced at Ski Cap's outstretched arms. These boys talked the way her own son did: out the side of their mouths, lips barely moving, a suppression of syllables. You had to lean in to understand, or as she'd do, get right up in Junior's face and say, "Open your mouth when you talk, how're you going to get somewhere in this world?" Junior, who'd dropped out of City College before the semester ended, telling her: "It's not for me, Ma. *Stop pushing.*"

Esme had long given up trying to follow the ever-shifting rivalries. The cause of each aggression, the need for dominance. She'd seen it plenty from her kitchen window. Fights breaking out, spilling into the middle courtyard, the *bweep bweep* of sirens, the thunder of running feet. Her own daughter sucker-punched. But not really, Esme thought. It'd been instigated They'd *gathered.* They held their phones up like tiny flags, to record the moment, proof of her subjugation.

Yesenia had begged her not to go, but Esme went anyway, marching into the guidance office, carried on a wave of feverish incredulity, *Have you seen her? Did you seen her face?*

The school counselor unblocked the You-Tube site and clicked play. It lasted twenty-three seconds. It was unbearable. The audio over-modulated and scratchy. The frame jammed with jittery faces, but it was clear what was happening: a loose circle ringed the fight, Yesenia center stage, or maybe it was the other girl and her fist that swung over and over, punching her daughter until she'd gone down in a heap.

Shame and helplessness flooded her chest, and for a moment Esme felt herself splitting in two, as if part of her had been tipped into a deep, bottomless well. The counselor told her it was her right to press charges, to seek further reprisal, but the thought of the police, the questions they might ask, and her own subversion—she'd paid a small fortune for her social security number—kept her quiet.

That afternoon she lay with Yesenia, their legs twined together, and Esme had rocked her. It was not often she thought of Enrique, the children's father. But she thought of him now, and somehow this assuaged her guilt, her uselessness. At least she was here, comforting their child, while he was *nobody*, not even a speck on the horizon. Esme stroked Yesenia's hair, but her daughter flinched, crying out, "Ay, stop mami, me duele."

"Sorry, mija. Sorry, sorry, sorry. Shh, shhh, shhhhh."

9

The subway doors opened. Someone jostled past, and Esme stumbled, bumping the boy in front of her. He turned, giving her a quick look, and she saw the wash of bright pimples on his forehead, he was no older than Yesenia, a child.

*Qué ridículo.* She was a grown woman, pues. Her legs stiff with fatigue, back aching, what was she doing standing. And with that, she stepped past the boy and sank into the empty seat.

It had gone quiet, the train idling in the station. Ski Cap pulled his legs together to keep from touching Esme, and the boy with pimples straightened, looking at a point above her head. He pulled out a short-handled brush from his pocket and began working it through his afro.

Yesenia used to swing her long, dark hair. She'd twirl and sway in front of the windows, the panes of glass turning to mirrors as night fell. She'd sing as she swayed, watching her reflection dance. Now, she kept to her room.

They were moving again, the train snaking out of the tunnel, rising above ground to find the night, and the city, far across the bay, was no more than a faint drift of luminescence.

*. . . nine dollars an hour*, the Chinese boy was saying.

*the one by Jay Street*

*. . . black pants, but to your waist, black shirt, button-up.*

The one with pimples said, *what, like church clothes?* His own clothes hung loose over his thin frame. Esme noticed a tiny hole where the waistband had come unstitched from his boxers.

*Gotta be black, to the waist.*

*You get a discount?*

*LeBron, KDs, Kobe . . .*

*That's tight.*

*Word, I got church clothes.* The boy with pimples snapped his fingers from the wrist and the action was near enough to Esme's face that she looked up, seeing his smile and the braces that caught the light.

On the video, the ring of boys had swelled, then broken apart. One of them lunged into the space where Yesenia had stood, his mouth open with laughter, silver teeth flashing before the image cut out.

Esme stared at the boy, studying his face, and there was something in his expression right then—she saw it and knew. There was no doubt, and without thinking, she reached out and tugged the boy's coat.

"'Xcuse me. You. Yes, you." He straightened, brushing her hand away, frowning at the strange woman who was glaring at him.

"You know my daughter?" Esme said. "Yesenia Nunez?".

His brow furrowed. He didn't answer, but she could see his mind working, sifting through a catalogue of responses.

She pressed on. "You were there, by to John Jay High School, when my daughter was beat up. I saw you on the YouTube."

A look of guilt flickered across his face, but just as quickly his face went flat with emotion.

She didn't like that he was standing over her, that her words had evaporated into air.

"Mamón, I'm talking to you," Esme said. "Yesenia Nunez. It was diciembre, I know. I saw you on the YouTube."

The riders were listening now.

The Chinese boy tittered, "She talking to you, son." Ski Cap laughed, "YouTube, you famous, nigga."

"Diciembre? Fuck I know about diciembre."

You was there," Esme insisted. "I saw you."

"Nigga's crazy, fuck she talking about," he said loudly, stepping away from her and crossing to the doors.

The train was pulling into the Smith/9th Street station. She glanced around the car. No one met her eye, but she knew they'd heard every word, their faces awakening as if nudged out of a dream. Ski Cap sprang to his feet and stood with the others, all of them adjusting and preening, oblivious to her now, as if something special awaited them outside these doors.

Esme's mouth had gone dry. She tried to swallow, but couldn't, her neck hot, her whole body stiff with indignation. The doors opened and the boys ambled off. She tracked their passage through the windows, then came to her senses, realizing this was her stop too. She shouldered her handbag, and ran for the doors, slipping through just before they slid closed.

She followed them along the icy platform, her heart pounding in her ears, down the long flight of stairs.

Out on the street, the inky darkness was startling and Esme felt momentarily disoriented. She braced herself against the wind, wrapping her scarf around her chin and mouth, her eyes on the boys as they cut through the drifts of snow toward Hamilton Avenue.

Junior used to wait for her on this corner, beneath the awning of Meep's Deli. He was eleven when his father left them. It was a routine he'd established without her asking, sprinting up through the inner courtyard of the projects to Garnet, Garnet to Smith, Smith to 9th. *Don't worry, Ma, I got it down to a science.* He prided himself on how quickly he could move, mindless of the dangers that might befall him.

Esme hadn't known Enrique was leaving them. He was meant to return in two months, three at the most. The border was fluid then. He was going home to San Andres, where they'd grown up, to visit his mother who'd become ill. But he hadn't returned when he was supposed to. Instead, Esme learned he'd taken up with a local girl. For months Esme was beside herself with jealousy and rage. But when he begged her to take him back, to be a family once more, she'd folded, sending him money to return to her. Then nothing. Not a word. One month, two went by, then a full year.

Two summers came and went before he called from Nogales. He'd just been released from a detention center, he told her, but she didn't know what to believe. All the days and months of uncertainty, the sheer loneliness . . . how could she be sure? Now he was in Ciudad Juarez breaking concrete, he said. Saving money. But how could she know for sure? It broke her heart.

Esme's head was bent against the driving wind, her boots crunching through ice and snow. Up ahead, the boys were no more than dark shapes moving in tandem. Black pants, up to the waist, black button-down. Hours of overtime, she'd saved and saved. Risked everything to fill out the financial aid forms, paid his remaining tuition, and still he refused. A job handed to him, but no, he refused her. Where did he go, what does he do, nineteen years old and she'd lost him.

She passed the recycling plant where men navigated their heavy carts up the ramp, and deep in the belly of the yard, a crane swung its claw, scooping scrap metal from a mountain of aluminum and steel. They didn't notice her, another bulky shape pressed against the night.

The boys were jaywalking across the wide expanse of Hamilton Avenue, forcing cars to slow, then brake completely, taillights splashing red across the slick, wet ground. And further still, beyond the avenue, Esme could see the white glare of stadium lights the NYPD

Command Unit had set up across from her building, a light so potent she could no longer open her shades.

At the corner, the boys were splitting up, Ski Cap and El Chino going in one direction and the boy with braces—the one who'd jeered, egging on Yesenia's beating, he was turning down another. Esme quickened her pace, hustling across the avenue.

It was a bleak, narrow block, absent of light, lined with shuttered warehouses, a methadone clinic, and a corner deli where a gold neon Modelo sign sputtered on and off. Esme was mid-block when the boy cut across the street and entered the store. She hurried forward. A figure stepped from the doorway. Esme froze, realizing it was Junior, his head down, looking at something on his phone. What was he doing over here, wandering around with his head down, his head always down?

She started forward, tugging the scarf away from her mouth. "¿Dónde estuviste?"

He looked up, startled to see her, and she watched him hide his surprise in a quick shrug. "Here, home."

"What do you mean, *'here, home?'* I left you money for the subway."

"I got hungry."

"Hay comida en la casa, stupid. I lied for you, me entiendes? Al director. He was ready to hire you and you treat me like this?"

"I told you, ma, I ain't no janitor."

She smacked him hard against the ear, once, two times. "Oh, no? Qué entonces. Quién entonces." She could feel her palm throb as he glared at the ground, silent. She shoved her hands into her pockets, hunching against a sudden gust that cut and swirled the night air.

She shivered beneath her jacket, then turned toward the store. "You know who's in there?"

Junior glanced back, looking through the plexiglass.

"Remember when they beat up Yesenia? That boy inside, he was there, watching. Laughing."

The boy stood in the center aisle, holding a bag of chips. He was reaching into his pocket, his pants drooping still lower as he withdrew a dollar and dropped it onto the counter.

Esme paced in front of the door.

"What're you doing, Ma?"

"Following him," Esme said, "that's what I'm doing. Following him to where he live. His mother, she needs to know."

Junior shook his head. "But a girl beat up Yesenia. Everyone knows that."

"So. She can know what kind of son she has. Who watches and does nothing."

"Mira, here he come now." The boy stepped out the door into the cold, his breath clouding the air, and he nearly collided with Esme who'd made up her mind not to move.

The boy frowned, but she felt no sense of recognition, none at all. *Oh, you don't know me,* Esme thought. And as he went to step around her, she put her body in front of his. She heard Junior say, "No lo haga, ma." But she could feel the boy's energy change, his eyes turning to daggers as he slammed her with his shoulder. Then Junior was between them, saying, "back the fuck up, nigga," and she wanted to shove him too, shove both of them, *You touch me, cabrón, eh? You tough guy?* But as quickly as the boy rose to fight, he backed down, his eyes on something behind her as he hitched his pants and stepped away. She glanced at Junior, then turned to see what the boy was looking at. A police car crawling toward them, its front wheel sinking into a pothole, the car bouncing on its shocks, then, without warning, a bright beam cut through the darkness and enclosed them in a cone of light.

Esme lifted her hand to shield her eyes. For a moment, she thought, *Yes, the police will deal with this boy, not me. It is my right.* She would take Junior and go. Yesenia was waiting. She reached for her son and felt him standing stiffly by her side.

Her whole body flashed with heat. The spotlight snuffed out, and she was momentarily blinded, white dots lifting and falling across the darkness. She heard the doors creak open, then close with a dull thud. She spun around, *where was the boy, that malcriado . . .* And she saw him there, just behind her, backlit in the frame of the deli window. But something was wrong, something in his posture—the slump of his hip, the way his hands were already raised, his fingers spread against the neon glow.

"Junior," she whispered.

"*Junior,*" she said again more fiercely.

And her heart, oh, her heart. Because they were coming, stepping over the icy ridge of snow, saying, *IDs, IDs, IDs.*

❖  ❖  ❖

*Mark Rubin*

# Coloring the Pigeons

They strut like heirs to a fortune,
neck and chest feathers puffed on the ready
for late morning mounts. To let them know
I'm here, I've learned to pool saliva
in my throat and coo like one of them.
I admire how they've made peace
with their low rankings among the swift
and beautiful, their contentment with crumbs.
With the finest No. 2 Kolinsky brush,
I paint them as they are, plain with everlasting
blends of iridescent green and blue mauve
grays, colors that hide in-born ancestral fear —
the five-egg pigeon omelet
or squab grilled on a bed of rice and mushrooms,
a meal for common royalty, for the poor
kings among us, and their queens
who would serve them.
I model my red, 2 a.m. bloodshot eyes
to better render theirs; my pale
tubular bones to rough in skinny legs
and feet callused from pacing back and forth
on concrete. Their need for me to paint them
is not unlike my own need
to be larger than myself, filled in
so as not to disappear. When gone,
to at least be looked for.

# Small Treasons

Somewhere, it isn't night & a body
moves across another without harm,
as if taking a knife to the sky, & we
can answer when a child asks where
the world goes when our eyes close.
Somewhere, we are sorry; I assume
for our silences. Bones ache & char
& must burn, somewhere, surely as
skin. Even our ghosts have left us.
There must be a place where hands
aren't cages & cages aren't gestures
well-intentioned but failing. Where
we love with more than body & hurt
& know when we have hurt. Somewhere, a less flammable history, at
least where the sparks fly upward
before falling back to ash.

# Overgrown

Tree branches have punctured the roof,
some curling back like horns, some submerged
like needles. Sitting at the edge of 13<sup>th</sup>, the street
they say the city goes downhill after.

It's the kind of house you throw rocks at
at the end of a movie. You're not crying,
you're fighting back. The rocks bounce off
the wood siding, an unsatisfying dent

as the dirt receives them with a thud. Throw harder,
aim less—break, window,
break—and let the glass shards pock
your carpet, or what's left of it
now that the vagrants and birds congregate.

Food distribution at the Kutupalong-Balukhali settlements. Photo by J. Malcolm Garcia.

J. Malcolm Garcia

# These Are the Stories I've Grown up with All My Life: The Rohingya Refugees of Bangladesh

## JANUARY - FEBRUARY 2018

My translator, Ousman, tells me he has worked with many journalists—TV, radio, print—and they all had specific requests. Get me this, this, and this person, they'd tell him. People suitable for stories they'd mapped out in their heads.

"Who do you want?" he asks me.

I've told him repeatedly that I don't work that way. I want to spend a few weeks in the Kutu-palong-Balukhali settlements, a refugee camp for Rohingya people fleeing Myanmar in Bangladesh. I want to hang out and let whomever I meet be my guides. Ousman, however, remains adamant. We should develop a detailed plan, sir, he maintains, as if without one his sense of himself as a translator and fixer would be betrayed. He does not just interpret, he arranges interviews. So, despite my objections, he shows me a piece of paper detailing how he has structured my days.

"Here are the people I've asked to speak to you," he says, a hand on one knee, his face leaning into mine, scowling with seriousness, his glasses perched on the tip of his nose. He reads:

A pregnant woman.

Schoolchildren.

A woman who just had a baby.

A raped woman.

"What do you think?"

Before I can answer, he raises a hand and goes on with what I presume is his idea of an orientation.

"Rohingya have two kinds of memory here, sir. Good memories and violence memories. The good memories are very distant. They are a like an animal facing extinction. Only a few remain. I was just two years old when my family left Rohingya State in Myanmar. I don't remember that time but I know the history. I know why we came."

That bitter history remains ongoing between the Muslim minority Rohingya and the Buddhist majority of Myanmar. Myanmar's military claims it is not responsible for the recent exodus of Rohingya into Bangladesh. It accuses Rohingya militants, who attacked a police outpost on August 25, 2017, for the unrest, asserting that the Buddhist-dominated military targets only insurgents. Human rights groups, however, contend that the military and the hardline, monk-led Buddhist nationalist group known as Ma Ba Tha—the Association for the Protection of Race and Religion—used the attack as a reason to annihilate Rohingya communities.

More than half a million Rohingya entered Bangladesh between August and the end of December 2017. By the time of my trip in January 2018, human rights investigators estimated that more than a thousand civilians had died in Rakhine, a state in Myanmar on the west coast where the Rohingya live, and possibly as many as five thousand.

Ousman's family fled Myanmar in 1992, long before the current crisis when more than 250,000 Rohingya refugees ran away from forced labor camps at the hands of the Burmese army. With the assistance of United Nations High Commissioner for Refugees and non-governmental relief agencies, the Bangladeshi government sheltered the refugees in nineteen camps near Cox's Bazar in southeastern Bangladesh. Ousman's family landed in Kutupalong camp.

Ousman remembers his mother telling him about the night the military came to their house, arrested his father and hauled him to a labor camp. *Ahmad!* a soldier called, and when Ousman's father answered the door, they grabbed him. Ousman's mother went to the village administrator, a Rohingya, and demanded he ad-

17

A graveyard at the Kutupalong-Balukhali settlements. Photo by J. Malcolm Garcia.

vocate for Ahmad, but he refused. *If I do what you ask, they will kill me too,* he told her. *They'll ask me, Do you want to be free or work in the camp? This man had no power. He just followed orders.*

Like others in the labor camp, Ousman's father split stones for ten to fifteen hours a day without pay, without a break. When people grew weak and were unable to work, the military threw them down hillsides. Men released from the camp told Ousman's mother that his father had been killed in this way.

After she received this sad news, Ousman's mother told her children, *We have to go.* The family left with more than one hundred other people from their village. They hiked four days to reach the Bangladesh border. Ousman's brother, Ali, ten years old at the time, told him the trek was the most painful experience of his life. As the eldest boy, Ali carried all their bags and helped his younger sisters while his mother carried Ousman. They just walked and walked. When they reached the border, Myanmar police stopped their group and started beating them with the butts of their rifles. Some men tried to stop them and were arrested. Everyone else cried and screamed for mercy and ran. Weeping, they paid boatmen to carry them across the Naf River that flows between Bangladesh and Myanmar. On the other side, they resumed their journey for two more days until they reached Kutupalong.

Ousman's family lived in a tent for three years while Ali and their mother built a small, mud hut. Ali cut down saplings to clear a space for their new home. They could not have a garden. The Bangladeshi government did not want refugees to get too comfortable. Yet, twenty-six years later, they remain in Kutupalong and the Bangladesh government continues to keep a tight control over the refugees. The Rohingya are trapped; they can't leave the camp without permission of the Bengali military, and they can't return to Myanmar.

More Rohingya come every day. The Kutupalong-Balukhali settlements now have a population of 600,000, making it the largest refugee camp in the world. As a boy, Ousman played beside a beautiful stream that ran through the camp and from the green grasses that lined the water he watched monkeys scrambling through trees. He walked barefoot and collected wood for cooking. The stream is his first good memory, but it no longer exists. Hundreds if not thousands of refugee families use it as a toilet and garbage dump. The clear, rushing water he remembers has turned green.

❖ ❖ ❖

Families living in Kutupalong have divided the camp, because of its vastness, into neighborhoods. The pregnant woman Ousman wants me to meet lives in Block 53. As I follow him to her shanty, I look around but have no idea where neighborhoods begin and end. I see only hovel after hovel of rickety shacks, dirt path after dirt path, trotting packs of dogs after trotting packs of dogs, and lines of people standing with no place to go, looking at me as I stare back at them.

The pregnant woman, Sanzida Begum, lays out a straw mat for us to sit on the hard clay floor. She then allows us to enter her home, a delicate square-framed bamboo structure. Black plastic covers the hut, blocking all sunlight except for thin slivers that penetrate exposed gaps in the plastic. A line of laundry behind Sanzida and a blanket behind it separates a space used by her mother-in-law, Asima Khatun, who now stands outside in the bright sunlight watching me through the door, a yellow shawl covering part of her face.

Sanzida is twenty-two, seven months pregnant, and the mother of a two-year-old girl,

Asman. She answers my questions in a soft voice, almost a whisper, facing me but without expression, leaving the impression that she is not looking at me but staring through me, her mind elsewhere. She folds her legs beneath her, demure, forthright, yet distant. From time to time, as Sanzida speaks, the light from outside darkens and I know Asima Khatun or someone else watching me has shifted, blocking the sun. Sanzida ignores the onlookers.

Before 2012, the situation was good between the Rohingya and Buddhists in Rakhine State, Sanzida tells me, but good in a less than good way: Buddhists would come to her village of Sawprang Rathidawng and take what they wanted, food, cows, chickens, without paying, but they did not hurt anyone and only took a little. They had the power to steal but they weren't violent or greedy. In that way, the situation was good.

After 2012, however, the Buddhists and police began looting Rohyingya villages of everything. Sanzida saw with her own eyes Buddhist teenagers enter her family's pasture, select the best ox and butcher it right there and no one could object. Sanzida watched her father sink into a

Sanzida Begum. Photo by J. Malcolm Garcia.

depressed, quiet anger. He let out their cows in the morning knowing that in the evening not all of them would come back. He didn't bother looking for the missing animals. He knew they had been taken by Buddhists and the military.

Sanzida remembers seeing Buddhist priests and the Myanmar military drive into her village with cases of Coca-Cola, kettles, and spices. They would butcher goats and chickens and eat all of it right there in the middle of the road as if they were on a picnic. The Buddhist priests had long knives, and the soldiers had guns. They sang and danced. Twenty, fifty, sometimes as many as two hundred priests and soldiers feasting on Rohingya livestock. Her family did not even have the freedom to watch. So fearful were they of their lives that they hid, and only in hiding did they observe the butchering of their farm animals. Rohingya men wept with humiliation. Some of them were forced to send their children to help with the cooking. Those that refused were beaten.

This was the life Sanzida learned to accept until August 26, 2017, when the military and Buddhist teenagers surrounded her village and started beating, shooting, and arresting all the men. Sanzida fled from her house screaming as shots were fired, and she saw two fall. They began singing a funeral prayer after the soldiers shot them.

The next day, the teenagers and soldiers returned. This time, they went house to house and brought out all the families and forced men, women, and children into a river. They then told them to bend over and stand without raising their heads. If one of them looked up, a teenager would place a heavy rock on the back of their neck. Even children were punished this way, wrenched from their mother's arms and made to stand in the water. Some men hid inside their bedrooms, but the military found and killed them. Other men were arrested and tied together and dragged onto trucks and taken away, including Sanzida's husband, Habiullah, and her father-in-law. Many trucks that day took away husbands and sons, uncles and cousins, grandfathers and fathers.

Sanzida wipes tears from her eyes. Outside her hut, I hear people speaking to one another and shouting for their children, and the children shouting back. Seams of light shift, the interior darkens and brightens as people peer through the door at us, obscure the light and move on. Through it all, I notice that Asima Khatun remains immobile, her body casting an oblong shadow past me on the ground.

"My husband was arrested," Khatun says from her post outside the hut. "My father, my brother, and my husband. From all those arrested that day, only four came back after seventeen days. Among them was my husband. He's sixty. They didn't want an old man. He saw one prisoner die. The military would only give this man a small cup of water. He asked for more, and the military shot him, removed his heart, stomach, and intestines, and put them on a table before everyone to see. They said, 'This is what will happen to you if you ask for water.' They still have my son."

Khatun stops speaking. Men lean over her shoulders, stare at me, and then leave, and I hear them resume conversations that had stopped while they paused to hear Khatun. Her tale, I'm sure, did not surprise them. However, in a place where there is little to do, listening to her talk to a Westerner provides a diversion. If they are interested in me at all, it is because I am new, different, but the answers to the questions I ask, I'm sure, are the same mournful stories they themselves tell and hear every day.

Like Khatun's son, Sanzida's husband was not among the four detained men who returned to the village. I presume he and the others remain in a labor camp similar to the one where Ousman's father was detained. Sanzida and Khatun and many other families waited seven days for their men to return.

"We tried to find them by waiting for them," Sanzida says.

But when the military destroyed a nearby village and fearful rumors suggested as many as three hundred people died there, Sanzida and the remaining members of her village decided to flee. They walked sixteen days to the Bangladesh border. Sanzida brought one change of clothes for herself and her infant daughter. She calls the slog to the border a horrible time. From the top of every mountain she crossed, from every hill she climbed, she stared back at her village more than one hundred times and did not stop looking until she could no longer see even the hint of a rooftop.

Here in Kutupalong, Sanzida has nothing. In the morning, she wakes up, feeds two-year-old Asman, and then stands outside in the sun to warm her body. She prays five times a day. As-

Asima Khatun in the yellow shawl looking inside the hut of her daughter-in-law. Photo by J. Malcolm Garcia.

man asks her for food, but Sanzida has none to offer beside the rice and peas the Bengali military delivers to the camp. Sanzida shushes Asman by singing to her. When she gives birth to the child she now carries, she will tell both her children the story of her village: When you were in my belly, the military attacked us and we were forced out and your father disappeared.

"If you lost your husband or son or wife, what would you feel?" Khatun asks me, peering inside the hut.

I don't answer. My fiancé, Olga Contreras, died two years ago from respiratory failure, the result of an asthma attack. We met in 2015 in Guatemala, and she would accompany me on reporting assignments. Despite the vast differences in our circumstances, just considering Khatun's question makes me feel the enormity of her death again, and I look away.

"I feel the same," she says.

Sanzida's thoughts remain with her husband. She dreams of him and her pots and kettles, her kitchen and her house. Her village had four big banyan trees and a pond. People rested beneath the trees in the shade. She sees the military and other bad things, and then she wakes up. She is always thinking of her husband. When she is cold, his memory warms her. She has a blanket, but she assumes that where he is, he does not. He has nothing to keep him warm, and she does not have him.

❖ ❖ ❖

As we leave Sanzida's shack, Ousman takes out his list, crosses out *pregnant woman*, and circles our next interview: *schoolchildren*. We follow a pebble-strewn path downhill that wends past bamboo huts draped with large, orange tarps. The tarps catch the sun, and I follow the blinking rays of light from one orange roof to the next, flat, dusty tarps stretching as far as I can see in the hazy air. A hot breeze feels like a tarp itself, stalling until it no longer moves, settling into a heavy weight holding in the heat, a burden for us to carry along with the load of Sanzida's story and the question Khatun asked me and the clay dust speckling our sweating bodies.

Ousman.  Photo by J. Malcolm Garcia.

"What did you think?" I ask Ousman.

"Of what?"

"Of Sanzida and Khatun."

"Sir, after twenty-six years, I know all the sad stories. I don't cry now. I feel pain, but I have no more tears."

We continue on, gravel crunching beneath our shoes, chickens and naked children scattering in front of us. I am a game to the boys and girls, a boogie man. They look at me, screech and duck behind blankets used as doors. Dogs roam between the shanties, sniff splashes of wet ground where people have shit and pissed, large pale worms wriggling in the feces, and the dogs raise a leg and then jog forward, their tongues lolling, the sun bearing down relentlessly.

"Sir, are you married?"

"No."

"Why not?"

"I was engaged, but she died before we could marry."

"And you've not met another?"

"No."

"You are like Rohingya, sir," Ousman says. "You are alone in this world."

❖ ❖ ❖

Ousman stops at a blue rectangular, cinder-block building. Two rows of boys and girls sit on a dirt floor, and a teacher stands before them at a chalkboard. With a pencil, he points to letters of the English alphabet.

"A, apple," he says, and the children repeat.

"B, boat."

"C, cat."

The students stop reciting when they see Ousman and me. I suggest we come by another time so we don't interrupt, but the teacher ushers us in. I am struck here as I have been in other countries by how I can barge in on someone without an appointment and be accommodated. I suspect this has to do with the more casual approach some countries have toward time than we do in the U.S. Also, I've learned that Muslim people take very seriously the treatment of guests, uninvited or not. Obliging them is an important part of their faith.

Ousman and I introduce ourselves, and the teacher, twenty-five-year-old Mohammad Shalon, repeats our names to the students. Mohammad tells us that he had not been a teacher in Rakhine State, but a university student. He fled to Bangladesh in October 2017. Once here, he felt that an educated person like himself should teach less-fortunate children. So, he started this school.

"You have walked in on our first day," he says. "I've not even given the school a name yet."

Mohammad teaches English, Bengali, and Burmese. He wants to include history and math, but there is only so much he as one person can do. I ask him if some of the students would tell me their stories.

"Of course, why not?" Mohammad says.

He turns to the students and makes my request. After a long silence, a twelve-year-old boy, Solim Ullah, raises his hand. Mohammad tells him to stand. Solim wears a dirt-smeared, pink shirt much too large for his slim body, and an equally filthy lungi, a type of sarong, a traditional garment worn around the waist.

"I remember the military came for us at night and the soldiers shot into houses," Solim says, speaking in a halting voice as if he were reciting a lesson. "My sister and her husband were arrested. The soldiers beat me with batons. My father was taken into our yard and kicked. Other people were tied together with rope and beaten."

Solim sits down. Mohammad points to another student, ten-year-old Rana Ahmed. Rising to her feet, she begins: "My house was burned. I saw the military shoot at people and I saw them cut other peoples' throats with knives, and I saw more people running away as I was running away. In my dreams I see people being kicked, people dying. Not always. Not in all my dreams."

Rana sits. Shabu Ullah, just six years old, stands. He tells how his three older brothers and father were arrested.

"That's all," he says and sits down.

It goes on like this. Student after student. Fifty-six of them who saw family arrested and beaten and disappeared. Who saw neighbors shot and killed outside their homes in gardens they had tended only hours before. Who heard shooting and screaming, and some of the screams stopped and others did not for a long time.

"I was asleep," seven-year-old Rogiya Ullah tells me. "I woke up to moving in the house. I turned on the light switch and a soldier stabbed me. I called my mother, *Please come. I have a bad pain in my head.*"

Rogiya sits down.

"Now I will speak," Mohammad says.

He tells us he can't stop thinking about the killing he saw. His head aches with these thoughts. Loud noises remind him of grenade blasts, of guns. If the noise is loud enough he runs, although in the camp there is nothing to run from, but he runs anyway. It never ends, that noise of killing.

More than eighty people were arrested by the Myanmar military in Mohammad's village. He hid in the toilet of his outhouse. For two hours, he crouched down ankle-deep in shit. It was better than dying. He misses friends he had known for years, some arrested, some killed. They had prayed together, eaten together, worked together, lounged in the shade together. Now he lives in the camp, and they do not. In the camp, when he is not teaching, he has nothing to do. He wakes at sunrise, prays, and then waits for the day to begin and end and tries not to listen to the noises in his head.

Ousman and I thank Mohammad and the students for their time. Mohammad follows us to the door, and the students watch us, immobile, their solemn faces revealing little. Mohammad takes my hand and asks me to visit him at his home on block 54, not far from Sanzida's shack.

"I don't have much here," he says. "When I sit on the floor, I am reminded of my house where I had a chair and ate at a table. The cow shed at my house was better than where I live now. It was better because I built it. It was mine."

❖ ❖ ❖

I am staying at Hotel Sea Crown in Cox's Bazar, about an hour's drive from the camp. Cox, a tourist destination for Bengalis, has one of the longest beaches in the world, stretching from Sea Beach in the north to Kolatoli Beach in the south. Families flock here, strolling onto the sand and renting reclining chairs for twenty-five cents an hour. At low tide, when the water comes no higher than their ankles, couples walk far into the ocean. The women remain covered from head to foot in body-length veils while the men keep their shirts on and roll their pants up to their knees. Teens and young men rent horses and four-wheelers and race up and down the beaches, the horses lathering in the heat, and by the time I return to the hotel, the beaches churn with activity and the shouts of tuk-tuk drivers offering rides.

The balcony of my hotel stands across from another hotel. I see curtained rooms and the occasional guest hanging wet clothes on a balcony. Water drains from the laundry, showering dogs rummaging in four garbage dumpsters in an alley below. I keep my drapes shut, feel odd about someone looking in on me as I have peered at them. The closed curtains darken my room, and I flip a switch. A dim ceiling light offers flickering illumination, and I think of Olga and how she would have lingered with Mohammad's students. She adored children. Her long red hair would dance between her shoulders as she laughed at their antics, and they would run to her, and she'd envelop them in her arms.

"*Que lindo!*" she cried in Spanish, *how cute!*

I'd get impatient. Once I had what I wanted, I was ready to leave for the next interview. However, when children were involved, Olga dragged her feet, hugging boys and girls and asking them questions and listening intently as if what they had to say carried profound meaning.

*C'mon, Olga,* I'd say.

*Shh! Malcolm!*

I would give anything to relive those years and I would not be impatient, but instead cherish every second, and these memories of another time far from here mix with the tragic testimonies I solicited today that have nothing to do with Olga and the beach and the beautiful sunsets at night glazing the sea and the people watching it, a pale orange, hands cupped over their eyes, *New families come to the camp all the time and we tell them, Please do not cry. We will go home one day. Then we think of the people we've lost and will never see again and we start crying because we miss them and in our sleep we hear them calling for us but they don't know how to find us,* and the voices from the camp grow louder, penetrating the laughter rising from outside, *The military beat to death four of my children and threw them in the river. My oldest son cried, Allah, Allah, Allah. My other son was just five. He screamed but was too far away to hear,* all these images condensing into the shrieks of frolicking families splashing in the waves and my own feelings of loss and regret.

❖ ❖ ❖

In the morning, mist layers the beachfront. Through a light fog, a tuk-tuk driver takes me onto Cox Road and out of town toward the camp. We pass shuttered stores, veiled and mysterious in the mist and morning darkness. Billboards promote *Diamond Coastal Milk* and mango juice. Colored lights blink above the closed doors of Captain Cox Night Show bar, and girls in blue uniforms walk single file to school, stepping around dogs asleep on the sidewalks beneath a banner of the prime minister, Seikh Hasina, "mother of humanity." We soon enter an area dense with palm trees, grass, and pools of water, and then the forest ends, replaced by empty beaches unfurling along the road, and sea gulls collecting on fishing boats marooned on the sand, while other gulls float above the flat and unmoving ocean, and the wet air tastes of salt. We turn down a side road, cross a bridge, and pass through villages of mud homes with roofs made from palm leaves. Boys pull rice in flooded fields, tie it in bundles. Lines of laundry form a mosaic of color above the fields, and mules stand ankle-deep in mud, twitching their ears against flies, and watch the boys work.

Soon the road fills with buses, cars, and tuk-tuks, and diesel fumes and dust and the garbage odors of Kutupalong bazaar replace the fresh, morning air. *Happy to have you amid us,* a sign reads as we enter the camp. Ousman meets us beside a stall where a vendor sells eggs and chickens, the chickens squirming by the side of the road, legs tied, wings flapping uselessly.

"Last night, many Bengali police entered the camp," Ousman says, sliding in beside me. "I don't know why."

We drive a few feet before we pause at a checkpoint. Bengali soldiers take one look at me and wave us forward. I notice a dozen men kneeling in the dirt, their hands cuffed behind their backs. Ousman suspects they are Rohingya who left the camp without authorization. Before I arrived, Ousman paid a forger to make a Bengali national identity card for him. With it, he can leave the camp and go wherever he wants, but he gets nervous. What if he's stopped and he says something that gives him away as Rohingya? What if a Bengali soldier recognizes him? Sometimes, he dreams of being chased. He can't see who's after him. He wakes up sweating and out of breath.

"The camp is like a jail," he complains. "When I leave it, I am always afraid."

❖ ❖ ❖

Ousman examines his list. This morning, he has scheduled an interview with a woman who recently had a baby. Her name is Sneu Arabegum, just nineteen. She gave birth to a boy seventeen days ago. She has two other children, a three-year-old and an eighteen-month-old.

When we meet with Sneu, she is holding her three-year-old while the newborn squirms on a blanket near her, opening and closing his mouth, eyes tearing but making no sound, his face wrinkly as crepe paper, eyes wandering, a sense of loss in his helpless wriggling like a turtle stuck on its back. Sneu adjusts his blanket, but otherwise ignores him. When I look at her, I can't read her face. There is no pleasure in her eyes and no sadness. No expectation of any kind.

Sneu came to the camp in August 2017. She has no memories of a happy time in her life. Her father died before she was born. Her mother raised her and worked her like a cow. When she was seven, her mother hired her out to families who employed her in their kitchens and farm fields. This was her life until she married at seventeen, and it remained her life because she did the same kind of work for her husband, Fardin. Her marriage was arranged, but she learned to love Fardin and had begun to enjoy his company and the routine of her life when the Myanmar military entered her village.

The soldiers, police, and Buddhist priests showed up without warning and made all the women and children walk into a lake. They told them to put their heads down in the water and Sneu asked God to save her. *See what is happen-*

Sneu. Photo by J. Malcolm Garcia.

*ing to us?* she said in her prayers. She was pregnant and felt a swelling pain in her legs the longer she stood. The soldiers kept her in the water from sunrise to late afternoon. Other women stayed longer. When the soldiers looked away, Sneu and the other women raised their heads only to submerge their faces again when the soldiers turned in their direction. *Leave!* the soldiers shouted at them. *Get lost! This is not your country!* As the day went on, babies cried from the heat and the fear they felt in their mothers' breasts, and the soldiers battered their small heads with the butts of their guns, and mothers continued standing in the lake with dead children strapped to their chests.

The military abandoned the village at midnight, leaving behind charred homes and a void of arrested men, including Fardin. Sneu and the survivors left for Bangladesh a week later. They wanted to leave sooner, but a military camp stood on the road to the border. The villagers waited for it to move and then gathered what clothes they had and trudged off to Bangladesh.

Sneu describes her time on the road as an "indescribable hardship." She was four months pregnant. She carried her youngest son and held the hand of her oldest. Some of the elderly people helped her. When they cooked food, they gave her a few bites, but no one offered to help with her children. Everyone was trying to save themselves. Who would she have helped if she were not pregnant and without children?

For four days she walked through mountain passes and dense forests, hiding at the slightest noise. What was that? The police? The military? At the border, the villagers paid a boatman to take them to Bangladesh. Sneu gave the boatman her gold nose ring.

She feels safe in the camp, but alone. When she wants to buy candy for her children, she borrows money from neighbors. Sometimes she walks to a free food distribution center and collects bags of rice, peas, and cooking oil. She sells the oil and peas for fish and vegetables. Her children can't only eat rice and peas.

"This is my life," she tells me.

She prays for Fardin every day. She won't remarry. Another man would not love her children as her husband had. She will tell her children about what happened when they are old enough to understand. She will talk about their father. He was not tall or particularly handsome, but he was gentle, quiet. He farmed all day. She worked beside him. Those were happy times, but those times are no longer.

❖ ❖ ❖

Ousman and I walk out of Sneu's hut into the glare of midmorning. Men sit on the hard ground talking and staring blankly at wherever their eyes roam: the ceaseless, flat plateau of orange rooftops, the children playing in the maze of pathways coursing like strands in an endless web, the meandering dogs, the other families who, like them, sit, talk and stare at nothing.

"Twenty-six kilos of rice for fifteen days is not enough. I have six children to feed."

"When I run out, I borrow from other families for about three days, and then the NGOs give us more."

"The camp is better than Myanmar, but we can't go anywhere. So we eat only peas and rice."

"If a doctor says, 'Eat meat and vegetables,' we tell him we can only get rice."

Listening to them, Ousman mutters, "This place, there is no escape."

❖ ❖ ❖

I forgot to bring water, so Ousman and I stop at a vendor. Bengali merchants offer Rohingya items to sell—chips, soft drinks, pastries—and collect most of the profit. Still, as the vendor tells me, it keeps him busy.

He waves us to a table and we sit and he brings us bottled water. His stall provides relief from the heat. The cool of the mud floor, damp from water he used to tamp down dust, penetrates my sandals. A boy sits at the end of our table, weeping.

"What is your name?" Ousman asks him.

"Abdul."

"Tell me why are you crying, Abdul? Why are you sad?"

Abdul faces us, his teary eyes as red as his

Another view of the Kutupalong-Balukhali settlements. Photo by J. Malcolm Garcia.

shirt. He looks down, rubs his hands on his pants, and sniffles. He tells us that he lives with his aunt and uncle. His aunt gave him rice for breakfast, but his uncle took his plate and told him he would not be allowed to eat because he did not get wood for cooking as he had been told.

"I'm hungry," Abdul complains. "My uncle beats and starves me."

"How old are you?" Ousman asks him.

"Eleven."

I ask Ousman to order a plate of rice and peas. When it comes, I push it to Abdul. He hesitates and then begins to eat with his fingers. Between mouthfuls, he tells us he grew up in Tulatoly, a village in the western part of Rakhine State. He was happy there playing football and helping his father in the rice fields. Then the military showed up one morning after sunrise and everyone began running, and Abdul saw his father fall and die from a gunshot. The soldiers torched their house and beat his mother and forced her back inside. His two older brothers were also killed. He does not remember shouting or screaming at the death of his family. When he thinks of that moment, he sees only people falling and dying.

I notice a man watching us and Ousman invites him to join us. He is Daid, an uncle of Abdul, but not the one angry with him. Daid is the brother of Abul's mother. Eleven members of his family were killed that day. He gives me their names:

Ayesha, 30, Abdul's mother, shot.
Kharul Amin, 35, Abdul's father, shot.
Ismail, 10, Abdul's brother, shot.
Robiullah, 8, Abdul's brother, shot.
Noju Mulla, 6, Abdul's sister, shot.
Easar, 4, Abdul's sister.

"She fell, and a soldier held her down and slit her throat," Daid says of Easar. "I am always seeing this."

He continues:

Forkir Ahamed, 65, Daid's father, shot.
Ambia Khatum, 55, Daid's mother, shot.
Nur Begum, 20, Daid's wife, shot.
Mohammad Anas, 2, Daid's son, head bashed in.
Fieyajd Bibi, 10 months, Daid's daughter, head bashed in.

"My children," Daid says. He breaks down. Between sobs he says, "I think I am going crazy."

The vendor brings him a cup of water and Kleenex. At another table, a man holds down a squawking chicken. He cleaves its head with one swipe of a knife, the head, mouth agape in one last squawk, falling into a bucket.

"My wife told me, 'Go to the woods,'" Daid says, speaking just above a whisper and wiping his eyes. "The military will kill men, but they won't harm women. I ran, and the military killed many of us before we reached the trees. Through some branches, I saw Abdul and ran to him and brought him into the woods, and when I looked back I saw my wife on the ground. She was not moving and I knew she was dead. After the military left, we buried our family. Then we walked to the border. At first, we all lived together, but then I remarried and Abdul moved in with his other uncle."

"How could you remarry so soon?" I asked.

"A man is nothing without a family," Daid replies simply.

"He has no family," Ousman says of me.

"I am very sorry for this," Daid says, taking my hand.

That he would think beyond his own misery and worry about me I find humbling and incredibly generous. I don't know what to say and in the silence of his concern I withdraw my hand and say nothing.

Abdul pushes his empty plate away. His eyes tear up again. He misses his father and mother. In his dreams, they rise from the ground and walk to their house. He does not see them after they go inside but he hears their voices calling to him. *Where are you Abdul?* but he can't reply because he is asleep. When he wakes up they're gone.

"For every person who comes here, they leave behind at least one dead," Daid says.

❖ ❖ ❖

Tonight in my hotel room, I collapse on my bed exhausted. All those names Daid gave me and still I know I don't fully appreciate what Rohingya people have experienced. How can anyone? Battering children dead with rifle butts. Even in Afghanistan, where I have spent most of my time overseas, I've not heard such stories. It's beyond comprehension. Even as we left the camp, Daid recited more names of the dead.

Fatema Khatun, 22, Daid's sister.
Sara Khatun, 20, Daid's sister.
Daid's nephew, 28 days old, no name.

Jashid Hossian, 35, Daid's brother.

I try to concentrate on the crash of ocean waves and the laughter of people outside, but a quiet has settled over the beach or perhaps my thoughts are too loud for me to hear anything else. Tomorrow will be worse. Tomorrow, Ousman has scheduled our interview with the raped woman. The accumulation of horror. I close my eyes.

❖ ❖ ❖

This evening, Sanzida remembers the soldiers. They came when only stars illuminated the ground. They destroyed houses by pouring gasoline over furniture and lighting it with matches. Near her house, one woman pleaded, *Please don't kill me, let me go, please,* but the military did not hear her. Sanzida did. She hears her in her dreams, sees the houses crumbling to the ground, and she wakes up crying.

She misses her old life. Picking rice, taking out the cows, playing with children. She and her husband, Habiullah, had fifteen goats and eleven cows. She misses her girlfriends and visiting their villages. They live in other camps now.

She wishes she could just talk to Habiullah. They've been married three years. She enjoyed going to the market with him, eating their meals together. Simple things. One day, Habiullah bought her a beautiful blue dress for no reason. Just to surprise her. It is for you, he said. She wonders why she does not see him in her sleep. Probably because he is still alive. He is not a ghost and can't enter her dreams. That gives her hope.

*What is he doing now?* she wonders.

❖ ❖ ❖

Teacher Mohammad Shalon lies on a straw mat and stares in the dark and sees nothing. He envisions his big, one-room house. Coconut trees provided shade. He grew potatoes, green chiles, and onions. He played football when he wasn't working and afterward sat on the steps of a friend's shop and talked until dinner.

He puts off sleep to stall the nightmares. He lost his infant daughter, Amina. His wife was pregnant, and the child was born in the woods as she hid from the military. His wife was very weak after the delivery. Other women helped her, whispering soothing words. It began raining, and they did not have umbrellas or warm clothes. Maybe the girl died because she caught cold. His wife buried her where she was born.

Had Mohammad died before all this happened, he would have lived a peaceful life. He finds that hard to imagine. He misses his cows, how he'd wake to the clang of their bells and their low mooing and the crowing of roosters and the calls of monkeys and the sound of a nearby river and the sight of his pregnant wife bringing him tea.

Amina. She was his first daughter.

❖ ❖ ❖

The following morning, Ousman and I enter the tent of twenty-five-year-old Roshida Begum and her sister-in-law, Hunsa. Roshida is the raped woman. She looks at me with flat, dead eyes.

"She is still disturbed," Hunsa says.

"And you?" I ask.

"I ran away but I am disturbed, too."

Hunsa gives me the names of the dead. Roshida faces her and listens:

For Ahmad, 70, Roshida's father-in-law and Hunsa's father. Shot.

Amina Saraway, 60, Roshida's mother-in-law and Hunsa's mother. Raped, killed.

Nur Fatima, 20, Roshida's sister-in-law and Hunsa's younger sister. Raped, killed.

Sarha Saraway, 17, Roshida's sister-in-law and Hunsa's older sister. Shot, killed.

Nur Begum, 26, Roshida's sister. Raped, killed.

Ruhru Khan, 28 days old. Roshida's son. Killed.

Abdul Haq, 28, Roshida's husband. Shot, killed.

"They are no more," Hunsa says.

Roshida turns to Ousman and me when Hunsa stops speaking, her blank, hard stare unchanged.

"I think you're very brave," I tell Roshida and regret it the moment the words leave my mouth. It feels terribly inadequate, almost patronizing.

"There's nothing you can say, sir," Ousman tells me. "These are the stories I've grown up with all my life. Just ask your questions."

❖ ❖ ❖

When the military entered her village, Roshida fled with other women into rice fields, while the men sought refuge in some woods, but the soldiers followed the men and shot them. They

Roshida. Photo by J. Malcolm Garcia.

then fanned out and set ditches on fire where people were hiding. Everyone was crying, running, and Roshida lost all sense of time until she couldn't move. Then she heard the shrieks of dying children and the shrieks of their mothers, and she held her own infant son and began screaming, too.

Soldiers dragged her and four other women into a house. Nine bodies of women they had raped sprawled on the floor. They raped the four women with Roshida one by one and slit their throats. A soldier ripped her son from her arms and smashed his head against the floor, once, twice, three times. Twenty-eight days old, skull crushed. Roshida raged like an animal, and the soldier beat her in the head until she fell. He tore off her clothes while four other soldiers gripped her arms and legs and a fifth soldier raped her. Then that soldier took one of her arms, freeing another soldier to violate her. It went on like this until all six men had done with her what they wanted. Then a soldier stabbed her just above the breast bone and left her for dead. Smoke fumes roused Roshida and she ran naked into the woods where a woman

and her daughter, hiding behind some trees, washed her and gave her clothing. The three of them stayed in the forest overnight before they felt safe enough to walk to another village, but it too had been pillaged and razed. They left and walked to another destroyed village. From there they continued to Bangladesh. Roshida would walk ten minutes and rest for twenty-five. By the time they reached Bangladesh, the wound in her chest had stopped bleeding.

At night, Roshida sees her son. He does not speak to her. Sometimes she sees her mother-in-law cradling her son. She is always thinking of the dead. She does not want to do anything. She can't complete the simplest tasks.

Roshida waits for another question, but I have nothing more to ask. There are no words other than her words, and they are enough. The violence against the Rohingya has been executed with a ruthless exuberance that in my mind has taken on the depraved aura of a psychotic circus, intimate and personal, stimulating its executioners to indulge their most perverse, sadistic imaginings and commit horror after horror without mercy or letup and that over time has no context, no reason, other than to terrorize and kill, and that leaves me speechless.

❖ ❖ ❖

As we leave Roshida's shack, Ousman's phone rings. A baby just died in the camp, the caller tells him.

"Come," he tells me.

We make our way along footpaths that lead to a rice field within the camp. Walking on the mud banks that divide the field into squares, we step past oxen plowing the flooded ground and boys striking their backs with sticks. From the field, we follow another path and navigate a series of narrow alleys behind a line of shanties. I am lost, but Ousman's determined step leads the way. A vendor watches as we emerge from the alleys into what could almost be called a street, and we walk downhill to a hut beside a sewage ditch where families crowd the door. I hear a woman inside wailing, and then a man emerges and asks us all to leave.

"I know the family," Ousman says. "They are friends of my mother's."

"I don't know you," the man says. "I am Jalal Hossain, the mother's brother. She is grieving, as you can hear. Come tomorrow after the child is buried."

"The baby is dead," Ousman tells him. "She can go to heaven. She has no sin. She's better off than us."

Hossain agrees. He tells us the baby, just six months old, had been sick for five days and had gone to a clinic four times for treatment, but the medicine did not help. He shows me a plastic bag with bottles of Moxacil and paracetamol and asks my opinion, but I shake my head. I'm not a doctor, I tell him.

Ousman and I join a group of men sitting outside the vendor's shop we'd passed earlier. A few feet away, two other men build a bamboo litter large enough to carry the dead infant to the camp's cemetery, a small plot of land on stony ground. Sticks pierce the graves like porcupine quills to deter dogs from digging up the bodies.

"In December, two adults died," one of the men beside us comments.

"Rohingya are dying. We have no food; we have no medicine," his companion responds.

A young man walks past. The father, Ousman whispers to me. He carries purple cloth for a burial shroud. Some of the men disapprove when the father pauses to offer assistance with the litter.

"He should be home grieving with his wife," they say.

The father overhears the criticism. Looking over his shoulder, his eye flat and cold, he addresses the men: "Some cry loudly, some cry deep in their heart. In my heart I'm crying for her. I feel sad. She was my first daughter, and she died in this camp. I can't bring her back. Everyone dies here. I have no child now. It's a bad place, but there's no other place for me because I can't go home."

The men say nothing. Then, after a long pause, someone comments, "Diarrhea from the dirty water here killed your baby. Our lives are hopeless."

"At least we have toilets," another man says, and then everyone joins in.

"Too near the water pumps," the father says. "Our shit gets in the water, and now this baby is dead."

"You can't call them toilets," Ousman chimes in. "All they do is dig a big hole for us to shit in."

"If a toilet-maker comes here, we must request, please don't make toilets near our water pumps. It's not good for our health. If they don't agree, destroy the toilet."

"No, they'll come back to check on it and will just rebuild it," the father says.

"The water pump must be deeper than the toilet," another man comments.

Ousman's phone rings. It's my tuk-tuk driver. He says the Bengali military are asking questions: Who are you waiting for? Who is he? Where is he in the camp?

Ousman looks at his watch. Almost seven. Foreigners, he says, can't remain in the camp after five. He doesn't know why. Security reasons, he supposes.

"Come," he says, tugging my arm, "you have to go."

❖ ❖ ❖

This evening, I sit on the deck of my hotel room and I listen to the ocean. I hear the waves breaking and taste the salt in the air. Rocking back in my chair, I read my notes, knowing that I should type them while the interviews remain fresh in my mind.

*Mohammad Jokoriy, 21, married three months ago. His father approached the family of the girl he wanted Mohammad to marry and told them that on the day of the wedding he would pay the family 1,600 taka or*

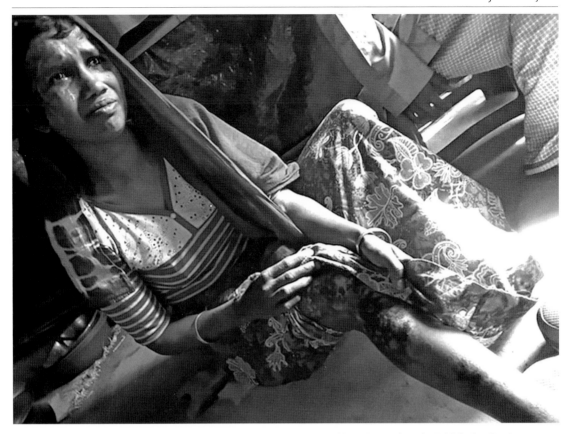

A woman left to die in a burning house by the Myanmar military in Rakhine State. Photo by J. Malcolm Garcia.

*twenty dollars. Mohommad did not know this girl, but since they've been married he has found her to be honest and a suitable wife. It is not ideal to have a family in the camp and he wishes for better things, but for now this is his life and there may be no other.*

*He was a rice farmer in Rakhine State, but then the August violence started and Myanmar soldiers sacked his village. To this day, Mohammad remembers the black smoke and the bad smell of seared bodies. Kuashon Village. The only home he'd known. A soldier's bullet took the life of his cousin, Ali Kharun, 25. A nice boy. Quiet. A farmer, too.*

I flip to another page and another and another.

*My parents died in a burning house. Soloma Khatum was my mother's name. Fojel Ahamad was my father.*

*The military launched rockets into my home and killed my uncle, Abul Kalam, and my aunt, Jahara.*

*New children come all the time. We are like older brothers to the new kids. We try to make them happy. We tell them we will go home one day, but I think I'll never see my home again. I cry. I miss my parents. They call for me. They don't know where I am. My father was Roshid Ahammad and my mother's name was Jonnot Araa.*

*I saw my brother, uncle, and grandmother die. I was not in the house but at the water pump. My uncle and brother were shot; my grandmother, a soldier slit her throat. I see them in the night. They get up and are killed again. My father was Soloman Shah, my brother, Abdul Haq, and my grandmother, Laila Begum.*

*Yes, I've seen babies clubbed in the face. I went very crazy. That's why I hit my head against bamboo to get rid of these thoughts. Everywhere dead bodies and blood. Many people cried, Don't kill me. My son went to the river to fish and the military cut his throat. He was tall and had a broad chest. He had a dark beard. He was very honest. Shoruson was his name. He was fifty.*

I get up, turn on my laptop. Staring at the ceiling, I listen to the ocean before I begin typing.

❖ ❖ ❖

In the morning I ask my driver to take me to the village of Teknaf, about an hour south of the camp, to view the Naf River. I want to see if Rohingya refugees are crossing today.

We stop to pick up Ousman at the camp and then we proceed south. The camp diminishes behind us, replaced by dry fields where cows

31

A woman bathing her feet in Kutupalong-Balukhali settlements. Photo by J. Malcolm Garcia.

stand in the dead grass and crows perch on their backs watching boys pick through garbage by the side of the road. A dog crosses the road, and a car swerves toward it, forcing the dog to leap in front of a bus, and the bus strikes the dog cleaving it in two, its two halves tossed above the bus, and cars zigzag to avoid the mutilated body, the front half of which lands on the road like a rug made from a big-game animal, its forelegs spread, mouth agape, eyes wide, still alive, before its head lolls to one side, eyes still open, and we along with other drivers stop and stare, "Oh my God," Ousman says, and covers his mouth, too stunned to say more, and we continue toward Teknaf as crows descend on the remains.

❖ ❖ ❖

The town of Teknaf teems with cars and tuk-tuks. Driving along a dirt road, swerving around cratered potholes, we bump and rock our way past thatched huts; straggling lines of women carry loads of food and laundry on their heads. The sun filters through the sparse branches of leafless trees, patching them with fleeting shadows.

We stop outside a butcher's stall on the edge of the river. The Naf stretches blank and flat before us, not even a seagull to interrupt our view, and we make our way onto a pier to better see the green hills of Myanmar, dimly revealed through a parting fog. I see no boats with refugees.

A Bengali soldier approaches us and speaks to Ousman. Ousman shows him his ID. They talk for a short time, the soldier glancing at me once, twice. Then he shakes Ousman's hand and walks away.

"He wanted to know what we were doing here," Ousman tells me. "I told him we are Facebook friends and I am showing you around Bangladesh. I said you will be returning to the U.S. tomorrow."

"Right."

"And you'll have no one to meet you when you get home?"

"Don't worry about me."

"You'll come back to Bangladesh? I don't think so."

"No, I don't think so."

"There are better ways to live in the world, but not for Rohingya. Will you say that in your story?"

I don't answer. A breeze rustles our clothes. We stand without talking, gazing at the coastline of Myanmar, where tragedies, I know, are unfolding right now in Rakhine State. Tragedies in real time, horrors I won't hear about but I'll know exist, as will Ousman. I turn to him, but he acts as if I'm no longer here. He stares across the water, dry-eyed and reflective, grieving.

❖ ❖ ❖

*Michele Wolf*

# Postcards at the Museum

The murderers had no fear of identification. Sometimes
The murderers were police. Vendors sold pop and sandwiches.
Sometimes, as prelude, a man was slashed, charred, or severed.
After the neck snapped, after the body's pendular swaying
Finally stopped, the mob of onlookers posed for the camera.
The youngest, age four, clad in a plaid summer frock,
Waited in front with other girls, just feet from the corpse.
One lynching postcard, 1916, signed "Your son Joe,"
Offers "This is the barbecue we had last night." Jotted
With brown ink, a cross shows where Joe stood in the crowd.

# Ghost Month

As if the others weren't also.

As if the moon, assuming a particular disposition, a certain aptitude,

      were the only measure.

As when the crabs, bloated with life, quicken their way to the beach-height,

that bed of split-straw and seaweed,

      to dig and scrawl,

          beyond the day's warmth,

to the dark-wet depository

         their instinct demands.


As if March were a breathing mouth and not a lamp

        baring the way upward.

Or August browning nonetheless under the early rains.


For you, we say, this bowl of basil,

champagne grapes upon their scaffold,

this white crane creased by the earnest.


What is it you seek but wonderment and delicious trouble?

That wooden stool with its finish worn bare?

The light that responds to the sound of our voices?

Take this house we burn it for you.

Can you see your grandson in the door?

The car with its wheels

      turned toward the curb to stop it from rolling?


Do not be saddened by the sudden decline of the pocket harmonica.

By the speed-wash setting on the digital machine.

Take joy in the smoke the world smoke it rises.

The night-market with its oils and cutlets.


Know that you are our recurring occasion.


That this is the expression of your coming.


That we have dug a hole and filled it

with sawdust and pitch

and set it afire and called it our longing.

That we have made ourselves into earthlight and season.

That we carry you forward into our changing,

and shall keep so till our wide-time is done.

Nathan Beard. *New Mexico Memory: Approaching an Evening Thunderstorm.* Acrylic on masonite. 18 x 18 inches.

*Liana Jahan Imam*

# Tore a Hole in the World What Did You Expect

We sit across from one another at a round bar table. We are necessarily far away. Don't touch knees. We eat careful, unmessy food: Parker House rolls and chopped crab salads and little squids stuffed with chorizo and cannellini beans. Each low-towered bite neatened and re-neatened with knives before liftoff. We speak to each other with this same kind of precision. We don't get anything on our hands, laps, or faces.

This is what I try to manifest, holding my phone in both hands, the unread texts from him piling up, three then five then eight. Extreme civility my only goal. He says what about Corner Bistro and I say okay.

Once we're already standing in line for a table I decide to say, "I actually thought we might meet at the Ace or something."

"Why did you think that?"

"I don't know, just thought it."

"Well, we could have."

You said your thing first, I don't respond.

Could I be offended that he made a suggestion that seemed wrong based on its conflict with an image formed in my mind?

Yes, I could be.

❖ ❖ ❖

Pickles slide out of the burger first. This is what always happens. The pickles never stay on the burger. The small little middlest eyes of the raw onion, I leave on the Styrofoam, always. The pickles I would like inside, but the pickles like the Styrofoam. The beer comes in handled half-pints, so we order four at once.

He keeps pointing out mustard at my mouth's corners and I run out of napkins to wipe it away and think of times when he wouldn't tell me, would rub it off himself and then lick his thumbs clean. Wonder vaguely what I'm doing here, what to say. Sipping the beers before had seemed nicely preemptive; getting ready, think-ing time. But we lost steam eating and now again are strangers, two years of estrangement, again, placed between us. This is why we needed salads, I think. This is why food with forks.

He wears his face with a beard now, which at certain angles makes it look all puffed out, though the messier haircut suits him, and the clothes, the henley that peeks out of his box-checked oxford, the sleeves all rolled up in each other. At our old hotel bar job he was always tie-and-vested, his face all clean. The way meeting under these kinds of extreme circumstances makes you think you know a person better. It was my first Manhattan job; didn't know you could dress up in a uniform and personality both.

"So," he says, "you're here for what again?"

"I'm just here. Just visiting."

"All the way from the great Midwest. I almost can't believe I rate a lunch."

"The actual West," I say, can never not say, why can I not just let him misinterpret me and leave it at that. "Do you even know where on a map Montana is?"

"What reason would I have to?"

I eat a pickle.

"Where are you these days?" I say, and he tells me still at JL, taking some managing shifts now.

"Moving on up," I say, best attempt at not shoving the leftover smear of ketchup and mustard on his plate into his absurd, absurdly earnest face.

"We should've gone there and gotten all the free stuff," he says, or I say, or both of us think without ever saying but know the other one is thinking it.

"I always think of you over in that part of the Village," he does really say, and the drop in my stomach shames me to death, and he goes on, "I love how scandalized you always were by the fact that there's a corner of Waverly and Waverly and Waverly."

"That corner is scandalizing," I say, feeling red, wondering how you can learn to be uncharmed by a charmer. Shoving the last pickles back into my last bite of grease burger.

"Barry Jenkins is filming a movie over there, some period Baldwin thing," he says. "They covered up one of the Waverlys with a Greenwich Street sign the other day."

"So dumb," I say, "Greenwich is so close." Though I couldn't remember if it was.

"Doesn't have such a cinematic three-way corner, though."

"So now he's just being historically inaccurate."

"You're unpleasable," he says.

I lizard my tongue all around my mouth, tasting mustard, one more round, and then clean.

"Thank you," I say, and mean it.

❖ ❖ ❖

Warm, unseasonably, so we go up on the Highline thinking Nola iced coffee, but the stalls are all gone, seasonally. We share one of the somehow still-pristine wood lounger benches, all connected to each other, and people-watch among the Eastern Euros all wearing their Canada Gooses already and peering past the piers to the coast of New Jersey like it's something to look at.

"What did you want to see me for?" I ask, can't not ask anymore.

He turns his face up to mine. We're in an old posture, him flush on his back and me elbow-propped, turned in toward him, close enough to feel breath.

"Why wouldn't I want to?"

"I mean, what's it doing? What difference will it make."

"Does it have to? Couldn't I just be selfish?" Glinty eyes and a shove of his shoulder into my side. That was never a problem for either of us.

I get up and go over to the railing, where in a while he meets me. The sky over the Hudson will soon start streaking creamsicle and we'll have to decide how to part ways.

"I just can't believe you ever left," he says. "You showed me all this stuff about New York. You were so good at it."

"And I'm not anymore?"

"It's its own thing now," he says. "Not like before."

He pulls me in to hug but I don't bring my arms up and he says, "Why isn't this fun?"

Having no way to answer except the oldest, dumbest way, I say, "Beer's weak in there. Let's get a real drink."

"Have to go all the way to the LES for that now."

"No way, there's tons over here. Santina? Oh, the Up and Up, let's go to the Up and Up."

"Nobody works at either of those places anymore," he says, starting to walk, his mind made already, like earlier.

"I think everybody that works there knows how to make us drinks. Come on, we can still name drop I'm sure."

But he says, "Nah, Joey's at Mother of Pearl today, that's better in the daytime anyway. All that glass."

Going downstairs to the 8th Avenue L all these people trot frantically when they hear the train doors beep open below, and even he speeds up, though we're at the end of the line and all the trains idle first before heading east again. We get one of the two-seaters at the end of the car, one of those so-rote behaviors I didn't even notice that's what I was looking for. I wonder if we have ever not made out in an L train. When we sit down our knees touch and we don't untouch them. Wonder how often people stay lovers because they know that without the lovering there is nothing much about the other person.

"Are you still playing basketball?"

He rolls his head around noncommittally. "It's been hard to find guys to pick up with."

"Never used to be."

He shrugs and the train starts moving and he looks around pleased, like the two were related. "Yeah, all these new guys coming through are so serious about the industry. It's like they never do anything else, just read all these cocktail books and memorize specs and look at *Eater* all day."

"As opposed to?"

"I dunno, having a life outside of work."

"I always thought people got this kind of food and bev job so their work could be life. Like, so you don't have to try so hard to distinguish."

"But then you just study all the time?"

This time I shrug and we're rolling to a stop at Union Square. "Probably doesn't feel like that to them. Probably just feels like being curious."

"Is that how you felt about it?"

"No, but I left."

He lets his eyebrows rise, though I can't believe this is new information to him, and say so.

"No," he says, "I guess it's not. I just didn't know people could admit things like that out loud."

I ask like what and he says, "Like what somebody might call giving up."

"Ah."

The train's still stopped and I crack my knuckles, re-roll the sleeves of my jean jacket. His phone's been one long vibration since we got to the station, long stream of texts. I try to remember if there was service down here when I left.

"Ladies and gentlemen. L train riders," says a real voice over the loudspeaker. "We apologize for the delay. A passenger is vomiting and needs to be removed from their car and taken care of. Thank you for your patience."

"The fuck was that?"

"The MTA has a new policy on radical honesty," he says, "after all the delay disasters in the summer."

"That part I knew about."

"I read that they announced a jumper once but I can't really believe that would happen."

"Because?"

"Because wouldn't everybody panic and freak the fuck out? What right does the train conductor have to remind me of my mortality and the inherent weakness of the human mind?"

"I think you got funnier," I say, and in a few moments the doors slide together.

"What did the article say?"

"What article?"

"How did it say people reacted to hearing about the jumper?"

He crumbles up his mouth, not wanting to say. "Well, it said they were like, all kind of horrified but ended up being quietly respectful of the delay."

"That makes a lot of sense to me."

"I don't get why."

"I mean, don't you think it's the same as when you're worried about something for a long time and then even finding out something not great feels really good compared to the not knowing?"

"Like what kind of thing?"

"Like I dunno, like finding out you've been cheated on, maybe."

His breath catches just slightly and he ducks his head into the collar of his Barbour coat, see-

ing that he's answered a question from another age, one I never knew existed.

❖ ❖ ❖

Joey makes Shark Attacks that cost us nothing and normal people eighteen or so dollars. It's just tiki punch that comes in a ceramic shark with Peychaud's dribbled all around the mouth to look like gore.

"Doesn't everybody who orders these know you can get the same thing in New Orleans for six bucks? And you get to keep the shark?" I take the rest of a daiquiri shot. "I'm sure the cost of a round of these washes with a plane ticket."

"Like you never left," Joey says, giving my head a little shove back, tender, asks, "What's the worst part about being gone?"

I sip my shark. He's quiet beside, sending texts again and pushing his snaiquiri around without drinking it.

"There's so many worst parts," I say, though I don't know if I believe that.

"Pick something," Joey pushes. He's lost his little paunch in the years I've been gone, brighter eyes, neater hair. Wonder what it was he quit doing.

"The worst part," I say, "is that all the people you never slept with are all still here and single and they're all fucking the new hostess someplace."

Joey shakes his head and his grin looks new too and he pours me a Zacapa shot, says, again, "Like you never left."

❖ ❖ ❖

Some amount of quiet drinks later he swivels toward me, says, "Doesn't this feel a little strange?" Arranging legs so both mine are between his.

"Which part?"

"That it's so easy to just be back like we were. All these same places."

"I don't know if it feels that way to me," I say.

But even so, nearing tipsy, what I want is to put my hands on his knees, to reach toward him with my whole body. Be easy. Wonder if there is anyplace at all we used to go we didn't make out in, all those public preambles to our messy little disasters of sex, falling off our small beds or bashing foreheads together in the drunk dark, knocking shins against the heavy kitchen benches at his Williamsburg studio, bruised all down my arms from getting caught, put back, held down grinning. Once on the M train to meet him at an opening someone passed me a help line card and I puffed up and said how dare you, I work in kitchens, which is something my girl-chef friends had to say all the time to explain the oven and cast iron burns on their forearms, though I'm sure my bruises looked nothing like burns and, frankly, though I'm sure I did need help, if not that kind.

"I wanna know what it's like out there," he says, as if he already forgot the other conversation he started, and maybe he did. I think this is the first time he's ever asked me. Joey's mixing drinks we asked for, rum old fashioneds, and I don't think I need mine, know I will drink it.

"It's really really quiet," I say. "Sometimes when there's a sprinkler on in my yard I think someone's trying to break in through the window. Or that it's like, lots of large insects."

"But it's really beautiful, right?"

"Yeah," I say. "Very beautiful." I feel exhausted. This question so pervasive and banal it's grown offensive.

❖ ❖ ❖

"I have a really good idea," he says when we spill out onto the sidewalk, the day now dusky and streetlights starting to twink on. "I've got mushrooms in the freezer at home."

I think back to this morning, my very high and particularized hopes, the fork-food and bright light of the Dory in daytime, and how I imagined sipping mineral water there and leaving the table without anything in my teeth and leaving him on the sidewalk near the Flatiron Building, and how the only excess I planned for this day was maybe possibly stopping in at the Opening Ceremony in the Ace's lobby and then making my way back to the L through the Union Square greenmarket, back to Janie's apartment and to Janie herself, who all day has not texted me one warning or one I-knew-you'd-spend-all-day-with-him or anything else, who simply gave me her extra keys as I was leaving and said she was closing tonight anyway, come back whenever.

We chomp hard stems and caps, wash the chalk of them down with Coke Zero, and wait for them on this huge blue sectional he didn't have before. A different apartment too than the one I knew him in. How did he afford it without roommates?

"That's a newish development," he says, and I notice the walls, mostly bare, and the bookshelves all sparse, things she'd taken with her. Which she, I don't ask.

We wait for the drugs and I pet his beard, something I had never done, something there never was to do before. He hated shaving all the time for that hotel job, but I loved getting to care for him, buying salves and soaps at Kiehl's, buying silk ties at the Housing Works thrift in Soho, where all the grannies took their husband's fancy accessories when they died. Loved sending him to work in his cheap Topman suits made nice by these small extravagances. I loved that fake person and could not reconcile myself to its foil.

I prop up on my elbow, look down on him like I always have. He's blinking and blinking, and I look where he looks, those stripped landlord-yellow walls starting to hover a little in front of themselves.

"How did you do it?" he asks.

"Do what?"

"Leave."

I lie on my side, twist into him, push hands through beard and lace fingers at his nape. "I just filled out some papers."

It was the truth, but he never believed it, resented me for what he thought was withholding, all the way back when I stopped serving and joined another restaurant group to become a junior maître d'.

But it really was that easy. You just fill out the papers and you don't think about the consequences. He couldn't figure out the second part.

It comes on heavy and the couch is an ocean or vice versa. We don't open our eyes because when we do we stop seeing direct into each other's damp brains, wound all tight together and becoming eagles and otters and giant flailed octopuses, bending and re-bending our knees in new ways to become one body through our clothes, snug in that tight uncontrolled singularity of hallucination or being in love or one and the same and even then, even in our lovely linked minds, I see myself trying to follow, asking him to tell me something, to let me watch him become whatever new thing he's going to be, knowing all the while he only does tell because I ask, because I make him. And later on, coming down, he realizes we left the door unlocked. He doesn't say it was me but we both know.

*Marsha Truman Cooper*

# Tendencies to Nest

A hummingbird covers
two eggs she urged
into a mudless cup the size
of half a walnut shell—

weaving and bending fibers
then threading them with spider
silk in the privacy of wood.

Some women still fabricate
baskets by interlacing
various strands of native grass
blended to make them smell
like vanilla, the bowls' formula
a mother-daughter secret.

For both nests the difficulty
arrives at the beginning moment,
a curling foundation
persuaded out of nothing
cooperative in the way of materials—

a gumption of initial loops,
first teaching words
about sacred vessels,
the opening beats of heart
inside a shell.

# Ode to Andrew McCarthy and Your Hand on My Thigh

"If I won a gameshow, I'd adopt a panda"
is the best pickup line I've heard in my life
        because it's not a line or a joke or a story
recounted at a party where they're out of chips,
        and who even makes punch for parties anymore,
except in the movies—and if movies are the guide
        to life, where we learn how to kiss, how to smoke
a cigar, how to tempt a lover in a Red Corvette:
        LA, 3 AM, the wind in your hair, down to your
breasts, braless under a low-v dress,
        stroking the driver who's your lover, he relents,
stops the car, the motorcycles circling around you
        because this is young love and everyone, *everyone*
must make way, and there's so many lights,
        and maybe we're not listening to the movies enough
because we're not in a convertible in LA,
        a young Andrew McCarthy stroking my thigh, no,
it's Christmas morning, not thinking about what
        comes next, speaking of which, I'd marry that man
who said, "If I won a gameshow, I'd adopt a panda,"
        no hesitation, travel to Chengdu with him or Ocean Park
Amusement Park, Hong Kong, home to
        Ying Ying and Le Le, and tourists and locals
supply them with an endless count of cardboard
        to rip, which is like a gameshow:
the grocery cart runs—you win a lifetime
        supply of Blue Moon Ice Cream or hot dogs,
and say *hello* to wiener bits and mac and cheese
        for lunch for the whole next year,
and what about those babes in sparkly dresses,
        the glitz and glamour of spinning that wheel,
letting it determine your entire fate,
        hoping it'll land on the boat or the trip to Paris,
but maybe what I want isn't the real-life pandas,
        but the things I cannot have, the things out of this world,
no not UFOs or the chocolate martinis on Mars,
        but that feeling, like how one night in Tallahassee
I chant my dead dog's name: *Buzzie, Buzzie, Buzzie*
        over and over again, and I feel him sleeping next
to me on the bed, and you've got to admit:
        some creatures really are irreplaceable,

and the once-in-a-blue-moon-nightly visits
        aren't enough, and I think about Andrew McCarthy
in *Mannequin*, how Kim Cattrall just comes to life
        for his eyes only, and he wants to keep holding
on to every moment, and maybe we do spend
        more hours of the day looking at someone
rather than listening to them, but what's the point
        if we can't feel their soft skin on our hands
every day, and can I just keep holding on?

NASA's Jet Propulsion Laboratory in Pasadena, California, provided this image of a dusty planet-forming disk first seen by the NASA Infrared Astronomical Satellite in 1983 and continuing to glow for twenty-five years, until it suddenly and inexplicably disappeared in January 2010. An infrared image from the Gemini telescope in Chile confirmed in May 2012 that the dust ring was gone. Courtesy of NASA/JPL-Caltech.

*Jennifer Key*

# The Horizon Has a Way of Disappearing

As a teenager, I was a babysitting *tour de force*. Like banquet halls in June, I booked early for big nights like New Year's, and I like to think I was good at my job. I could color and read books and play games with the best of them. My favorite child was Sammy who wore cowboy boots with his pajamas and pronounced squirrel "whirl" as he excitedly pointed out the rodents in his backyard. Never before or since has the Domino's deliveryman been greeted with such fanfare as when Sammy spied his approaching car. And when we weren't ordering pizza, I made dinner and gave baths and wrangled children into bed not too much past their bedtime.

As I grew older, I saw that none of these things or even my pleasure in them meant that I would be a good mother. In fact, I grew pretty certain I wouldn't be. When I asked myself what I liked so much about babysitting, I had no good answer except that it was make-believe. As an unhappy teenager who hadn't been invited to homecoming, I enjoyed pretending to be someone else, and an adult with a home and children was about as different from my life as I was then exposed to. It looked like happiness. Make-believe often does. It's not so different from looking at a house fashioned out of a barn and imagining your entire existence there would be fortunate, which is how my marriage began years later.

In truth our first home had once been a small horse barn, and our bedroom stood in what had been the hayloft, a steeply pitched room tucked under the eaves of the tin roof. Among the house's charming features was a narrow, twisting stairwell, which struck me as magical, nearly turret-like, when we'd looked at the rental, but seemed less so upon move-in with actual human-sized furniture. However, the private backyard, once a fenced horse paddock, that initially enticed me with its thorny labyrinth of rose bushes proved even more useful when our septic backed up and

for showering we had to resort to hosing ourselves down outdoors.

I watched the black tulips open that fall and the pear trees break into lace and leaf in the spring through the French doors in our bedroom that opened to a small, splintery deck. Over this balcony and through these doors, my husband Greg and our friend Adam hauled our double mattress before our wedding. It was in this picture-book room that my experiment in cutting-edge birth control procedures lasted precisely one year. It did not make for an auspicious start to our sex life.

From its very commencement, our sex life had not been one for the books. On our wedding night I took a sleeping pill and passed out mid-rollick. *Coitus interruptus*. Didn't everyone think of Latin class on their wedding night? Of course it would get better! It had to, yet I wound up on Nuvaring after a honeymoon of ouchy sex marked by much starting and stopping and the strategic reconfiguration of our bodies like assemble-it-yourself components of an Ikea bookcase. All this under the gauzy mystique of a mosquito net shrouding a canopy bed.

"Am I hurting you?" my husband asked.

Here I'd been worried about the dread honeymooner's disease, which left one of my friends sidelined and sobbing in a shallow few inches of bath water in a Key West hotel a decade earlier. If I'd paid closer attention, I might have learned something about worrying about the wrong thing.

❖ ❖ ❖

I was prescribed the Nuvaring at my first doctor's appointment as a married woman when my doctor suspected that condoms may have been the culprit for our less than transcendent honeymoon. Dr. Bannon came highly recommended by my college roommate, to whom Dr. Bannon had been recommended by another college friend, and so on, until everyone I knew from our college who migrated to Washington seemed lucky enough to be in on the secret of Dr. Patricia Bannon. She was, as my old roommate described, a firecracker: outgoing, sharp, warm, and funny. As she stood to greet me from behind her desk, she pushed her tortoiseshell glasses to the brow of her head, where they anchored a mass of long hair. She leaned in to listen when she asked a question. I adored her from the first, and it was to her I confessed that sex hurt. I hadn't intended to reveal what I considered a personal failure, but the doctor was so genuine and, well, normal as she sat across from me during my initial consult that I found myself confiding in her. I wanted her to be my best friend or big sister or at least my next-door neighbor. She would address the pain, of course, but there was something else she wanted to say, too.

"I know you just got married and it seems like you have a lot of time, but if you want to have children—if that is something important to you—do not wait too long. You can wait a little, but don't think you have all the time in the world. I see it every day," she explained, "couples who wait too long."

I was twenty-nine, and this was to be the first of many fertility pep rallies held in doctors' offices, from Washington, D.C., to Dallas to North Carolina over the span of twelve years. Did I believe Dr. Bannon? Yes. To this day, she remains the kindest, most empathetic, and confidence-inspiring doctor I've ever seen, but I wasn't ready to act on her advice.

"All you smart, young women," Dr. Bannon said when I named my friend who'd recommended her practice. I was surprised to be lumped into a group like that, and I was surprised at how flattering it felt. It was one of the few moments in my life when I actually felt young or smart, and that was a sorority I liked belonging to.

What I remember from that tony office: walls full of framed baby portraits and then joining me on the elevator ride down from the office a pretty twenty-something woman in whatever jeans were *de rigueur* that season, her mother and blond toddler in tow. She was the kind of woman I spent a lot time in those days wishing I were: she took up only the right amount of space in the right spaces.

"What did the doctor say?" her mother asked.

The young woman stared at the seam where the elevator doors closed. "Positive," she said.

Her mother gently prodded, "Aren't you happy?"

❖ ❖ ❖

The Nuvaring was cold from being stored in the fridge, and it held the cold even as my husband's thumb and forefinger compressed its circular shape into a translucent figure eight. It was a springy plastic loop implanted with birth-control hormones designed to be worn internally for three weeks every month, and I stockpiled them from my father-in-law, an ob-gyn swimming in samples, so that a phalanx stood at the ready in their silver foil packages beside a twelve-pack of Diet Coke.

The trick was to apply just enough pressure to hold it in that exact figure eight while you shoved it inside yourself. Naturally, the ring tended to spring back to a circle about the size of my middle finger and thumb forming an "O." The mechanics and angles of pushing it in on my own were damn near impossible, which is how my husband came to be enlisted in the task. Naturally, the drug enclosure leaflet made the process sound simple, as though your whole life you'd been manipulating little plastic bracelets into dimensions just right for vaginal insertion.

As much as insertion hurt, it was the easy part. The real difficulty started then, and this problem was twofold: keeping it in and taking it out. I can't explain how these two challenges didn't cancel each other out. After all, the ring's tendency to slip out would suggest an ease of removal that did not exist. This was precisely Nuvaring's perversion of reason. While taking a walk or out on a ride, I'd feel its descent, creeping centimeter by centimeter, until I could think of nothing other than remedying the situation, and I'd return to the semi-privacy of a horse stall, expecting to find the circle free-floating in my underwear like a ring that slipped its planet. If a slip of plastic was this uncomfortable I couldn't imagine part of a baby, say a head or an arm, wedged there.

Although I would've spent half my time hiding in a dim hay-sweet corner of a horse stall as I pushed the plastic loop back inside my body, when it came time for the ring's monthly removal, it anchored inside me with a vise-like lock. This procedure required that I brace myself flat on our bed, naked from waist down. If Greg had been drilling my tooth for a cavity, it couldn't have been more clinical.

Here's how my husband described it: you wouldn't know where it went, though there obviously weren't that many options, so you had to fish around, your finger hooked to latch onto the loop.

What I remember: how sore I was from all that rummaging around. The more he tried, the more it hurt, and the more it hurt, the more my muscles clenched and the longer it took. Once Greg scratched me with a fingernail and I yelled at him. Here he was he was doing this thing to me so that he could do other things to me.

Greg says he doesn't think about that these days and mainly remembers feeling sorry for me as I contorted and twisted like an extra in a Civil War surgery scene. Towards the end of the Nuvaring's tenure in my body and our marriage, I undertook these procedures on my own, asking Greg to remain on the other side of our bedroom door.

But all the trouble seemed worth it. Birth control was serious business, despite Dr. Bannon's admonishment not to wait too long. Two of my friends fell pregnant while taking the pill, one industrious couple working with only a single ovary and testicle (as the husband bragged one wine-soaked night). In this climate, pregnancy loomed like a threat that required constant vigilance, a scourge like bed bugs in a youth hostel.

The sensation of watching my friends prepare for children was the feeling of being left behind as the school bus whisked away from the curb while I was running to catch it. Only I didn't feel panic or worry at being left behind, and that in turn worried me. I certainly wasn't yelling after the bus for it to hold on. *I'll catch up with you at the next stop* was the strategy when we missed the bus as kids, and if we were lucky, someone's mom would rev her Country Squire LTD down the block after Bus 5. Now nobody was gunning the engine to catch up. After all, we—or *they* to be more accurate—were the mothers and the Country Squire was a wood-paneled relic from another century. Instead, I remained on the street corner waving to my friends as they turned the corner without me. I was happy for my friends' joy—this thing they wanted coming to pass.

"I'm excited to meet him," my friend Liza said of her unborn baby, as though she were off to a mixer and not a scheduled C-section.

❖ ❖ ❖

What kind of woman is afraid to have children and simultaneously afraid to make the decision not to have them? After all, I like kids and am concerned for their welfare. It's perplexing even to me that these feelings haven't simplified the decision I ought to have made long ago and ironically may have made indirectly. For years my friends offered me their children's outgrown baby clothes and strollers, supplies that mushroomed in closets like lavish provisions of small regimental armies. Then they stopped offering.

When I listen to myself protest that I actually like children, a defense I find myself mounting to strangers who ask if I have children, it seems almost nonsensical that I haven't establish a small cottage industry of childbirth ala Michelle Duggar. "I really like children," I'll hear myself say. "I do. I really do."

When my friends' babies arrived and grew into small people, I too was excited to meet them. I found myself caring quite a lot about them and genuinely anticipated Halloween photos and pictures from summer camp. Not for the sake of politeness did I ask whether they like their teachers and how their soccer game went and which dinosaur it was that haunted their days and nights. For about a decade it seemed that if I weren't hearing about dinosaurs then I was learning whether one American Girl Doll or another was sufficiently outfitted for her ice-skating excursion.

Wasn't it the milk of human kindness I felt when I couldn't bear to see Liza's small son plead and sob behind his baby gate where she'd deposited him for a time-out?

I was supposed to be helping Liza with her toddler and new baby while her husband traveled on business. "Please, Liza," I called downstairs. "He said he's sorry." When she peered up from the foot of the stairs, the look she laid on me was one hauled from the deep when all other reasonable looks have been exhausted. Some help I was. She didn't have to say, "Don't make me come up there."

Max and I held hands through the bars.

❖ ❖ ❖

Two years earlier when Max was just a baby, I met his mother at the mall so that I could watch him while she got a haircut. The small tyke was tucked in his stroller, and as I pushed him from Nordstoms to Belks, Max acquired a fan

47

club to rival a boy band's. I simply had no idea that other people—women—flocked to babies with the frenzied devotion of pre-teens. In all the times I'd seen women with babies in public, it never occurred to me to stop and ask about their offspring. In my mind a baby resembled a fragile package carried from one point to another, and with any luck as simply and directly as possible. It would not occur to me to stop a parent on such a mission.

"Excuse me, madam? Yes, you, who have not slept through the night in over a year and whose breasts may be, this very moment, weeping milk onto your blouse. May I inquire as to junior's health, sex, and name?"

"How old is he?" one lady asked instead during Max's mall outing. She strained over the stroller's edge to glimpse his tiny fists clutching the blanket as he slept.

"Oh I don't know," I answered and walked away. She expected something I couldn't provide: specifics. When people ask a baby's age they want stats down to the day, week, and month, but I hadn't paid attention to the passage of time the way I should have.

❖ ❖ ❖

When we visit a new church, it's the first question asked.

When I get my hair cut.

When we move.

When I show up for jury duty.

On the airplane.

At parent-teacher conferences when I taught.

With my jaw an unanswerable O in the face of the dental hygienist.

Balanced on one leg as I peel off my swimsuit in the locker room at the Y.

Mind you, it's a reasonable question: nobody asks it out of inconsiderate motives, and I hope I never answer unkindly. Surely there are questions I ask in all innocence that needle others, but when I asked my husband if he were routinely, even daily, asked whether he had children, the only time he could remember that happening was once by a new boss who happened to be Mormon.

❖ ❖ ❖

When Greg's brother and his wife asked whether we would be the guardians for their three children "should something happen," we were flattered and readily agreed. I think

Greg and I discussed possible logistics at least once in all seriousness. Later, because it seemed incredibly improbable that his nephews and niece would be orphaned in such a dramatic fashion and we could hardly fathom ourselves cast as their caretakers as though we'd woken in a Dickens novel, Greg and I laughed as we imagined inheriting three gangly, monosyllabic teenagers in one fell swoop. Boarding school sounded like a good answer.

The more telling details are that I forgot birthdays and we often opted to stay home rather than travel to see them over the holidays. I had to admit I wasn't even a passable aunt. Or friend.

Greg and I left Washington a few years after Liza had Max and stayed away too long. The next time we visited, he enforced a strict "No Girls Allowed" policy in his room, and now he is a shaggy-haired tween who could—heaven forbid—father a child of his own before I reach my own verdict as I inch toward the shady side of my thirties.

❖ ❖ ❖

Once, drunk while my father was dying, my mother slammed past me on the stairs. I was five minutes late to feed the horse. "Your father and I worry about something happening to us when we can't depend on you," she sputtered over her shoulder. When I asked my father if he worried about my dependability, he denied it, but then isn't that what most parents would do, especially one who didn't feel much like fighting on his death bed? Then there is the alcoholism, genetic, which, like a natural disaster or act of god, seems to have happened to our family while I was away at college, and from which there has been no rebuilding twenty years since.

❖ ❖ ❖

Maybe it is because I'm concerned about this suggested lack of reliability that I worry so much. My friends with children did not appear to fret over the future with anything like the devotion I marshaled. My contemporaries forged ahead, populating the planet, baby names and birth orders growing fuzzier until each new name served only as shorthand for another gift unsent. Could my worry be an attempt to outwit my own sorry inclinations? My in-laws used to tease me that I would be a terrible worrywart of a parent. Even my golden retriever wore a life jacket around bodies of water vaster than a bathtub's.

But then there's the worry that isn't about me and my ego. It's the clichéd worry of whether it's fair to bring a baby in to the world. Cliché or not, it's a legitimate concern. These are conversations it's best not to discuss among your friends with kids. They've thrown their lot in with the living and there's no looking back now. I admire them, really, their optimism in the face of one miserable certainty: people are ruined in many indescribable ways and intent on harming, sometimes brutally so, other things. I do not excuse myself from this human foible.

I wish I didn't see the world in these terms, but no amount of religion—or yoga or poetry or scenic views of granite cliffs that plummet into the Pacific—has been sufficient to shift my outlook. I certainly don't think there's anything admirable about it, my tendency to look at life like an ingrate refusing the world's extravagant gift, but the fact remains that even if I discount human cruelty and stupidity, the only ending any life is writing is death.

To wit: my golden retriever has been dead four years now, and our adored Adam, who navigated that precarious move into our first place, has been gone for nearly seven. These are the horrible things that happen when you're trying to live your life and love the people around you. Adam and his curly-haired wife had two daughters, both as beautiful and brilliant as their parents, and the last time I saw them they were sitting side by side on a plank that secured the edge of their father's grave.

❖ ❖ ❖

When I consider having a baby it's because I'm worried I'll want one some day, but the threat of regret still hasn't been enough to convince me to pull the trigger.

"So this is the year of getting pregnant!" my latest doctor decreed a year ago when I asked about getting pregnant at my age. I've been a cheerleader and a teacher and know what it is to want something for another person more than she wants it herself.

❖ ❖ ❖

Not long ago my husband and I had a pregnancy scare when a condom tore, and the fact is

it was a scare and not some nascent hope that sneaked up on us when we weren't looking. In that moment and realization I turned out to be who I always was. Could there be anything less miraculous?

"You probably weren't going to get pregnant anyway," Greg said, trying to reassure me, but somehow, illogically, it was a horrible thing to hear: the finality of his statement. What was the point, after all, of announcing a thing that wouldn't happen?

So many cares taken not to be careless, and now this, I thought. The accuracy of my husband's statement sharpened to knifepoint, an understanding so decisive it amounted to fact. No longer did I feel doubt's powerful undertow. To have the matter decided in a moment after years of leisurely appraisal was a shock in itself.

I either was or was not pregnant, but we would never know once I took the emergency birth control pills my father-in-law phoned in for me. It was the middle of the night, too late to call anyone other than family, and anyway the revered Patricia Bannon's status as my doctor had been lost to my peripatetic decade as a failed writer and professor. It was a decade in which much had been lost, including my father and friends and my vision of myself as a person with reasonable hopes for a productive future.

On the Midwestern plains, pearl-handled in moonlight, my mother-in-law, awakened by the phone, must have checked the clock and calculated what her son already knew: there would be no grandchildren, a hope they'd banked on. Children promised a future recognizable from here. How many cocktail hours had they spoken of it in their living room glittering with crystal?

I leaned against the shower door while Greg stood on the other side of the glass. This man I'd married, so boyish he had to be reminded to brush his hair, wanted to be of use, but all he could do was watch and hold my towel. Now he was off to the all-night pharmacy. His manners even then kind to a fault: "Can I get you anything else?"

After he left, I lay on the bed, damp from the shower, and counted the blades on the overhead fan until I was numb with numbers. Too late I saw that what one added could be divided endlessly until all that remained were parts of the whole. I'd spent my adult life waiting to become someone else, someone who felt different about motherhood and babies, but the decades of my adulthood hadn't transformed me into a new person. Sadly, they only made me more cautious. All the years' designs dissipated. No more the chatter of what I now knew had always been a fiction: children long ago dreamed into being and already named—that invention a marriage hinges on, for the idea of children can float for years in a couple's imagination neither happening nor decisively not happening.

It was my body again. For a time my husband and I had shared it; that was all. I turned the fact first this way then that in my head. How to explain once wanting to be married with children and now not, one decision erasing the prudence of the other? No prescribed rules governed my decision to marry, only expectations I followed precisely as dance steps with the finale always the same: a husband reeling me in for the big dip.

The destination had been clear: a yellow doorframe of light I walked toward, never asking myself whether I wanted to live inside in that house. To choose to be on the outside looking in—who could be that brave? And who was to say I still didn't have time to change into the person I planned to be, someone more like the young woman stoic about her fate on the elevator, my go-getter friends, or my mother before she lost her way?

Anyway, here *he* was, my husband, more generous than I would ever be, returned in his pajamas and overcoat, his hand emerging from the rustle of a plastic bag to offer me the only power of choice he had to give. He'd made that embarrassing phone call and gone out into the night to insure my freedom. From what, I still wasn't willing to say.

❖   ❖   ❖

# The Pope's Chair

The man who brings the new cherry wood tables to our door
says that in a few days he is delivering a chair to the Pope.
Today, these end tables.
Soon, a pontiff's humble, but emblemed seat.
In the bedroom doorway, he is all nodding patience
when we exclaim that one table is higher than the other.
He withdraws to the hall
and, while we measure and re-measure each dimension,
he waits, carefully folding the blankets in which the tables came.
And when we confess that it was all an optical illusion,
he comforts us: "I saw what you saw."
He is delivering a chair to the Pope
and the peace that comes to him with knowing that,
shines down then on us.
It is the way small miracles happen—
the cup by the dentist's tiny sink
that refills just when you need it;
the bus that takes a detour
bringing you much closer to where you want to go;
the child in the stroller, who,
on a day when a sad thought clouds your mind
so you don't even see her at first,
smiles at you with her whole heart
as if she has been waiting for you.

# Viewing Service

From the Philippines, my cousin FaceTimes me, shows me

the coffin in Tito's bedroom. I stare at my phone
trying to say anything, but nothing follows. All I can think of

is that I don't remember the Bisaya word for head,
          for body. After a minute, the FaceTime video moves
into the dining room. My parents

appear on the screen and grin, as if ready for a selfie—*Hi, Yan,*
they greet me from oceans away. My mother's eyes
          carry sacks beneath them, souvenirs from jet lag

and weeping. Flies hover behind them over a plate
of sliced mangos.

And I think: What is the Bisaya word for fly, for fly home
          now? I notice my parents are glancing
at the corner of the screen, where a small box contains

          their image. Dad runs fingers
through his hair. Mom straightens her blouse. They were
once children on this island, nibbling

on banana-leaf rice, their shoulders rubbing
against other shoulders on the Jeepney. Now, they only fly

home for the funerals. I take a screenshot of them. I try

to remember the Bisaya word for remember. After we hang up,
I type up a message in English. I won't press send. I will
think about Tito. His rice-white teeth, his hairless arms.

How he told me stories about ogres and white ladies,

how, on the microphone, he'd sing: *talk in everlasting
words and dedicate them all to me,*

how, at the airport the last time I saw him, he walked

slowly with bones heavy and burdensome as a church.

*Virginia Konchan*

# Investment Circle

My stance on high-risk portfolios:
if you fear what you desire being
forbade you, why would you
ever ask? No, I'm not in the
camp of being able to survive
denial of the one made for me,
because that's all I want:
Jesus swinging from the
chandelier, wielding a
tantrum of blades.
He knows the score.
He knows that if you keep
scrolling down through the list
of emojis, they just get progressively
more mad, or sad. Getting older is
like that. No way of dodging the bullet
of sentimentality. What else is an archive
but a carefully curated love letter to
past worlds, bound for obsolescence,
gathering dust or mold? I won't lie.
I love a good gift shop, perusing
replicas of the actual paintings
on ties, postcards, and mugs.
*Quelle heure est-il?* Good question.
Why don't you tell me? Oh, wait,
you can't. You're chained to finitude,
but the way you move your body is gold.
It will only be once, and it fits mine like
tongue-and-groove flooring, like love.

Stephen Brook. *Food to Go.* 2017. Acrylic on canvas. 39 x 39 inches. Courtesy of ARTicles Art Gallery.

# Girl, Freckles

Girl, freckles, bruises, presses her knees together and tries not to let her jeans touch the gummy stain on the lip of the plastic seat as she traces the cool metal logo on the zipper pull of her suitcase and perches her forehead against the bus window, a heart-shaped patch of fog extending and receding under her nose, the glossy lenses of her sunglasses failing to cover the bruises blooming across her cheeks that an older woman tries not to stare at as she drops her quarters through the stainless steel maw of the farebox and shuffles down the aisle, her heartbeat accelerating like a bouncing ping pong ball, her thoughts piling up on one another like overeager baby animals—*This is new, this is different, I knew today felt special, maybe could*—until the girl shifts her suitcase from her lap onto the aisle seat and coughs and looks at her hands.

❖ ❖ ❖

Girl, freckles, messes with the radio in her car and the airbag explodes in her face and all in all she's fine but not so much the man lying in the street leaking blood from his ears. Girl, freckles, goes out to buy Hawaiian rolls and boxed ham the way her boyfriend likes it (thickly sliced, flavored with smoke) and drives into a man at a speed that separates his left femur from his tibia and cracks five of his ribs and his cellphone and his skull, though all she sees is a substance that resembles in color and viscosity but couldn't possibly be blood, she wasn't capable of that, he must have been carrying some sort of juice or syrup, so many fruits are red these days, she tells herself as she accelerates away, back over the bridge and onto and off of the turnpike and down narrower and greener roads until she's standing on the banks of the old abandoned pond, license plates in one hand, wad of bloody napkins still in the other, watching the water settle and wondering what else made the car hers, wondering if the pond is still abandoned or if it ever had been at all. Girl, freckles, bruis-es, deploys her suitcase and pretends to cough to keep an old woman with an old friendly face from sitting down next to her and asking questions like she knows she will, that face of hers all old and friendly and witnessing and alive.

❖ ❖ ❖

*What a unique crime, staring*, the woman thinks, her face warming, sweat beginning to tickle down her sides—*you exist in one of two discrete states, caught or not caught, living free or dead, no moment where it could go either way, no chance of escape, certainly no trial of one's peers, so who's the real victim here*, she tells herself, tells herself the girl is no better than the rest of them, rude and self-centered and commandeering a seat certain people might consider a treasure after a day slash week slash lifetime of, say, standing in the crosshairs of tenth-graders and squeaking out unit circles and trig identities on a whiteboard, and has just rolled onto the balls of her feet to relieve the pain in her heels in a way she hopes doesn't look fake but also isn't too subtle to notice when the bus succeeds in punching its way back into traffic and she goes flying forward, just catches a handrail in time to avoid the lap of the man in gray sweatpants tweezing dried plant matter out of an Altoids tin onto translucent paper and grinning and saying things like, "I had a misplaced youth," to the lady across the aisle and shouting things like, "Fuck you!" at the bus driver, to which the woman says nothing because she doesn't hear, is too busy clutching the handrail and trying to blank her senses, *La la la la la la la, la la la la la, how embarrassing*, she thinks, scooting one foot then the next down the aisle, *two unfortunate events in one day, and right in a row, maybe I should cut my losses and get off now and walk the rest of the way home, if only my feet could handle that, ha-ha, handle, and we're talking about feet, no, that's a bad one, don't say that out loud, just walk to the back and stand, back equals farthest from doors equals warmest, and sitting is killing us anyway,*

*sitting is a drug, sitting should have its own aware-
ness group, Women Against Sitting People, Women
Against Sitting Humans, People Against Sitting
Suicide, no, definitely not that, don't even think that
one out loud, just walk to the back and stand and
get off and see if there's mail and try to ignore the
empty walls and remind self to go to Target tomorrow to buy something nice, something artsy, something with copper maybe, or wool, tomorrow will be
different, remind self to cancel Amazon Prime, remind self to remind self, remind self self has been reminded—or,* she thinks, giving in to the thought
zipping around her head like the electron of a
hydrogen atom—*or, could stop in the aisle, next to
the girl, could say, Hello, or, Hi there, say, Is anyone
sitting there, say, I might just be a stranger to you,
but there's something I would like you to know.*

❖ ❖ ❖

Girl, freckles, high school, wears two bras
sometimes and thinks about kissing a girl once,
at homecoming her junior year, to try to make
the blonde soccer girls in her French II class
uncomfortable, but mostly goes out, when
she goes out, with older boys on sports teams,
ones who have learned how to hold her hand
in public and announce she's pretty and suggest night swimming at the pond or studying
at her mom's house, where she finds herself
spending a lot of time vis-à-vis her bedroom
window staring out across the dark cul-de-sac
at the Christmas lights duct taped to the gutter of the house behind the basketball hoop
into which a University of Kentucky Wildcats
Men's Basketball basketball had so often been
lobbed over her head by her neighbor who,
before growing nine inches and sitting down
with coach to talk seriously about his future
in sports, would spend Saturdays drawing
chalk mazes and looking for tennis balls behind the rec center and playing paper football
with sugar packets at the IHOP with her, but
who grows nine inches and learns to dunk and
flies away to college to try to dunk on other tall
boys and drink when he wins and drink when
he loses. Girl, freckles, bruising, speeds away
from the man bleeding expensive post-doctoral
Ivy League blood onto the smooth white reflec-
torized paint of the crosswalk, "Just tragic, the
loss of such intellect, of such a mentor, a husband, a father, a friend," they whisper at his
service, all but the young woman wearing blue
and standing at the back of the hall who says,

"Good riddance." Girl, freckles, bruises, emp-
ties her checking account at three ATMs and
takes the 28 to the SL1 to the airport and flies
to Alaska, where she walks along the shoulder
of Old Nenana Highway and practices smiling at the birch trees as she climbs the steps to
the old wooden farmhouse and knocks on the
door and informs her old college friends how
right they were to settle down, how ready she
is to get away from that whole city thing, how
important those good old days in college are to
her and surely still are to them, though none of
them really remember that much that well anymore. Girl, freckles, leaves after two weeks of
the dirt and the wind and the pigs and the styrofoam seat of the outhouse always being satu-
rated with the urine of the school children visiting the (real live!) organic farm, in the night
with seven jars of preserves and all the bread
and an old .303 Enfield she wraps in a Gortex
coat and clutches to her chest as she hitchhikes
south to a town on the coast where she moves
into a basement she can afford to rent because
she agrees to pay in cash and because, Alaska,
where she grows tempered and dry and learns
to eat fish and aims the rifle at the face of a bear
that noses open her tiny window one night but
realizes just before she pulls the trigger she forgot to steal any bullets.

❖ ❖ ❖

*What you should know,* the woman thinks,
tightening her grip on the railing as the bus
whips through a turn, *is that while I might just
be a stranger, I'm here for you, woman to woman,
no matter what, you don't even have to move your
suitcase, I can stand, my feet are fine, you don't
even have to look at me, we can just talk out loud in
proximity to one another, sports or math or birds or
weather or work or shit, as in talk shit, as in about
the man who's responsible for those bruises, don't
ask how I knew, there's not time for that and this is
about you anyway, you poor integral of a thing, let
me guess—you were struggling, he was not, he had
family money, a family job, director of something or
other in whatever industry, waste management, say,
and you always thought he was kind of full of it but
then again he could quote the volume of a garbage
truck just by looking at it, just by hearing the sound
its muffler made as it idled at a stoplight, not that
you had any way of checking if he was right or not,
anyway, he was the one who suggested moving into
the city proper because he could afford it, but you,*

*you had to tutor after work and on weekends just to pay your half of the rent, just to pay for your half (and wasn't it more) of the groceries you had to shell out for at Whole Foods (because where else could you walk or even dream of parking), no wonder when you got home you just wanted to crash on the couch and eat bagels and watch* The Daily Show *and laugh at whatever Jon Stewart was saying about* Fox News, *but this man of yours who called you his, he didn't fail to notice you never laughed like that at anything he said, and he sat there picking the varnish off the wicker chair and clenching his teeth and feeding that awful thing growing in his brain until some random Tuesday in March when you got up to go to bed and happened to see the time on the DVD player behind his head and cursed and he jumped up and raised his hand and you threw up yours and closed your eyes and waited, but he just stood and stared over your head and left you there blinking tears and trying not to think about the dream you'd once had where a stranger had walked up to you and pointed a gun at your face and you'd thrown up your hands in exactly the same way, as if your fragile bird bones could ever endure a force like that.*

❖ ❖ ❖

Girl, freckles, bruises, tosses her suitcase onto the aisle seat to deflect a presence she deems risky in her life and flies to Alaska and watches her freckles fade in the reflection of her cracked phone screen. Girl, freckles, hits a man with her car and runs because there are too many things she can't do as a manslaughterer, like applying to grad school or growing raspberries or lying in the grass watching airplanes and geese, which she loves, and is definitely going to start doing soon, once a week at least, Fridays or Thursdays or the warmest day of the week, or the coolest depending on the season, maybe she'll take up cycling or rock climbing or both, time may as well be infinite, this whole thing is a blessing, really, she tells herself as the airplane quivers and she tightens her grip on the armrest, clouds erasing the topography of British Columbia below in wispy, unforgiving strokes—a reminder that, the minute this all blows over, she has a life to start living. Girl, freckles, calls down to her boyfriend in the basement that she's going to the grocery store and rolls her eyes when she hears him curse, though not at her, she doesn't think, yeah, there's the thump, he'd just missed a shot and smacked the fat rubber end of the pool cue against the floor and it had bounced and torpedoed a new blue pockmark into the ceiling, which she laughs about a little as she walks down the stairs, not her security deposit on the line, but stops on the bottom step when he slaps the cue ball onto the table, stands there and watches him line it up with the green ball and splay his fingers and hook his thumb and glide the cue back and forth over his knuckle, stopping its tip the same miniscule distance shy of the glassy surface of the cue ball each time in such a delicate display of attention she finds herself imagining what it would be like to be that ball at that moment—he'd looked up when she'd walked in, had already been watching the stairs, had tossed the cue aside and opened his arms all where-have-you-been-all-my-life before sweeping the balls (irreversibly!) aside and picking her up and setting her down on the table and kissing her lips and neck and pushing her gently back, which she would allow until she was almost horizontal before flexing the muscles in her core and sitting up and looking him in the eye and finally getting to be the one to say, No, I think I'm going to do my own thing right now, I'm just going to go to the store like I said I was, but hey, you want anything, to which he would blink and blush and stutter something about Hawaiian rolls and boxed ham—until the crack of resin striking resin drags her back to the world and the words "no" and "myself" and "later" set her running back up the stairs and through the kitchen and out the door. Girl, freckles, dabs at the corners of her eyes with her thumb as she inches her car out of its spot and through the exhaust-soaked slush and turns the radio to FM 102.9 Spanish or South American or Latin music, she doesn't actually know the difference, the discerning nuances, simply savors how far away the music feels, how the order and duration of the notes are the product of a destination to which she lacks coordinates or even a continent of origin but wants to go and dance barefoot over tiles made from a material mined from the earth and hardened with fire as she sips something colorful from a glass she holds out while she dances, away from her body, far away, so far away from this road and her steering wheel and the Dunkin' Donuts and the lady in the next car driving with her knees as she types with both thumbs on her phone. Girl, freckles, runs up the basement stairs and out the front door and down the sidewalk and almost makes it to her car before she hits ice and crashes into an aluminum streetlight pole. Girl, freckles, bruising, holds a slab of Starbucks napkins under her nose and smacks the radio power button and tries to turn up the volume to fifty like she used to in her mother's minivan on her way to her high school in the suburbs where they paid to sandblast graffiti from the bathroom stalls and it never smelled like stink bombs or soggy bread as she sat through French II for the second time or stood in the auditorium lobby staring at a flier for girls' soccer tryouts, but hits a pothole and turns the volume up to fifty-two, fifty-one, forty-nine, fifty-one, forty-nine, forty-nine, forty-nine, can't hold her hand still enough, no, this is not her fault, not this time, the manufacturer should have put groves on their knobs to increase traction or included fewer volume levels as to render each one less sensitive, flies forward in her seat and has killed a man. Girl, freckle, lies pirouetting with consciousness on her bed after nosediving into the northern Pacific and catching a life ring and hanging on for dear life as her crewmates haul her up and carry her inside and lean their cold faces over hers and ask her not to die, lies there sucking in their humid breath and the metallic air and listens, not dead, not yet, simply too cold to ask for or care about another blanket.

❖ ❖ ❖

*So, no, of course I don't blame you for being afraid to sit next to another human being, you of all people know what humans are capable of, and besides, sitting leads to talking, and talking leads to honesty, and honesty leads to suffering, ha-ha, just kidding, just a little film joke to lighten the mood, but then again, is it all that untrue, is not honesty kind of what got you into this mess in the first place, you poor hundred and eighty degree angle of a thing, let me guess, you convinced yourself it was time, that he was the one you were going to let in, and on some random evening, sitting under a tree on the esplanade tearing dandelion leaves into tiny squares and secretly hoping he couldn't hear anything over rush hour traffic and was just nodding to be polite, you told him everything, about your dad, your learning disability, your trouble with food—how it started with the websites and the mirror in your room, where you learned to hide your meals and how much water you had to drink before going to the doctor, the trip to the hospital and the program, the meetings, the writing down of everything you ate and the*

*progress you made, the setbacks, the standing on the bank of the river with your scale in your hand and how you held it and held it and held it and threw it in and watched it float and wished it would sink, how you drove to Target and found the bath section and stood at the end of the aisle fingering shower curtains and soap dispensers and how you threw the shredded pages of coupon catalogs out your window as you drove home, bagless and shouting about snow and singing Jingle Bells—and he just smiled and kissed your head and told you you were beautiful and must have known then, somewhere in the dark folds of his brain that protected his evil things from the light, he could keep you down as low as he needed you to be.*

❖ ❖ ❖

Girl, freckles (kind of), spends her last twenty dollar bill on tampons and vitamin D capsules and pads up on the sixth of the month to the kitchen where the husband of the couple who owns her basement is making coffee and stands in the doorway studying the holes in her socks and says in a tiny voice, "I need a little longer this month," hears him set down his cup and spoon and flinches when she feels his hand on her shoulder, her hip, her lower back, contracts her limbs and opens her mouth when he tries to kiss her and he bites her bottom lip and takes her hand and leads her into the hallway and halfway up the stairs before she yanks her hand away and runs back down to the basement and curls up behind the hot water heater and waits to hear the whine of the wooden steps under his weight, but they're quiet, quiet, quiet, so quiet she's not surprised when she runs into him in town a week later and he stares right through her, not surprised when the first of the month comes and goes again without notice, and so she stays in her basement, though even with a window large enough to accommodate an alarming percentage of a bear's head it feels more like a cave sometimes, not that she's ever lived in a cave or seen a cave in person, though she did read about one once, in a book about men and women in yellow plastic suits cutting open dead monkeys in a room not that far from the nation's capital in an attempt to identify a killer virus that may or may not have spread from a man who'd inhaled particles of dung when he'd hiked into a cave to photograph elephants, but even a baby elephant would have trouble getting much more than its trunk through her window, so she thinks she's safe. Girl, freckles (ish), steals a pair of skis off a porch and learns to ride them down from her cave (sans elephant) to the lightning-struck aspen where she buries them in the snow and walks the rest of the way to town because the skis are bright orange and obviously stolen, obviously belong to the boy she sees smoking (sans skis) near the docks in a neon green and yellow striped Volcom jacket, and she wonders how he affords cigarettes, and she wonders if there's a way to ski uphill, too, but is afraid to ask anyone, What a fool, they would say, And hey, where did you get such nice skis? Girl, freckle (barely, the one on her eyelid that's probably just a mole), watches men hoisting sacks of dead marine life onto the docks and follows the one she hopes makes the decisions to a restaurant and tries not to shake as she forces a smile and a nod and a wink and talks, touches, begs until the man removes her hand from his knee and says, "Okay," and sends her the paperwork and teaches her how to run the winch and boom and play bridge and make a bed, which she lies on sometimes in what she calls the morning and stares at the ceiling and wonders, despite herself, about the man in the crosswalk on River Street, whether he'd recovered fully or if she'd doomed him to a limp or a wheelchair or scars, though scars wouldn't be the worst, some people like scars, scars can be sexy, probably, she tells herself, shakes her head and swallows coffee and tries to shut off what she calls a brain as she reaches over the gunwale for the dredge, against which she clocks her skull on her way into the ocean before ending up back on her bed, life ring still clamped between her arms, temple still dribbling blood, still too cold to speak or even shiver, her crewmates's words and the thrumming engine and the rattle of steel distilling into a single saccharine tone, so simple and warm and forgiving and everything she needs from the world, *Beautiful*, she thinks, *the way things happen like this*, and as the faces and walls and ceiling dissolve to gray she closes her eyes and floats in her sheets and listens to her tone, just lies there and listens, listens, listens until it begins to tremble, growing louder at first and then softer, then louder and louder and louder until the door crashes open and too many people come rushing in, shine lights in her face and count to three and lift her up and carry her out, and she tries to sit up but two gloved hands hold her head in place and she tries to raise her arms to free her head but her left wrist is handcuffed to the stretcher and she closes her eyes and tries to die as they slide her into the back of the ambulance but they slam the doors and crank the heat.

❖ ❖ ❖

*But just listen to me, going on while here you are in the middle of a getaway, here we both are, really, I admit there are some things I haven't told you, but there's no time for that now, this is about you, and who am I to slow you down for even a second, you poor brave asymptote of a thing, no, I'll just walk by, stand in the back where it's warmest, get off and see about the mail and practice drawing circles on junk mail and pretend I never saw you behind those sunglasses at all, but allow me one thing, one little thing the world may never acknowledge but we can carry together, can remember when we think we're alone,* and as she walks by she says, without turning her head, her voice just barely louder than the acoustics of the city, "You're brave for doing this," and the girl, freckles, bruises, stares.

❖ ❖ ❖

# A Portfolio of Poems from *After Earth*

*Winner of the Tampa Review Prize for Poetry*

Michael Lavers received the 2018 Tampa Review Prize for Poetry for *After Earth,* which is forthcoming in 2019 from the University of Tampa Press. Pre-publication comments are glowing. Sidney Wade writes, "*After Earth* is engrossing, delicious, fulfilling, delightful, learned, surprising, riveting, powerfully broad, movingly deep, and beautiful." Lance Larsen praises its creation of "lyrical worlds both wild and domestic, with one foot in the tradition reaching back through the Romantics to the Ancients, and the other in the hurly-burly of right now." Jacqueline Osherow says, "These beautiful meditations, by turns celebratory, funny, mournful and elegiac, make an exquisite, lyric truce with the human predicament." We are pleased to include a selection of poems as a small preview of *After Earth.*

# Cosmography

In one, a cesspool stirred to lamentation.
In one, a vacant palace and a throne
deposed by air that would step down
if it could be mere breath again. In one,
all hours coalesce, like insects hatching
on a standing pond, while in another,
they make a single-file break for it
over the barbed-wired hills. No stars in one,
or else no moon, or else no sun, or else
two suns, stabbing their spurs into the earth.
Some just like ours, except for wind, and rain,
and some where starlight drips like resin
from cracked wood, and gravity relaxes
its long tenure on the leaves, and someone
makes a greenish fire for us from the firs.
The one where silver moths will cover you
like cloth until your shivering has stopped,
then fly, blushing, away. The ones where
I can find you, and the ones where I run
through the dunes, calling your name, hearing
the darkness take it, and the boiling sea.
One with a fountain. One with a cloud.

*Michael Lavers*

# Eclogue Hidden in the Trunk of a Tree

We are heading to the border on foot
with our son who is very ill, pausing only
to write this note to you and hide it here
in this dark wood, the spot agreed upon,
uncertain if you will receive it. Guards
patrol the mountains, and always now
there is the smell of smoke, and winds rise up
bringing the black leaves off the trees in sheets,
a sound like the tearing of paper. Last night
the bits of quartz that caught the moonlight
blinked this warning to me as we walked:
*Turn back. They're waiting for you up ahead.*
*The world might seem to hover on the cusp*
*of clarity, it might appear that new*
*transmissions will start creeping through the chaos*
*any day, a harmony that will reveal things,*
*transcendent things. But no: the universe*
*has long outlived its usefulness. This is the end.*
I pass this message on to you, and then
must go: the dark gesticulating willows
know where we are hiding, and conspire
in semaphore. The time may come when we
will see each other, but until we do,
beware: the stars, the roads, the swaying weeds,
the white geese bathing in a brackish pond—
all things conceal and are not what they seem.
The clouds may look like clouds, but don't
forget our enemies control the wind. In rain
and spreading shadows they slink through the world.

# The Task

At least once, let us try to approach the center of the real problems.

I mean the real ones.

Such as why, when you did not ask to be made, we insisted.

As if you will never taste evil, dear child, and know only the grass, the way it sags just before cutting, thick and heavy with dew.

As if that much sufficed.

No—we walk on the roof of Hell, the boards are brittle and thin.

Not only thin, but missing in patches. Suffering flickers, unceasingly there.

You will be tempted to seek your revenge on the world, or demand consolation, or believe that it's all a mistake—that you belong somewhere else:

a city of green leaves, light wind, stars watching us greedily. A stable horizon. All things known.

But rejoice: we are here. So we stand. We go into it, a place which eludes description: good days, bad days, days drifting like smoke through our ravenous arms.

I hold you, but only as much as the sea holds the hull of a ship: always lapping against it, and never discerning much more than an outline, a bright mass with somewhere much farther to go.

Some sea will lie always between us.

Rain falls, and I can hardly believe it.

I promise you, this is not poetry.

A luminous wind fills the mountains and valleys, melting the high snow, and stoking the aspen like pillars of fire.

The swaying maples creak and snore. A blithe hawk doodles on air.

We have so little time.

I don't know if you'll find me again at the end, if there is one, or how soon you'll get to lie down.

All I know is your task is immeasurably great. It cannot be accomplished, yet it cannot be avoided:

persist, little heart. Straighten up, shoulders. Move, legs. Go forward. Bear yourself over the ruinous world.

*Michael Lavers*

# The New Arrivals

There was a crowd there, waiting. Everybody
stared, the way you do your first day
in a strange place. And the sun was up now,
and the last stray stars of Capricorn had fled.
One of the new arrivals looked at us and said:
"Please tell us, if you know, which of these paths
leads to the mountain." And my guide responded,
"you think we belong here, that we know
this place. We don't. We're strangers too.
We also just arrived, just barely before you,
but by another way, a way so steep and rough
that this new climb will feel like rest."
But they'd already paled: they had noticed
I was breathing, that I had a body, that I lived.
Like when a messenger, holding an olive branch,
brings news some far-flung town has longed for,
and gets sighted from the gate, and thronged,
that's how they crowded me, as if forgetting
they were dead already, and that now the only thing
they had to do was go, and become beautiful.


*Purgatorio*, Canto II, lines 52-75

Michael Lavers

# The Suicide Angels

Like poppies bending down
to clear their heads of rain—

too swayed by emptiness
to rise again—

some lay, heavy
with reasons, on our lawns,

some washed up on our shores
like sad sea cows.

Maybe they'd traced perfection
to its edge

and jumped, hoping
to trade

the Church of the Everlasting
for the Church of the Fleeting

and Plain.
In time, and as if stoned

on gravity, they rose,
smelling like burnt perfume,

all bright like soil after rain,
all darkly bruised.

Assure us, we said, others
remained happy

to mourn you;
that those you left do not miss

temporal form,
or that perfection too

has its material.
Tell us such bliss, for most,

is bearable,
that we can hoist the burden

of a happiness
without variety or end.

But they had not come back
to comfort us.

They simply moaned
like struck bells

when we shook them,
and then walked away, leaving

their greasy prints like thieves
on everything—the skylights

and the pears, the mirrors
and the decorative spoons.

Robert Ross. *Pause*. 2017. Oil on canvas. 42 x 48 inches. Courtesy of ARTicles Art Gallery.

# The Metairie Loop

She was knee-deep in CVS Pharmacy's trash because she and Tim had fought, and after they'd fought she'd needed a distraction. Of course, Lora's Dumpster habit was one of the reasons they'd argued, which made it perhaps less than ideal when she looked him straight in the face and lied about her evening plans, but there she was, sorting through receipt paper and plastic wrap, the emotional echoes of Tim's voice bouncing around the sticky six-foot top-loader.

She'd driven all the way to Metairie, where Tim lived, but not to apologize. As far as she saw it, she had nothing to apologize for. Tim lived alone, but he never invited her over anymore because Metairie had great Dumpsters, while where she lived with her roommate in the Lower Nine had nothing except a Rally's and a couple dollar stores. As if a lack of invitations could dissuade her from the hunt.

The pharmacy trash was a bust. She didn't need her headlamp to know that. The light hung around her neck, its single eye pointed unseeing toward her sweating cleavage. Only April and the New Orleans humidity was already starting to get to her. She tore into one last bag near the bottom, picturing a crushed package of individually wrapped peppermints, bloomed-chocolate candy bars, maybe a couple tubes of an unwanted color of lipstick. What she got instead was a thick, sugary liquid that coated her hands and oozed onto the refuse below. The smell of spoiled milk and vanilla filled the container. Melted ice cream. She tried not to let her gag make a noise. Just on the other side of the Dumpster's discrete privacy fence, unknowing, late-night customers slid past. Silently she located a bag of bathroom trash and wiped her hands on the used paper towels, taking care to avoid a rolled-up sanitary napkin.

Lora had a system. A loop of stores she used to check on her way back to the Lower 9 from an evening at Tim's. Before Tim, she'd never spent much time in Jefferson Parish. It reminded her too much of the sort of things she'd moved to New Orleans to escape: vinyl siding and monoculture lawns, wide parking lots in front of box stores. "What's wrong with vinyl siding and monoculture lawns?" Tim had once demanded during a different fight, to which Lora shouted back, "The northernmost Caribbean city!"

Before she'd started with the Dumpsters, Lora had eaten the same food her roommate Tansy did: organic, South American super grains, almond milk, home-cultured kombucha. She and Tansy worked for nonprofits, which gave them the do-gooder double whammy that came from working for the community and living off a penny salary. Healthy Hearts, the community kitchen where Lora worked, paid her well enough plus a free meal when she was training new volunteers. She and Tansy grew tomatoes in pots on the front porch. They composted. Tansy thought her Dumpster diving was crazy too.

"I can't even imagine all of the nitrates you're putting in your body," she had said shortly after Lora's first time on the loop. Lora had been rinsing garbage water off of five shrink-wrapped pre-cooked hams. "Your salt and sugar consumption. You know you'll have cancer before you hit fifty." When Lora didn't stop, she put it more succinctly. "You're getting fat."

"Waste not, want not," Lora had said.

The box of baby wipes she kept in her car removed most of the spoiled ice cream from her hands, but she could still feel some of it deep in the crooks of her fingers. In her pocket her phone buzzed. She didn't answer it. Only one person texted her this time of night. She could see the turn-off to his apartment from where she sat in the pharmacy lot. He'd be long home by now.

The seeds of the argument had been sewn earlier that day at Healthy Hearts while Lora trained four new volunteers. She was always training someone new. They came from all across the county to spend a few weeks or months working at the kitchen to serve a rotating troop of men and a few families from the neighborhood. Healthy Hearts had their regulars, but some men she saw once or twice and then never again. Eventually their features blended into one pan-human face. The line of patrons and their trays shuffled by. At a pause, she met one stooped man's eyes.

"How you doing?" he asked.

"How's it going?" she replied with a smile.

He had a tangle of an ashen beard and stretched-out skin that had seen too much sun. Long ago someone or something had broken his nose, and it had reset a little crooked. He breathed through his mouth. She offered him a choice of vegetarian or meat lasagna.

"Where you from?" he asked. He must have assumed she was one of their visiting volunteers. She told him she lived in Holy Cross, right up by the levee. He tilted his head. "But where're you *from*?"

Her smile became that stretchy plastic. "Where are *you* from?" she asked.

He crunched his shoulders until he stood a little taller. "Went to Abramson High."

That meant nothing to her. All the schools had gone charter and been renamed after the storm. The man waited, eyebrows raised, one hip relaxed against the buffet table.

"I grew up in Michigan," she admitted, which produced a satisfied smile.

"Yeah. You didn't look like you were from here."

She wanted to know what he meant by that, wanted to know exactly how, after these five years, she didn't look like she belonged, but the man had his eggplant lasagna and was already moving down the line.

Later, when she recounted the story to Tansy, her roommate said, "I get that question all the time. Mostly white people wanting to know if I'm Chinese or whatever."

"Are you Chinese?" Lora asked.

Tansy smacked her upside the head.

But the encounter with the man still bothered Lora. She inspected her reflection in the CVS parking lot. In her hole-infested diving t-shirt she raised her shoulders and lowered them and raised them again. She wiggled her toes in her grungy diving sneakers. She considered the line of her eye makeup, her eyebrow piercing, trying to see what the man had seen. All she could see was Lora.

She'd first come to New Orleans in 2010 to visit Tansy, who'd been placed in one of the latest charter schools as her Teach For America assignment. "I have serious problems with this system," Tansy had told Lora as they toured the classrooms, the tile floors so new they were still off-gassing. Lora didn't know if Tansy's problem was with private charters or the TFA system, but they had graduated college into the employment freeze left in the recession's wake. Lora was an unpaid intern at a nonprofit that recycled wheelchairs in northern Michigan.

It was a warm February day as they walked home from the school through a neighborhood of brightly colored duplexes that, to Lora, looked fit for ocean-side royalty. Pink wooden shutters, ornate finials, upper-floor porches. Stray cats ran out from under parked cars. Mardi Gras beads decorated the wrought iron fences and nearby trees.

"I feel healthier just taking in this brightness," Lora said.

"Those beads are super toxic," Tansy replied, then pointed. "Watch out. The sidewalk gets bad here."

Lora returned to New Orleans again after the vice of Louisiana's summer heat had relaxed. Then it was a third trip. Then a fourth. Tansy had finished her volunteer corps tour of duty and was working part-time as a film crew gopher when Lora asked if she could stay a little longer than her previous visits.

"How much longer?" When Lora shrugged, Tansy frowned. "That's how people get stuck. Look at me. They don't call it the Big Easy for nothing. She just opens up her legs and takes us all in."

"I'm not sure I'm okay with that analogy," Lora said.

Of course it wasn't a big easy. It was the opposite of easy. The cost of living was easy. Finding a good band on Frenchmen was easy. She had her pick of eccentric jobs unheard of in northern Michigan. Carnival float fabricator or urban gardener or guide for a haunted French Quarter tour. The hard part was the government, the condition of the streets, the bicycle accidents, the poverty, the black-mold-trauma in every building. She was a white, privately educated, post-Katrina transplant. The hard part was living in this body when she wanted so desperately to finally belong somewhere.

Sometimes it was easier to just disappear inside a front-loading Dumpster and slide the door closed.

Tim called her Dumpster-diving disgusting and dehumanizing. He had tried all sorts of tactics to get her to stop. First he offered her a loan. When she turned that down he said, "What if we go grocery shopping and you pick out whatever you need. My treat." Like she was a college student again and he was her father.

After that he developed subtler tactics. At bars he paid her tab when she was in the bathroom. When she demanded the bartenders refund his card, put the charges on hers, they told her their machine couldn't do refunds.

"Cash then!" she yelled and waved her Visa like a pistol.

She never asked how much Tim got paid for his job in the CBD, because it was up in the area where all the numbers were basically the same. Having grown up on his mother's EBT card, the appearances of wealth were very important to him. He was the only person she knew who ate more natural foods than her and Tansy, back when she'd worried about those kinds of things.

They'd met at the co-op a year ago while waiting for the dispenser of sprouted almonds to be refilled. He'd been wearing a very fashionable tie. The blazer looked custom tailored. To fill the time, she'd said, "My roommate told me almonds are the least energy efficient food humans can eat. On account of water demands."

"Is that so?"

He grinned as she filled a brown paper bag with five pounds and his lips revealed a metal arc of late-stage braces. She was smitten from the start by the contrasts of fashion and dork.

When he stopped inviting her over, he said it was because Metairie was too far out of her way, plus he liked the ambience of her house in Holy Cross. Next, he wanted to cook her dinner. He said he needed to practice his culinary skills, brought all the ingredients to her house and with it made three times as much food as two people could eat. When she boxed up the leftovers, he refused to take any back with him.

"If you don't eat it, I'm just going to throw it out. I hate leftovers. You can keep the rest of those ingredients too. I already have flour and butter at home."

He'd figured out how much she hated to see things go to waste.

That's what killed her. Food rotting while people in their city went hungry. She saw it every day on the faces of the men at work. It was more than that, though. She thrilled in the repulsion other people felt toward garbage. It felt good to do something that most folks she knew wouldn't dream. Like move to the Lower Ninth Ward. And then there was the puzzle of what to cook with what she found. Like one of those kitchen reality shows. What would this week's food challenge be? Make a dessert without eggs. Make a dessert with forty eggs. Winning didn't mean beating the competition. It meant beating the system.

Tim had a different system he was trying to beat. Childhood left its scars on everyone, even Tansy.

After the pharmacy Dumpster was the discount grocery. Situated midway down a strip mall beside a pizza joint that reliably threw out full pies, the grocery was one of Lora's favorite stops on the loop. Nearly everything came canned or boxed or wrapped in plastic, even the produce. The practice drove Tansy crazy. Lora loved it.

When she cut the motor behind the store, she could hear movement through her open car windows and tensed. She'd rehearsed what to say if someone ever caught her in their trash. She knew, rationally, that anyone who took out the garbage wasn't high enough up on the food chain to care about a white girl sorting through expired Hostess packages. Tim, on the other hand, seemed able to conjure half a dozen horror scenarios out of thin air, each one more irrational than the last: a rabid possum; a bag of HIV-positive needles; a drifter serial killer. She was pretty certain the only thing that might attack her in a Metairie Dumpster would be a bad bout of dysentery. Nonetheless, she got quietly out of her car. Then came the voice.

"Don't shoot. I'm just getting some grub for my chickens."

To her surprise it echoed from the interior of the trash receptacle. A man in a headlamp appeared at the Dumpster's side window. She flinched when, for a moment, the light blinded her, before the man apologized and flipped his lamp downward. The beam cast shadows over his dark, curly hair, brown face, and humidity-fluffed beard. She stood frozen, unsure what to do. She'd never run into another diver on her route before. Under his gaze, she became very aware of her body, her keys clenched in her hand, the distance to her car door.

The face disappeared from the window and returned with a cardboard box brimming with brightly colored packages of food: packs of bacon, a half-crushed loaf of wheat bread, a container of pineapple juice, and a five-pack of bratwurst. Lora'd been craving bratwurst all winter, had hoped that the upcoming Memorial Day might yield something at one of her stops, but German food wasn't especially popular down here in Cajun country. She kicked herself for wasting time on the fruitless pharmacy Dumpster instead of heading straight here. She might have arrived before this man and those brats would have been hers.

"You feed your chickens bacon and sausage?" she asked. She felt like a pirate beaten to his own buried treasure.

The man's hands that dropped the box of finds onto the asphalt were calloused and dirty. And yet, Lora thought he was younger than her, maybe mid-twenties.

"Not chickens. Goats," he said, changing his story with little concern.

She didn't know quite what to say to that either. She didn't want this man here, on her loop, in her trash. She'd come out tonight to escape, to be alone. She forced her voice all cheery and said, "If you need more, someone told me to go over to Kenner. Chalmette's usually picked over."

"Good haul tonight," he said.

"The best area is Slidell, but I don't like to make that drive unless I have to."

"It's a terrible commute," he agreed.

He lowered a second cardboard box, this one full of plastic-wrapped vegetables. In the beam of the nearby loading dock floodlight, she realized to her surprise that she knew him, or thought she knew him, though she wasn't sure from where. Perhaps she had served him roasted vegetables or explained a kohlrabi as he walked down the serving line. "It looks kinda like a Pokémon," one Healthy Hearts patron had told her when she showed him the untrimmed plant, but it had not been this man.

He dropped yet another box of food out the Dumpster window, then a fourth, before pulling himself out too. He kept his eyes on his finds. Lora wondered whether he was wor-ried about her stealing from him or if it was something else dragging his gaze downward. Gesturing vaguely behind him, he said to the asphalt, "All yours."

She stood slack in front of her beat-up sedan, now even less sure of what to do. It felt rude to climb in before he left. More than rude, it would be humiliating. She couldn't stand anyone seeing her so desperate as to scrutinize another person's leftover leftovers. Being seen wanting, begging. Like this man was. She was ashamed now for wishing she'd beaten him to the Dumpster. He probably had a girlfriend, maybe several young, hungry children. Chances were, she'd seen the whole family at the soup kitchen. They had fewer families come through than they had single men, which would explain why this man stuck out to her while so many others faded away.

Insects stippled the beam of the floodlight as the man walked in and out of the wash, carrying his boxes to a dark truck beyond. His green foam flip-flops slapped against his heels with every step. Flip-flops. For climbing into Dumpsters. Lora found herself wondering which public school he had attended. What charter school his kids were bussed to. She'd started to ask Tim where Abramson High used to be, the one the man at Healthy Hearts had gone to, only Tim had gotten upset before she'd had the chance.

Tim knew everything about the Crescent City. He knew the history of the ritzy Lake Vista neighborhood's star-oriented cul-de-sacs and the explosion and ebb of the punk music scene. He knew the economic reasons for why plantations on the Mississippi were so long and narrow, and he could tell her without a beat dropped which neighborhoods in which wards were historically black or historically white. He could tell her what they were before the storm and what they were now. She snapped up every sugary, Domino-encrusted morsel he offered her. She didn't have the badge of birth. She needed his knowledge. With knowledge came belonging.

She loved Tim for other reasons too, of course. Tonight he'd brought her a bottle of her favorite wine. She didn't drink often at home because it was so rare for her to find any on her route. He'd unloaded a full grocery bag of ingredients onto the counter. Rice, spices, something wrapped in brown butcher's paper.

"I'm going to make you boudin," he'd said, his smile now proudly free of the late-stage braces. That smile alone could make her laugh for the rest of her life. "My grandmama told me to share this recipe with no one."

While the rice steamed, she stood at the counter working on a fruit salad. He came up behind her and rested his chin on her shoulder. She wore a spaghetti-strapped camisole. She could feel his breath on her bare skin.

"Hey," he said in that soft voice. It was his version of *I love you*. She said hey back.

"I have this image in my head," he said. He was always telling her about fantasies he had of their future: a house with orchids in the window, the electronic chirp of hummingbirds in the fruit trees. They never argued in his fantasies. "We own a place in the Garden District and Grandmama comes to visit. She's sitting at our kitchen table and you bring her a plate with a single, overstuffed sausage steaming on it. She says, *Lora, this boudin looks like heaven*."

It was rare, him talking about his family, his history. He never told her when he was going to stop by his mom's or how the visit went after he did. She'd only met the woman once, the distance of a wide restaurant table between them. She couldn't remember him ever mentioning grandparents. And what was boudin, but the poor man's sausage, protein augmented with grains when there wasn't enough meat to make a proper bratwurst. He had never eaten boudin in front of her, never relished the New Orleans traditions they promoted in the Quarter. Yet the rice was steaming. The spices had been mixed. Maybe that seemed small or strange, a boring everyday moment void of special energy. Romantic gestures rarely seemed significant, Lora thought, to someone who didn't have the context. A person couldn't observe something from the outside and experience it on the inside at the same time. That's where love was. One hundred percent under her skin. People on the outside simply didn't get it. Just like people who didn't climb into a Dumpster couldn't understand those who did.

Because it wasn't always daydreams about the Garden District. The argument that evening had started when he had opened her fridge and spotted the seafood salad on the top shelf. She'd never even heard of seafood salad before she'd found it behind the Wal-Mart. Imitation mayonnaise. Imitation crabmeat. Tim knew all of her strange finds from when he was a kid. Pickle loaf, ham in a can. She was telling him about the Abramson High man from that afternoon, the one who knew just by looking at her that she was a transplant. Tim touched the plastic container like it was the ghost of his long-vanquished childhood. Then he closed the refrigerator and said in a quiet voice that scared her:

"You can't do this any more."

"What harm am I doing to you?" she wanted to know.

He said, "Do you understand the difference between shopping secondhand for pleasure and shopping secondhand because your mom only has twenty dollars for back-to-school clothes, shoes, notebooks, supplies, and gas to drive you all those places? Do you understand the difference between backpack camping and living in a tent? Who cares if some old man thinks you're an outsider. You *are* an outsider. Coming from somewhere else sounds so easy. I would have shot a man in the back to grow up where you did. Without all this mess."

"That's not funny," she said. She envied his belonging. She didn't like to know the ways he envied hers: a bored teenager reading Mercedes Lackey under her high school desk. Soccer fields and child-safety play equipment and the mall. Pick them up, put them on the moon, and they'd have looked the same. A person might not even notice the lack of oxygen.

"You fly down for one St. Anne's parade, you baptize yourself in glitter, and you think you're one of us?"

"That's not—"

"You weren't here for the storm. None of your friends who work at your little kitchen were here for the storm."

Which she knew had been exactly what the old man waiting for his lasagna had meant, too.

The Dumpster diver loaded up his last box of food and then turned to her, as if waiting for some acknowledgement, but of what she wasn't sure. She felt like she was missing something important in the back alley's semi-darkness. He looked at her and she looked back. Her white self and his black self standing beside a ransacked Dumpster. She felt in him a desperation. He wasn't desperate-looking because he was beside a Dumpster. The desperation came from somewhere else, the line of his mouth or the wideness of his eyes as he watched her.

71

For the second time she became very aware of her body, the stretch of skin, her own vulnerability. Almost as quickly, she became aware of that awareness and felt ashamed. It became harder and harder to make eye contact. When at last she couldn't look at him at all, he seemed to give up waiting and climbed into his truck without a word. She was glad to see him go. Glad to have the trash and the floodlight and the mosquitoes and this corner of night once again to herself.

As the vehicle swung around and sped off down the empty back lot, she caught a glimpse of the red scrawl of his Louisiana plates and the sticker on his back bumper. It was the one Healthy Hearts gave to each of their visiting volunteers.

Infuriated and inside the Dumpster, Lora was determined to find something of value her former volunteer had missed. An individual pack of croutons even, something to prove to herself—she wasn't sure what. The image of the bumper sticker had replaced Tim's voice in her head. For that, at least, she was grateful. She trained a dozen new volunteers a month; she couldn't be expected to recognize them all if she ran into one in a side-loading Dumpster at the back of a discount grocery. Her image of a girlfriend and five kids evaporated. Of course she could remember him now, a jazz clarinetist who had played for their lunchtime crowd. She'd invited him back a few times before asking if he wanted an internship. Their patrons had loved him. The young man had shaken his head.

"Internships are for rich, white kids to get a taste of the old unpaid labor market. We got enough of that legacy here as is."

Lora threw trash bags from one end of the Dumpster to the other. Her thumb pushed through something squishy and she continued angrily on. She felt tricked. She'd been sorry for him! And he was just standing there, waiting to see if she'd recognize him. How could she? Four interactions half a year ago. He hadn't had that beard then either.

She might not have been born here, she might not have been around in 2005, but she'd paid her sweat equity at Healthy Hearts. She voted in the local elections. She relinquished her sales tax. She'd registered her car, even bought legal brake tags, even though everyone else told her it was a government scam and pointed to a guy they knew who sold them on the cheap. She didn't want to be a transplant. Deep in that identity-generating part of her, she was a New Orleanian now.

Lora straightened and grunted in satisfaction, a brown plastic container in her hand. There. The musician had missed a tub of peanut butter. The pleasure of his failure dulled her embarrassment. But as she inspected the list of ingredients to see how much sugar had been added, she became aware of a long crack along the side of the container through which slick peanut oil seeped out. She threw it back onto the pile, wiping her hand on her pants. Then she picked it back up. In the mess underneath the peanut butter, somehow unblemished, sat a single, shrink-wrapped, sweet potato.

Within the confines of the Dumpster echoed the sound of a vehicle approaching and the slam of a door. She froze, stooped over, one hand resting on the root vegetable. Her headlamp was still on, but turning it off would draw even more attention. Footsteps approached. A flashlight. The musician, she thought. He'd come back to chew her out for forgetting him.

"Just getting some grub for my chickens," she called out when the footsteps stopped.

"I thought you were having a girl's night with Tansy," replied Tim. His torso appeared at the window, well-dressed even at midnight behind a discount grocery. His voice was as quiet and his expression as unsmiling as it had been when he'd opened her fridge to find the seafood salad. Even when they fought, Tim's anger was never loud. She straightened, but otherwise didn't move. There was nowhere to move to. She was caught.

In all the time he had railed at her and undermined her, he had never followed her on the loop. He'd never even asked to come, which meant she'd never had to bear him seeing her as she was now, knee-deep in mercantile dross. No one had ever seen her like this, in fact, not a store employee, not even the musician-diver. Tim, too, flinched as her headlamp scanned him, but when she turned hers off it was too dark inside the Dumpster for her to make out the intricacies of his expression. She perceived only blankness, and it was enough to know he saw in her that same desperation that she had seen in the younger man, that he was regarding her with the same pity and sadness. She understood now how misplaced those feelings had been. Knowing did not help hold her together. Who in history had ever truly desired to be pitied? Who could love and pity the same person at once? In the darkness of the steel container, she glimpsed a mother at the church resale shop buying back-to-school sneakers for her son. She glimpsed the customers at the front of the discount grocery, buying sugar-enriched bread and antibiotic-pumped beef. Visible, but still to her inaccessible. There was Tim, who would not stop looking at her the way he had looked at the rescued tub of seafood salad. She

felt more than saw him take a step back, which is when she picked her feet out of the sea of plastic bags and moved to the Dumpster window with a hand outstretched.

"Sweet potato?" she offered. Her smile had no teeth.

He did not need a sweet potato. He could buy himself a hundred sweet potatoes with just the cash in his wallet. He did not need it, but he took it from her and he rubbed it on his too-nice shirt the way one shined an apple. He held the vegetable with one hand and he did not walk away.

❖ ❖ ❖

An alley in the shanty known as El Basurero. Photo by J. Malcolm Garcia.

# El Basurero (The Dump)

I sit in an office of Francisco Coll School with teacher Sister Gloria Xol. A breeze blows a paper off the table. I pick it up. An electric bill. I give it to Sister Gloria. She reads it aloud. If the school doesn't pay one hundred dollars within thirty days the electricity will be shut off.

"Money makes our lives difficult," Sister Gloria says.

She offers a resigned smile and shakes her head and puts the bill aside. Through the open office door, I watch a group of children chasing one another in the courtyard. Their voices bounce off concrete walls. Above the walls, I see the vague tips of skyscrapers of downtown Guatemala City thinly veiled by a brown haze and no more than a ten-minute drive away.

Sister Gloria teaches fifty third-grade boys and girls and finds them a very hard group of children to handle. The small classrooms exacerbate their bad behavior. The children sit too close to one another. The slightest thing sets off a fight. A look. A bump. That's all it takes. They erupt, explode, start yelling and hitting. She has twelve students who can be very violent.

Take this one boy. He beat a classmate one day. He lives with his alcoholic stepfather and mother. The mother told Sister Gloria that she hits him with a wire cable when she gets fed up with him. She wanted to send him to a boarding school but couldn't afford it. How do you handle a boy like this? the mother demanded. With violence.

Sister Gloria told the boy what his mother had said, and he started crying. He spoke about his mother's punishments, how much they hurt. Sister Gloria told him that the way he felt when his mother hit him was the same way students felt when he hit them. She thought she might get through to him, but he didn't change. He remains aggressive. He gets no support at home. The boy's grandmother worries that his mother will lose control and beat him to death. Sister Gloria would like to get into the hearts of both the boy and his mother and remove the

Sister Gloria Xol teaching a third-grade class at Francisco Coll School. Photo by J. Malcolm Garcia.

pain they cause each other but she does not know how.

"Your grandson is a child of God and deserves a chance," she told the grandmother.

❖ ❖ ❖

I learned about Francisco Coll School on a previous trip to Guatemala. In 2015, the *National Catholic Reporter* asked me to cover the country's presidential election. I'm a freelance writer. I had worked with the *NCR* editor when I worked for the *Kansas City Star* newspaper years earlier.

After the election, my Guatemalan translator introduced me to a friend who volunteered at Francisco Coll. I had been a social worker before I became a reporter. The lives of poor children interested me, and I asked to see the school.

Named after a Spanish priest and saint, Francisco Coll opened in 1995 as a grammar school. Next door, International Samaritan administers a middle school. Most of the students of both schools live in a barrio beside the Guatemala City garbage dump, the largest landfill in Central America. The Dump holds more than a third of the country's trash and provides work for scavengers who recycle as much as a million pounds of trash a day. In the process they expose themselves to toxic fumes, hazardous materials, and landslides of garbage that have been known to bury scavengers alive.

My translator's friend and I followed a school administrator through a network of alleys choked with sacks filled with bottles, cans, and other recyclables collected from The Dump. Mattresses buttressed shacks cobbled together from corrugated metal and discarded boards. The remains of buckling hovels laid untended beneath the dark smoke of trash fires. Sagging lines of laundry offered a bit of color.

We stopped at the shack of a single mother and her three daughters. The mother was working in the landfill. The daughters were home. The two youngest girls attended Francisco Coll. The infant daughter of the eldest girl fussed in her arms. Piles of damp clothes covered the floor and their mildewed funk told me they were ruined. The older girl explained that she was sorting the shirts and pants for the school to sell at a bazaar. She did not look at me as we talked. She held the baby away from her body and did not look at her either.

"We're trying to help this family," the administrator said after we left. "They are a tragic case. The father is in jail. The girls are his children. He committed incest. The baby you saw is his child."

The next morning, I left for the States. I told my editor about the school. She agreed I should write about it. In April 2016, I returned to Guatemala.

❖ ❖ ❖

Sister Gloria Xol introduces me to the principal of Francisco Coll, Sister Gloria Marlena Guadron Castillo. Sister Gloria Marlena has a pleasant smile that does not conceal the worry lines around her eyes. She tells me she is almost as new to Francisco Coll as I am. She came here in January, just four months ago. The lives of the children in El Basurero, The Dump, as locals call the barrio, shock her. Her childhood in El Salvador was so different. Families were poor, of course. People earned at most less than a dollar a day but violence was rare.

As a young girl she wanted to build her own school for poor boys and girls. At the time, she didn't like her teachers. They yelled at the stu-

dents and provided textbooks that looked one hundred years old. She thought she could do better. You know children and how they think adults are incompetent, she says.

Her ambitions changed when three nuns with the order of Dominican Sisters of the Annunciation of the Blessed Virgin came to her village outside Santa Tegla, El Salvador. The sisters called a meeting. They discussed living a life devoted to God. Afterward, they went house to house and asked families to send their children to Sunday school. Sister Gloria Marlena was among the children who attended.

At sixteen, she joined a weekend spiritual retreat and read a biography of the saints. Their simplicity and concern for others moved her. Perhaps she was an impressionable teen. She only knows that when she finished the biography she decided to devote her life to God. As a young nun, she served in remote parishes in El Salvador and Guatemala for eleven years before her superiors transferred her to Francisco Coll.

For the past few weeks, she has focused much of her attention on three orphaned students, two brothers and a sister. When they were small, their father was shot in front of the boys. Recently, their mother was murdered. The older boy, a sixth-grader, has vowed revenge on his parents' killers.

What does she say to such children? Sister Gloria Marlena asks. Vengeance is not yours to give? You should pray? Do they even understand what prayer and faith mean at their age? Is prayer as real to them as a gun?

"Before I came here, never did I ask myself these questions," Sister Gloria Marlena says.

❖ ❖ ❖

After school, Sister Gloria Marlena escorts me to a building about a block from the school. Here, lay teacher Juan Pablo Rivas tutors students in math and Spanish grammar. He volunteers Monday, Wednesday and Friday, from two in the afternoon to five. He sees about 40 students. The work drains him. Some of the children have poor hand and eye coordination. They don't understand the simplest things. They don't sit still. Their moods fluctuate like a breeze, one moment gentle, the next blustery.

This afternoon, as I look on, he gives his students a composition exercise. He wants them to write an essay about the meaning of honesty.

Principal of Francisco Coll, Sister Gloria Marlena Guadron Castillo. Photo by J. Malcolm Garcia.

Perhaps the word will make them reflect on values and their own behavior and that of the adults around them. Perhaps they won't understand and won't complete the assignment. Juan Pablo waits. He never knows with these children.

*My life,* one student writes. *Sometimes I'm really happy and sometimes I'm really sad. With my Mom I'm really happy. But on the other hand my father is no longer here but I am really happy with God and my family too.*

Another student begins her essay, *My name is Jennifer and I would like to tell you about my life. My life is happy, nice, but sometimes it is sad and at those times I don't want to be without my father. He was shot. I would like to be a dentist or a doctor or a vet. I adore my family but want my father. I want to be somebody in life. That is why I need to study so I can look for a nice job and help other people and so I'm able to take care of everybody else.*

Still another student offers a wish list: *I would like to do more things in my life such as going to the country. I'd like to go alone to the video games and I'd like to be able to have boots. I would like to tell my parents thank you because they are the ones struggling and suffering to support the family. I have an* *older brother who helps us out. I have a teacher who loves us very much and I have never had such a nice teacher before.*

The essays sadden Juan Pablo. Such a tragic world. The stories remind him of a six-year-old he once tutored. The boy got involved with gangs. He picked fights. Juan Pablo asked him to leave. He hasn't seen him since.

Then there was this girl. Twelve, maybe thirteen. Juan Pablo helped her as much as he could but she had problems at home. Sometimes she lived with her father, a gang member, and sometimes she lived with her mother and grandmother, alcoholics both. The girl got very violent. She tried to act older, but she was just a kid. A kid with problems. She got into too many fights. He doesn't see her anymore either.

Other students give him hope. Like nine-year-old Francisco. Francisco is doing well. He stays off the street. He comes from a very poor family but his mother and older sister support him. He does his school work.

"Would you like to meet him?" Juan Pablo asks me.

He calls Francisco's name. A boy emerges from the classroom. His stained, orange T-shirt hangs off his slim body like a rag suspended

77

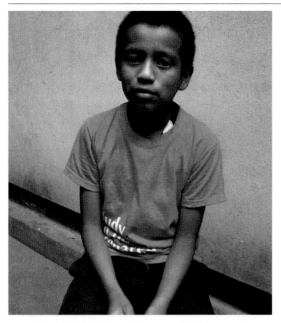

Francisco, a nine-year-old student at Francisco Coll School. Photo by J. Malcolm Garcia.

from a hook; his blue jeans spill over his sneakers. He sits beside Juan Pablo, head down. I imagine he wonders what he has done to be called out of class. I introduce myself and apologize for making him nervous. OK, he says, and shrugs, showing a nonchalance I suspect he does not feel. However, as he answers my questions, Francisco relaxes. He enjoys talking about himself.

He tells me he lives on a big, quiet street. Not much traffic. The steep street twists and turns. It gets slippery when it rains. Yesterday it rained and Francisco's house flooded. It was very wet inside. When it does not rain, Francisco rollerskates but the bumpy pavement makes him fall too much. When he skates on smooth roads, he really gets going.

Francisco likes school because he's good at math. He has not yet memorized his multiplication tables. When he does, he thinks he'll like math even more.

This week in Francisco's catechism class, Sister Gloria Marlena read a Bible story about a robber who got caught. The class talked about how no one should take things from other people. If they need something, they should pray for it, Sister Gloria told them. A friend of Francisco told Sister Gloria he prays for his mother to stop beating him.

After school, Francisco sometimes helps his mother at his grandmother's tortilla shop. His grandmother has not been feeling well so these days his mother runs the shop. Francisco mixes tortilla batter and daydreams about becoming a firefighter. He doesn't know why. Maybe all the smoke rising from the ovens makes him want to be a firefighter.

"What do you think?" he asks me.

❖ ❖ ❖

When Juan Pablo dismisses the class, I walk with Francisco to his home. We stop at a shack patched together with aluminum siding, wood and blue plastic tarps. He knocks. No one answers. He tests the door. Locked. His mother, he says, must still be at the tortilla shop. He crosses the alley and raps on the door of a neighbor who watches him when his mother works.

A young woman answers the door holding a baby. Francisco introduces me to her. Carmela. She is nineteen. Her two younger sisters peer around her. I recognize them all. The girls I met on my first trip. The incest family. A toddler and a baby sleep on a mattress on the dirt floor. Carmela's. She notices me looking at them. Her boyfriend is the father of that one, she says pointing to the infant. She doesn't mention the father of the toddler. Her two teenage sisters, Cindy and Jaqueline, still attend Francisco Coll. Carmela dropped out a long time ago.

"There are no opportunities here," says Carmela says of El Basurero.

Just the other night, two men stopped her with a pistol and took her money and cell phone. Jaqueline has also been mugged. Ten times in two years, she says. Sometimes when she walks to school. Other times on the bus. She cries talking about it.

Three men stopped Cindy and her mother one time. The men had guns and demanded money. Cindy and her mother had a little change. The men took it and let them go. Toward the end of each school day, Cindy has trouble concentrating. She thinks of the walk home. Alone on the street. She walks fast.

"My sister was mugged," Francisco says.

She was walking to the store to buy some underwear and a guy stabbed her in the belly. She was seventeen. She lived. She stayed in a hospital for a long time, though.

Another time, Francisco continues, a shooting took place in front of his house. He looked through a crack in the wall and saw a man bleeding from his right arm. The man took off. This happened maybe two years ago.

"You were never mugged," Carmela says.

No, Francisco agrees, looking a little downcast. Then he pipes right back up. He doesn't worry about being mugged because Sister Gloria Marlena told him he should only fear God.

❖ ❖ ❖

The next morning, I return to Francisco Coll and sit in on a social studies class taught by Sister Carlotta Merida. Sister Carlotta grew up in San Marcos, Guatemala, and worked in Africa for twenty-three years before she returned to Guatemala in 2015 to care for her ailing mother. In Africa, she spent most of her time in Cameroon. Ivory Coast and Rwanda, too. She had never seen such poverty. So much desert land. The people could not grow food in the parched soil. Children starved. Guatemalans at least can get something to eat, even if it comes from the landfill.

What do you want to do when you grow up? she asked a Francisco Coll student one afternoon. I want to be a professional killer and thief, the boy told her. She knew he didn't know what he was saying. He was reflecting the life around him. Still, he surprised her but she did not criticize his choice. She did not say, professional killers are bad. They'll go to hell. If she did, she'd only alienate him. Many of her students' parents are thieves, prostitutes and gang members. They are flawed but no matter. Children love their fathers and mothers.

Instead, she asked the boy more questions: What else would you like to be? A policeman? He agreed a policeman would be fun.

Sister Carlotta wants her students to understand the meaning of respect, love and truth. Don't steal. They know that one. That's easy. Many of them have been mugged. They know what it's like to be robbed. She gives them a goal once a week and asks them to explain what they must do to achieve it. This week she assigned her students two goals: avoid saying bad words and show respect to your teacher. One student told her he had behaved well in his math class after he was sent to the principal for fighting.

This as an accomplishment, Sister Carlotta told him, write it down.

The boy who wanted to be a professional killer has changed, too. He sits still in class. He stopped hitting other kids. He doesn't get

Lay teacher Jessica Gomez teaching composition to fourth-grade students. Photo by J. Malcolm Garcia.

up and leave without permission. Who knows what his future holds.

❖ ❖ ❖

Lay teacher Jessica Gomez instructs a fourth-grade composition class across the hall from Sister Carlotta. On this morning, she tells the class to list the main characters of the day's reading.

"Then we'll work on our writing and our vocabulary," she says.

Jessica graduated from Francisco Coll about six years ago. Her mother, Altagracia Arevalo, is the school janitor. Jessica has seven siblings. She never knew her alcoholic father. He died when she was young. Her mother came from Jutiapa, Guatemala, near the border with El Salvador. She moved to El Basurero before Jessica was born, in search of work.

When Jessica completed high school, she decided to become a teacher and chose to work at Francisco Coll because she understood the students. She had been one of them. Besides, a teacher's salary is so small, where else could she live but the barrio? People around here know her. She has never been mugged. Muggers respect her for being a teacher. Some of their siblings and children might be her students.

"What's the main character?" Jessica asks, shaking a rattle to get one boy's attention.

"Where do these characters live? A farm, a town?"

The boy grabs the hair of another boy and wrestles him to the fllor. Jessica breaks them up. The first boy walks around the class making faces.

"It's not nice for you to be out of your seat," Jessica tells him. "Where's your book? If you don't work, I'll send a note to your mother."

"She'll beat me," the boys says.

"Then sit down."

Jessica glances around the classroom. She doesn't see Francisco. Sometimes, he doesn't show up. In the beginning of the year, Jessica confronted Francisco's mother about his absences. She told Jessica that Francisco was tired from helping her in the tortilla shop. Some mornings she lets him sleep in. Jessica told her she was also was tired but she still did her job. Francisco had two jobs. To help his mother and attend school. Francisco's mother agreed and sent him to school the next day.

Another student, Stephanie, reminds Jessica of herself. Stephanie's mother works in the landfill, leaving Stephanie to care for her three younger brothers and a sister after school. Stephanie feeds them and puts them to bed. Jessica cared for her younger siblings, too, when her mother toiled in the landfill.

"I'll give you five more minutes to finish the assignment," Jessica tells the class.

The two boys who had been wrestling tap their chests, their fingers spread into Vs. They stop when Jessica shakes her rattle. She has been having problems with them. They want to join a gang. After school, she sees them wandering the streets alone.

Another student, Aracely, also can be difficult. She does not pay attention, talks back. Aracely has five younger sisters. Her father is an alcoholic. Aracely and her siblings don't have enough to eat. Jessica brings Aracely's mother food and encourages her to send her daughter to school.

That is how her life will be different from yours, Jessica tells her.

❖ ❖ ❖

In her office next to Jessica's classroom, Sister Gloria Marlena considers a sketch drawn by an eight-year-old student. A stick figure of a girl holds a gun. The girl drew gang insignia in the stick figure's dress. Jesus stands on the other side of the page, a crucifix above his head, yellow to make it shine like the sun. The stick figure and Jesus hold a rope. Jesus is trying to pull the stick figure to his side.

The student had been absent from school for days until Sister Gloria Marlena visited the student's family and begged the mother to send her to school. She was a bright girl, Sister Gloria Marlena said. The mother agreed she was bright and that she should attend school but still the girl stayed home. Sister Gloria Marlena hounded the mother. The mother never attended school. She didn't understand its importance. Eventually, she relented and sent her daughter to school.

Sister Gloria Marlena considers the picture.

Let Jesus pull you across, Sister Gloria Marlena told the student. Don't be afraid.

❖ ❖ ❖

At noon, the recess bell rings and all the students run out of their classes to the courtyard. Sister Carlotta serves snacks from a wagon. I see Cynthia, the daughter of the man convicted of incest, take a box of M&Ms and sit on a stone bench. I join her. She eats one M&M at a time. She offers me one.

"Have you always lived here?" I ask her.

She shakes her head no. Their first house stood near the landfill but not as close as the house they have now. It flooded all the time. The dirt floor turned to soup. They put a mattress on the floor and she, her mother and her sisters slept together. In the morning, they ate rice and beans. Sometimes, they ate only vegetables. The mattress, dampened by the mud, smelled and got cold. Every morning they put it outside to dry.

They have a better house now. It has good doors. The first house didn't have doors at all, only a piece of wood to cover the entrance. It fell off all the time. When she has a house of her own, she wants it to be like this house but bigger with very large doors.

"I met you last year, do you remember?" I ask.

"A little," Cynthia says. "You did not stay long. Sometimes foreign people with NGOs come by and look at us and don't stay long either."

Cynthia likes to read books her mother finds in the landfill. Some of the books look new, others are dirty and torn. She enjoys stories about fairies and nature and animals. She draws the characters. Tigers are her favorite animal. Their fur has lovely coloring. So wonderful to look at. She'd like to be an artist.

Even more than reading, even more than drawing, Cynthia enjoys spending time with her mother. Her mother has dark skin and is not tall. She can be very easygoing but sometimes she gets quite angry if Cynthia and her sisters don't make dinner and clean the dishes afterward.

Cynthia once had a lovely dream she shared with her mother. All of her family were reunited and happy. They lived in a delightful house. She remembers this dream fondly. It made her mother smile.

She looks forward to seeing her father when he's released from jail. When he lived with them in their first house, Cynthia's father let her play with a friend outside. Then he went to jail and her mother brought her and her sisters to El Basurero and Cynthia never saw her friend again.

She does not know why her father is in jail. She does not know the father of Carmela's first baby. No one in the family tells Cynthia anything. Her mother and Carmela say, Stop asking questions about the baby.

She pops an M&M in her mouth and chews in silence.

❖ ❖ ❖

An hour passes. Recess ends. Some of the boys and girls drift into the classroom of Sister Gloria Xol. This afternoon, she teaches math.

Sister Gloria: Attention! Sit in your seats. Put your food away right now and copy the assignment on the board.

15-8 x 2 =

2x15 + 2x8 x 2 =

Sister Gloria: Who doesn't understand? I will explain. Multiply 8x2 subtract from 15. If you have 15 minus 16 what do you have?

Boy: Negative one.

Sister Gloria: Good. (to another boy) Did you copy everything?

Boy: I don't have a pencil or pen to write with.

*She gives him a pencil.*

Sister Gloria: Be sure to give it back. Pay attention, this will be on exam.

*A boy throws a pen.*

Sister Gloria: What are you doing? Why aren't you paying attention?

Girl: I don't have a pencil.

Sister Gloria: What are we going to do if we keep forgetting your things?

A boy sings a rap tune: *I never asked to be born, and death's no question/The sun's still shining off the same old lessons/Then why does life feel like an educated guess?*

Sister Gloria: Pay attention!

❖ ❖ ❖

I leave Sister Gloria Xol's class and follow Altagracia Arevalo, the mother of teacher Jessica Gomez, through the barrio in search of truant children.

"I feel bad for the boys and girls whose parents work all the time and are not around to support them," Altagracia says. "They have to work, I understand. I have to work, we all do. I'd rather not but that is not possible. My two sons, both mechanics, have been laid off. Another son lost his job at a chocolate factory. I am still supporting my family."

Altagracia labored in the landfill for twelve years. Twelve years, one, two, she says shaking a finger at me. She earned just a a dollar a day collecting and selling glass bottles and cans. Some things she kept for her children, clothes and shoes. Once or twice she found a hat to block the sun. She competed with children, little ones not yet teenagers, who could stoop over longer than she could rummaging through the garbage. One boy ate something and died. She almost died, too. Years and years ago, when she was three months' pregnant, she picked up an open can of rancid meat and ate it. Doctors pumped her stomach.

Altagracia stops to confront a boy pushing a wheelbarrow holding another, smaller boy, sound asleep.

"Why are you not in school?" Altagracia asks.

"I have to watch my brother," the older boy says.

Altagracia asks the boy where he lives. He takes her to a shack beside a gutter flush with gray water and a dead puppy. Altagracia pokes her head through an open door. A woman washes plates in a bucket. Chickens settle on a bed beneath a bare lightbulb. More chickens cluck on a sack of clothes beside a wood pile.

"You need to get your son to school," Altagracia tells the woman.

"I know, but I needed his help. Last night's rain flooded the house."

"School is important."

"I know. I want my children to learn something in life. To read and write so they can find work. I am allowing them to study. I just needed their help today. I worked seven hours in the landfill yesterday. Today, I'm not feeling well."

"Did you eat something you collected?" Altagracia says.

"No."

"Good."

The woman says she only gathers bottles and cardboard, not food. She earns about six dollars a day. Saturdays she stays longer and makes a little more. Her husband died in 2007. A mugger shot him in an attempted robbery. Since then, she has been with other men. It's good to have a man in the house for protection, she says. Men, however, come with a price. She has eight children, ages twenty to a year and a half. She is pregnant now with her ninth child. The father, like those who came before him, left her once she became pregnant.

"A woman is one thing for men," she says. "A baby quite another."

"You get pregnant and they don't want you, is that it?"

"Yes," the woman says.

"You make excuses," Altagracia says.

"No," the woman says. "I talk about my life."

❖ ❖ ❖

Back at the school, Cynthia stops Altagracia and me. She shows us a pencil sketch she drew of a two-story house and a door almost as tall as the house. A large tree provides shade. A branch curves over the roof of the house and turns into a mountain on some distant skyline. Cynthia remembers seeing a house like this when she was small. It's one of her first memories. She made several versions of the house before deciding to save this one.

"I like it very much," Altagracia tells her.

"This house would never flood," Cynthia says.

At two o'clock the children leave for the day. They stream out of the school and pass a thin, muscular man throwing glass bottles into barrels. He wears sunglass to protect his eyes from flying glass. His name is Ramon Gonzalez. He fills one barrel and starts in on another and then loads them on a pickup to discard at a recycling factory. He earns less than one dollar per barrel.

Cynthia, a student at Francisco Coll School, displaying one of her drawings. Photo by J. Malcolm Garcia.

Ramon tells me he drove a garbage truck but quit after a few years. Collapsing mountains of landfill trash almost buried him alive more than once. The landfill is a living, breathing monster, he tells me. Every so often something sets it off and it needs to feed. He prefers tossing glass into barrels. Safer.

❖ ❖ ❖

Francisco returns to school the next morning. He had skipped to help his sister sweep rain water out of the house. His grandmother remains ill and his mother took her to the hospital. She won't tell Francisco what's wrong. She cried when he asked her. He said a prayer for his grandmother and continued sweeping the water. It whooshed out onto the street and rolled back inside. Francisco used a bucket, scooping it up and tossing it as far as he could. Still, the water drifted back. His mother, he said, praised him for his hard work. After school, he'll help her in the tortilla shop. He invites me to join him.

❖ ❖ ❖

The tortilla shop stands at the end of an alley near a closed gate. Behind the gate, piles of junked cars provide homes for feral cats leaping from hood to hood. I see Francisco's mother, Christine Ixcoi, flattening dough and tossing it between her hands before she drops it into one of two wood-burning ovens. The ovens give off an intense heat and she steps back and wipes her face with an apron and then notices Francisco and me waving smoke from our faces. She embraces Francisco and offers me a chair.

If her mother was well, Christine says, she would be working in the landfill sorting through garbage from eight in the morning to about six. However, her mother is not well. This morning, Christine took her to the hospital. A doctor said she had ovarian cancer. He told Christine to try homeopathic medicine. She does not know where she will get the money.

Christine moved to El Basurero with her mother in 2009 because it costs nothing to live in a shack. Otherwise, she would never live here. However, El Basurero is not so cheap that she has money left over for medications.

"The life is not easy," Christine admits.

Her first husband left her when she became pregnant with her daughter, now twenty. The father of Francisco and his seven-year-old brother also left her. Young men do drugs on the street, she complains, and their families say nothing. They are poor and too preoccupied with their poverty to discipline their children. Christine is also poor. Her shack floods. She, Franciso and her daughter share a mattress at night. They eat every day but it is not enough.

Of her three children, Francisco, she says, is the most even tempered. He helps around the house doing chores. He has good eyes and sees everything through them, the good and the bad things in life. She hopes he has a life far different from hers. She hopes he attends high school and graduates and gets a job. She doesn't care as long as it's not in the landfill, not in the tortilla shop, not here.

❖ ❖ ❖

While I am with Francisco, Sister Gloria Marlena receives a disturbing phone call. The mother of a student tells her that her nephew and his friend were killed while they sold candy on a bus that morning. Chiclets. Shot by two robbers. Sister Gloria Marlena can't believe it. Why? They wanted their money, the woman tells her. The woman's voice has no feeling. She sounds as dead as her nephew.

Why did the woman call? Sister Gloria Marlena wonders. What did the woman think she could say? Did she want help? Help how? Perhaps the answer is that there is no answer. Sister Gloria Marlena's job is to listen, offer support and pray. She can always pray.

❖ ❖ ❖

Twelve-year-old Fernanda Mayen sits outside Sister Gloria Marlena's office. Fernanda left her composition class to use the bathroom without permission. Sister Carlotta sent her to the principal.

Fernanda lives in a part of El Basurero that has an empty bit of land where she and her friends play. She has good friends but no best friends. People move too often to have a best friend. As much as she likes playing in the alley, Fernanda knows she has to be careful. Some people bully girls when they see them alone. They throw rocks at them, grab their dresses. They drink and get high and chase them.

On sunny days, she spends as much time as she can outside. Her house is ugly. It's a mess. Mud everywhere from a flood. Everything is

83

A child in an alley in the shanty known as El Basurero. Photo by J. Malcolm Garcia.

so dirty. A rug absorbs much of the water. It squishes beneath her feet. It stinks.

Fernanda lives with an uncle and aunt. She does not remember when her father died. Her uncle told her he was mugged and shot. Her mother died near their home when Fernanda was in second grade. Not in this neighborhood, another one. Sometime at night. Her mother had been working in the landfill. A friend found her body in the street. She had been shot. Fernanda stayed with her uncle when her mother worked. That night, he told her she would not be going home.

She thinks she has a picture of her mother but she doesn't know where she put it. Her mother had red hair and was a little fat with fair skin, her face darker than her arms and legs. She was really fun. Her mother never hit her. She talked a lot. She liked to gossip with friends.

Life without her mother has been hard. Sometimes her uncle eats before Fernanda gets home from school and doesn't save anything for her. He gets angry all the time. He's angry about the rain and how it flooded his house. He threatens her. If you get anything wet and dirty, I will pull your pants down and beat you with my belt. If she goes to a store for school supplies, he yells at her. You're always spending money. Fernanda's uncle is a big man. He works with trucks and has strong arms good for beatings. He hits her brothers a lot. They attend fourth and sixth grade. The older brother wants to buy a gun and kill whoever killed their mother. Her uncle tells him to shut up about that. Fernanda thinks her uncle likes being angry.

She enjoys school. The neat and tidy buildings so much better than her home. Of her classes, she enjoys math the most. The math teacher sings little rhymes. *Two plus two is four / not one numeral more.* Fernanda wants to be a teacher so she knows all the things her teachers know.

After school, she feels sad. She knows she has to go home. Sometimes, her uncle lets her do her homework. Other times, he has her do chores. He doesn't care if she attends school or not. Her aunt always asks about her grades. Fernanda likes her even though she yells a lot, too.

One night, Fernanda dreamed about her mother. She was dressed in white. She and Fernanda went to the bathroom together. When Fernanda finished, her mother was gone and Fernanda woke up.

❖ ❖ ❖

In the morning, I ask a garbage man near my hotel if he will take me into the landfill. He agrees providing I give him a tip and don't mention his name in my story. I meet him again hours later after has finished his trash route.

I pull myself into the cab and we drive past Francisco Coll School and El Basurero to a pitted road. The road descends into a gravel trail that winds into the landfill. Visibility shrinks from the dust we churn slaloming around deep holes. We turn into an area filled with idling garbage trucks. I watch men hauling sacks of recyclable material larger than their own bodies off their trucks. They run, feet dancing for balance, the weight of their loads propelling them toward a row of lean-to shelters where recyclers sit beside weigh scales.

The garbage man parks and gets out of our truck to drop off his recyclables. He has been

A recycler bagging what he has collected. Photo by J. Malcolm Garcia.

A child in an alley in the shanty known as El Basurero. Photo by J. Malcolm Garcia.

picking up trash for twelve years. His brother, also a garbage men, got him the job. No prior work experience required. The garbage man can't read or write. He's lucky to have job. He starts at two in the morning and finishes at six four days a week. He'll do this work for a long time. Rest of his life, maybe, who knows? He's only twenty-six, but it's steady work.

We wait for a recycler to weigh the garbage man's sacks of cans and glass and bundled cardboard. He makes about a dollar a pound. Trash unsuitable for recycling he'll dump elsewhere in the landfill. People from El Basurero will sift through it. Maybe they'll find something he missed, who knows?

The garbage man collects trash in mostly residential areas. He sifts through the garbage for recyclables and other things. He has found gold chains, shoes, and furniture. He keeps the shoes and wears them on the job. He found two guitars once. Good shape. He can't play but he kept them. Maybe he'll learn to play. He collects metal shelving, cabinets, even refrigerators, all of it recyclable.

The landfill trash rises high as mountains, the garbage man says, pointing at one towering mass of refuse. After a hard rain, however, these mountains can collapse, burying trucks and people.

The garbage man points at dark shapes circling the sky. Vultures.

"For us, the landfill is life," he says, "but it is also death."

❖ ❖ ❖

My last week in Guatemala. A Thursday evening. I am watching a televised soccer game. A photo of the landfill interrupts the sportscast. A massive heap of garbage fell, an announcer says. At least 24 garbage pickers are missing. The soccer game resumes.

I call Sister Gloria Marlena.

"It's very bad," she tells me.

Her voice shakes. She had been teaching catechism. The cell phones of some of the children began ringing. Then all their phones were ringing.

Mother! Mother! one boy yelled, the landfill caved in and washed away the people!

He ran out of class. The students and Sister Gloria Marlena chased after him. She doesn't know yet if any students were in the landfill. She can't imagine what families must be feeling. The only thing she could do was stand with them outside the landfill and wait for up-

El Basurero residents working inside the landfill. Photo by J. Malcolm Garcia.

dates. Eventually, she walked home alone and prayed.

❖ ❖ ❖

In the courtyard of Francisco Coll the next morning, somber children stand in small groups. They don't speak. Their weighty silence cuts off everything, even the noise of the recycler Ramon Gonzalez, still throwing glass bottles into barrels despite everything that has happened. Sister Carlotta holds two candles and asks the students to remember and pray for the dead. She tells me that families remain lined up outside the landfill waiting for news of a husband or son, brother or wife, grandparent or sister.

The father of one student is missing. Three other students lost their grandfathers. A stepmother of another student also died. A former student was buried alive. Everyone called him Chico. Fifteen years old. His body hasn't been found. His parents worked in the landfill but got out. His father was trying to hold him but Chico was sucked in. It was like a whirlpool. Everything spinning down. Chico's father yelled, Chico! My Chico! but could not save him.

❖ ❖ ❖

I accompany Sister Gloria Marlena as she walks through El Basurero to check on families. At one house, a girl tells her that her grandfather was taken out of the landfill barely alive.

"My family is OK," another student tells Sister Gloria Marlena.

He points to a shack.

"The grandfather of that family, he's missing," the student says. "There's no news. The family went to a hospital, but he was not there. They have looked for him all night. The police have stopped looking for him in the landfill."

"We'll drop by again to see if you've found him," Sister Gloria Marlena says.

One boy tells her his mother was supposed to be in the landfill but went into labor and did not work. She named the baby Lucky.

❖ ❖ ❖

Sister Gloria Marlena and I return to the school. Just outside its gate, volunteer Angela Hernandez stops her. She had been in the landfill when the garbage gave way. It happened in a flat area.

"You're working and the next thing you know you sink down," Angela says.

She was scared. She ran. The noise. It sounded like some big animal chasing her.

Angela has worked in the landfill since she was seventeen. She is fifty-six now. She has been sucked down into the garbage twice. The second time, she sank so deeply only her head stuck out. It took a half-dozen men to pull her out. She survived but survived for what? She has no other job. She puts in twelve hours a day sorting and picking and selling trash. It is the only work she knows, that and volunteering at the school cleaning toilets for food.

"I think forty people are missing," Angela says. "One day of rain and this happens. Imagine what it will be like during the rainy season."

❖ ❖ ❖

In the school courtyard, I see Cynthia and ask about her mother.

"Alive," she says.

Her mother was leaving for the landfill when she heard people screaming and wailing. Then the noise of ambulance sirens drowned their shrieks. Cynthia was home. She heard a really big bang. She worried her older sister Carmela might be in the landfill. Carmela was running errands but Cynthia didn't know that. She couldn't sleep until Cynthia came home. Now she knows everyone in her family is safe. She will sleep today. Her mother gathered ten sacks of aluminum cans before all the upheaval. The cans will support the family until the landfill reopens.

❖ ❖ ❖

The older brother of Fernanda Mayan, the orphaned student who lives with her uncle, saw the landslide of trash. He told Fernanda that a mass of garbage dragged people down into the ground. He started running. He had never seen anything like it. Like a roar. He shook. He could not stop crying.

Fernanda tries not to think about what happened. Her uncle says it is part of living in El Basurero. She worries about her brother. What will he do now? How will he earn money for the family if he can't work in the landfill? Fernanda's uncle wants her to drop out of school. Find a job, he tells Fernanda. I know a paper factory that needs workers.

❖ ❖ ❖

A child resting on what his mother has recycled. Photo by J. Malcolm Garcia.

Students in class at Francisco Coll School. Photo by J. Malcolm Garcia.

Sister Gloria Marlena eases her way through the students and stands alone in a corner of the courtyard. Every day she urges parents to support their children's education. What does that support mean when they can die in the landfill? When will this happen again? How many more families will the landfill take? How many students?

She looks at me but does not expect me to answer. In her prayers, she puts the children and their families in God's hands.

She turns to me.

"How many will continue to fall through his fingers?"

"Do you question your faith?" I ask.

"No," she says. "I question my strength."

❖ ❖ ❖

Francisco stops me as I leave the school. He says he was with Juan Pablo, the tutor, when the landfill caved in. His mother had been selling tortillas to street vendors. Her brother drives a garbage truck and she called him. He was OK. Francisco was glad. Not long ago, his uncle told him a story that a gold mine lies at the bottom of the landfill. Whoever looks for it will not come out. His uncle told Francisco to study hard so he can get a good job and not be tempted to work in the landfill and search for gold.

Yesterday, before the landfill collapsed, Francisco earned ninety points on a math quiz. Maybe he'll get one hundred points next time. You never know, he says. He's hopeful. He knows not to wonder about such things now. Today is a sad day. Maybe tomorrow will be better. You never know.

❖ ❖ ❖

*Carolyn Guinzio*

# Is This about Absence?

They put cameras on the collars
of cats, and cats cut through fields

where chimneys that act as graves
of houses stand among the bulbs

that still push up around them.
The edges of the bricks have been

rubbed round by cats. The cats
pause to clean their paws. They roll

in the weevil-riddled leaves
that drop from the same bleak oak

each October. There are soft ashes
in the ashes' system of roots

that harden like paint on the faces
of the cats whenever the rooting-

up ritual occurs. They know
what they were. If you turned

for one last look, where on earth
would it fall, the gaze to end all?

# Ravines

Forgive me :

        I  repeat  myself


It is not       only light   we want     we like

                                the word

                    silk

Unadorned

      with  in sensible

but for the covering        adornments      the sensual

                                full of holes

                      a silver poly-

ester lace   head cover for mass


A creaking       confessional

door        A protracted penance


Whisper this

sentence

before you

          I'm here how do I

                leave how do I live

here I'm here and I want

                        to leave I will not

  speak how do I

leave I will not drink I will cover

             my eyes I

     will wait in the dark until

                      I can leave I won't open my

eyes I don't know how to breathe

leave:


Before you breathe:


A caustic      silver

              flavor

laced in the plain

          bread   threads

               a path

on the tongue

        so to speak

    cutting    holes    in
        words
and other   vestiges
           of the intellect

A caustic     silver
           sound
A garish     silver    forgive

me   I       repeat     myself

Robin Perry Dana. *Soliloquy*, from the Watershed series. 2017. Archival pigment print. 36 x 24 inches. Courtesy of ARTicles Art Gallery.

## Nadia Villafuerte (translated from the Spanish by Pennell Somsen)

# The Salt Frontier

They told you that fire inhabits the south, but you didn't believe that the heat could be so ferocious. In the distance, in some lonely places, the sun is an almost invisible veneer, *almost* because in reality you can make out a dense thickness, a hot ember that deforms the shape of things. Pueblos in the south are given to poverty, to ignorance.

The jeep glides down the only highway. There is a sound of melancholy bluesy blues. You are far from your own country. You chose to wander from place to place, led only by your will and that of your camera. The camera is like an extension of your eyes, of your hands, of the impossibility of capturing that "something" that you still haven't found.

Farther away, the jetty appears motionless. You have arrived at an hour in which the sunset is the main event. A sunset is the same over every ocean, you think. Maybe it's your mood: Gary Moore with his agony of blues coming from the speakers, or perhaps the four beers you drank, but you could swear that this sunset isn't the same. At least you maintain the capacity to be amazed. It has to be because you're in the Pacific.

It's called Paredon. A village of fishermen. One of those places that coyotes speed through in their motorboats carrying illegals from Guatemala to Mexico.

The tires of the jeep are strong enough for this type of travel, you say to yourself, as you drive with some difficulty on what isn't exactly a road, but rather the beginning of a labyrinth which splits off into nearly impassable puddles of mud.

It seems that the pueblo has been laid out with one main street, the only one paved, and has chaotically spread to all sides. *Given to poverty*, you repeat, reminded of the phrase, and, seeing the desolate misery of the houses, you feel a stronger desire to leave than to convince yourself to stay.

You can see the place with your nose: most of the patios have shrimp drying in the sun, thousands of tiny red shrimp whose salt you want to taste. Smelling with your eyes: a trench enters your body carrying its lukewarm acid juice of decay. Yes, poverty is detestable. A writer friend of yours hates it, hates poor people, and underdeveloped countries like this, places like Paredon that probably are never even imagined on the other side of the world. Like the suburbs or the Rwandans that swarm everywhere although they never communicate with each other beyond certain gestures of long-distance compassion. It isn't necessary to go to Africa to comprehend the crude beauty of misery.

In any case, you are moved. It's inevitable. It seems that the south, this small uncapitalized, monosyllabic word isn't the real border but an error, a historical horror. Is it possible, in spite of everything, to witness, how to say it, a magnificent sunset? You have already seen too many. Nevertheless, it isn't the sunset that bewilders you, rather that it's flagrant beauty is displayed so arrogantly before a place so deplorable, so lyrically sordid, infested with shrimp, fish, disreputable dives, drunks vomiting in the middle of the street and naked girls with vacant stares trying to capture frogs in the filthy mud puddles. You look for images and you see that there are more than enough. That's how art is but what are we going to do? Art serves to denounce tragedy and also to conceal it. It's a way to behave cynically, without shame. You know it. It's moving, it moves you, it could move others but it won't help anyone. A photograph doesn't give people money or drainage or even paint to cover the walls.

You think of the twenty rolls of film to be developed into contact sheets in the dark room.

You think of selecting those images that don't echo those of your other trips: Prague, France, Ireland, the coast of Spain, so that you don't repeat yourself with the same apocalyptic vision that at times you detest but that remains in your retina like a shadow. Then, emerging in bromide and gelatin the enlargements of images that exist, of places you travelled on foot, images that you held back because there are places like Paredon whose profound sadness leaves a deep wound. Finally, after looking up friends that will help you, and visiting the director of some distant museum, one far from this place, you will mount the exhibition: a series of ten-by-ten photos revealed on the wall of your solitude. You'll call it "Southern Border," a dry title. The country itself is irrelevant.

There is no beach because it is a dead sea, a sandbar surrounded on two sides by arms of the sea.

You saw the poster at the travel agency: a typical office photo that, nevertheless, didn't promise luxury tourism, rather an example of a typical place. The concrete wall holds back the ocean. This is the perfect angle: the backlighting highlights the drowsy, rhythmic swaying of dozens of launches that stir up the green slime. Some of them are clustered together as if they were voices chatting in the middle of the afternoon.

You're not looking for that image, in fact, you're sick of it: you are certain that beyond tangible things there is a soul that sprouts up or simply doesn't shine in the light. A flock of black birds cross the fragment of sky.

You don't stop. There is something uneven, agitated in your breathing. It isn't that the pueblo is big, in fact it's so tiny, that any one of your friends would have turned around saying, "There is nothing interesting here." But you have always gone against the flow and you are in or have decided to come to a place none of those friends could even imagine, a place that in spite of how it looks throbs with life wherever you look. You go where there is no money. To a place where the world could begin anew. Paredon burns in waves of heat, its scarred walls are full of political propaganda for candidates that have certainly never been there, the trees are unknown to you, exotic flowers bloom in patios, on dirt roads and smelly trails that end at the breakwater which is soaked with filthy water.

You devour what you see, it nests in your brain. You walk along the shore but the villagers don't stop their work. People come and go retrieving their catch and their tools. It's impossible to make out any symmetry in the houses

or in the only market in the port. It's actually its disorder, its randomness that makes the place disturbing. The men and women only look like themselves, destiny here is largely a question of luck, of hope. It looks as if you are engrossed in a photo that fascinates you, an enormous one; troubling, convulsing, powerful and sad. What is that woman thinking, the one who without a tremor in her hands cuts open an enormous fish? Who does he love, the black man who watches the calmness of the horizon? Bicycles come and go. Children come and go. A young man wearing inexpertly applied make-up and dressed like a *quinceanera* walks down the middle of the street while the group on the corner make fun of him, jeering and laughing uproariously.

Your friends already know that you live minimally: you don't look for a hotel, maybe food, a night drinking in a tavern, a cigarette while you listen to the unending liquid songs of crickets and frogs (this is something that you don't hear in other places) or while you lose yourself in the geography of a good dream.

This time will be no exception. You have no idea where you'll stay. There isn't a beach with solid sand on which you can lay your sleeping bag and sleep.

So you'll look for the house. In the darkness you finally arrive at the end of the road and see a light, as if you were a fisherman who has unloaded his tiredness in the nets and walks naked closer and closer to the flickering lighthouse. You rub your eyes. Is the house getting closer or farther away?

A woman opens the door. You explain, in your clumsy, stuttering Spanish, something about your work and your reason for visiting. She doesn't care. She laughs with an open mouth to reveal perfect white teeth. It's as if her teeth were unreal, as if instead of talking she too stuttered, doing poor imitations of a likely response. You say that some boy told you about the house. "She can rent you a hammock," the young man said with his marked accent. You couldn't see her face with the light behind her. But surely this is the house, the last one.

"I'm a photographer from a distant city in a far away country, " you say, because it is unlikely that she knows where Moravia is or that other ports like hers exist.

But, in truth, you aren't from anyplace. To say that you're Czech is a social convention. Until twenty years ago it was even forbidden to lay claim to your nationality. You fled. In truth you were born when you began to photograph the gypsies and wander with them: travelling without stopping to different corners of the world, finding in each one of them the recurring themes of fantasies and places of rest. A permanent exile, to end only when you die.

The woman looks at you with the trust and warmth of her decency. You don't feel the hostility you encounter in cities. She says, in a perfect but curious Spanish, that you should put down your things, that you will sleep in the corridor in one of the five hammocks. You don't understand her very well; she speaks as if she is shaking or striking certain sounds. But you understand that she hasn't said no, that her brilliant black eyes have allowed you to enter, to pass a few nights in this Paredon of no one.

She wears a robe which shelters the humid odor of her breasts. Until now you haven't explained to yourself why you haven't been able to live with a woman. Nothing, however beautiful it was, has been able to divert you from your one obsession, the camera and the world or the world and the camera? Which conceived which?

This young woman has flustered you very quickly as if she were an image that you had searched for and finally found within millions of possibilities. You have organized your life with a rigor that is almost military and religious. You take refuge in the thousand negatives that you arrange on a table as if they were, in reality, a world unto itself without frontiers, nationalities or names, a silent sepia territory hiding screams and words. You aren't tied to anything, money doesn't interest you, nor comfort, your relationship with nature and humans doesn't go beyond those moments dedicated to shooting pictures. You didn't even tremble when you placed your watch if front of the camera to document the exact moment in which the first military tank arrived in your country. Your country. And so why in the hell does your skin shiver when you hear the woman approaching you? Why, at an age when all you seek is good photos, good health, deep sleep, does this person show up to confuse you, this woman with her eyes like waves, her robe covering her.

You divine her curves, you feel your way as if you were in the dark room touching the bottles of liquid developer. She indicates a dilapidated chair, "Idiot, sit down," you tell yourself,

"Maybe she wants to talk even though you won't understand much."

She tells stories that would seem unlikely if she didn't tell them as if they were everyday occurrences. Yesterday they found the bodies of two men that drowned. They abandoned their life jackets in the middle of their journey and began to swim, they became exhausted, they went numb before they could take their last strokes.

You hear her speak of the growing violence along the coast, of a notorious murder committed by students who, for a change, left the dead man on the beach, as if the sea was a depository whose salt would erase all signs of rottenness. Or as if to make the sea understand that not everything it contains is beautiful. That anecdote and others make it clear that the women is an expressive storyteller with a prodigious memory. But you probably don't understand the significance of this collection of stories, they only serve as an excuse to listen to her and watch her movements.

The robe is loose. Her body dances inside of it. It ought to be very late already, you've both had several cups of coffee. You would like to photograph her, not with the clarity of her features but blurred, nebulous and naked, with her back to the camera and the world, lost in diffuse greenery, barbed wire in foreground, protecting her from you.

"Until tomorrow, what am I saying, in a short time," she says as she leaves. You ask the time but she tells you that she doesn't have a clock, that she uses the radio to know the time, it's that now she doesn't want to turn it on because her husband is sleeping. And then she is gone leaving an emptiness in you that hurts like an incision in your stomach. Her long thick hair falling on her naked shoulders is no longer in front of you. Nor the mouth which seems to have desires instead of lips. Nor the dark eyes brimming with who knows what passionate words. Nor the teeth suggestively appearing with her light smile.

She has warned you to put on repellent for the nighttime mosquitos. It's impossible to use the sleeping bag. There is no wind or even a fresh breeze and the little air there is smells of salt. You realize that the hammock is not what you expected, it's like a fishing net in the air in which you can't get to sleep.

One hour, two . . . How many hours until dawn?

It was the coffee, the bitter coffee.

Later you hear her. You hear them. The other hammocks are empty. You walk brushing up against the corridor wall until you reach the window. A weak light, you don't know where it comes from, manages to illuminate the shapes reflected in the mirror of what appears to be an armoire.

The woman, what did she say her name was? is lying on her back. The man has opened her as if she were a fish receiving the smooth, sharp blade of a knife in it's guts. You can hear her pant, softly but rhythmically. You want to be the man whose odor makes her moan. Love is also a version of a crime. Why does your photographer's vision make you see everything as if it were a close-up? Why do you have to capture the surface of things with an intensity that hurts your eyes? And why to you have to suffer over something that has nothing to do with you? Then you realize that you have spent sixty years in desolate places and that, images like the one you see now, are already a lost paradise.

You feel hot blooded, with a hot body, and a hot mouth wanting to satisfy, bury, immerse yourself in the skin of the woman far from your frontiers. One doesn't love collarbones or muscles of the other but rather skin, which is the boundary one longs to cross. The skin, another frontier. You don't even feel the mosquitos leaving their tracks of blood. You have come to the pueblo of a distant country only to confirm you are close to desire now that your age only asks for good sleep, a good photograph and good health.

When you see so much beauty concentrated in one place you have to leave, to do something yourself, to act for a change. But it's too late. The scene has left you empty. It has destroyed your first camera. You've roamed different countries shooting photos of gypsies, or immigrants from various parts of the world. You have avoiding owning things. Even the possibility of a home, of a place to return.

When there is nothing to photograph it's time to leave.

You return to the hammock, leaving behind the lovers that are still delving in each others bodies to a point of exhaustion. For the first time you are afraid of the dark, it suffocates you. Because of that you gather your few possessions and you leave, wanting to get out as

soon as possible. One day, one night, a fraction of a minute can be enough to break down our interior worlds. One can be a city inside and outside the armed warrior who begins the battle.

You want to learn, not just repeat yourself. What are the hundreds of images that you carry with you in rolls of film but the same: ordinary people who flee, leave, die, who ravage their lands? Didn't you know that deep down that what you were looking for photographing pueblos, ports, cities, was an image of yourself? And finally you have found it in a place that doesn't even aspire to be a pueblo, in a house that doesn't even have plumbing, in a small woman first wrapped in a bathrobe and then naked, writhing like a fish that jumps in the net trying to breathe.

To hell with all that, with exile, with war, with the darkroom! You start the jeep, you lose your way many times because there is no way to see the muddy road at night or what might be the beginning of dawn. Before you leave this Paredon of no one you go to the pier. You take the film cannisters from your backpack. You walk toward the shore. You feel that you are on the edge of an abyss. You want the sun to come up. Slowly a faint stain appears and begins to spread itself across the sky. And then, one by one, you let fall the films that you were going to develop, carefully, in the winter, over there in the silent room in Prague.

The rusty train car with four Central Americans huddled on top falls.

Two men looking through a hole in a chain link fence at the long road ahead and the warning: HERE GUATEMALA ENDS AND MEXICO BEGINS fall.

A boat of inner tubes in which an entire family crosses the river falls.

Two buses full of deportees fall.

The woman sitting on the steps of a sordid hotel on the Guatemalan border falls. She falls and with her, her exhausted lost look falls.

The itinerant market ten kilometers from the border falls.

The border police drinking beer with a whore fall.

A lonely cross in the middle of the highway falls: there died two sisters before they began their long journey to the north of the country.

The barbed wire falls.

The fences fall.

The immigration kiosks fall.

The abundant, tropical foliage of the abandoned south falls.

And, inevitably, your dream of being a photographer, your photographer's eyes, your horror of being a lonely man fall.

The woman and her moans fall and her small body vanishes as if it were sand.

It's likely that for today, you won't want anything, you think.

And while the film cartridges begin to float away the sun rises. Faster and faster.

❖ ❖ ❖

Heike Mueller. *Lady 3*. 2018. Oil on canvas. 20 x 16 inches. Courtesy of ARTicles Art Gallery.

## Paul Lindholdt

# Swaddled in Rose Silk

*"Sometimes even good Homer nods off."*
– Horace, *Ars Poetica*

A while ago I read a poem that said no one wants to talk about heroin anymore. Too déclassé, too many dead, too many who survived the ordeal now gone to seed. A bit of psychic shrapnel surfaced when that poem soaked in. A jagged shard that had lain embedded and suppressed in memory's equivalent of the inner wrist, that vulnerable site sad people slice when they hope to go away.

Heroin put my natal city of Seattle on the map. Its favorite psychedelic son, Jimi Hendrix, got busted for carrying it into Canada, before he killed himself at the age of twenty-seven with booze and barbs. Kurt Cobain emerged from a cocoon in the depressed mill town of Aberdeen, made it big on MTV and in *Rolling Stone*, then swirled clockwise down Seattle's deepest drains. A taste for junk likewise claimed Layne Staley, the singer for Alice in Chains. Multiple others from the haunts of rock and roll have perished from the powder, celebrities too numerous to name.

Even before my teenage introduction to the stuff, I saw its casualties stalk the streets, as Ginsberg phrased it in *Howl*. One friend on hands and knees heaved and swept a gutter with his hair. Another moaned from hepatitis C, liver inflamed, his life saved only by the ACA. Ginsberg was most interested in mental illness in his poem. Now a consensus is building that addiction is a disease, that we need to assist people to heal before they have a chance to become strung out.

In 1993 the *Seattle Times* reported, "The lead singer of Nirvana was on heroin when he shot himself in the head, renewing speculation that Seattle is a hotbed of heroin abuse, particularly among grunge musicians and fans." It's a white-bread habit, costly and select. And while Big Pharma and seedy physicians are fueling an epidemic of legal drugs, heroin remains a major player everywhere, in large part because synthetic opioids nurture penchants for its sweet sensation.

On the bright side, junkies, unlike the run-of-the-mill speed freak or drunk, rarely turn fierce, even if they do resort to property crimes to gather objects they can pawn. They hurt themselves, but rarely others. Several European nations are regulating heroin, effectively legalizing it, acknowledging addiction as a disease.

Seattle seems ready to follow their lead. In a single day in January of 2017, three people on Aurora Avenue died of heroin overdoses and a fourth had to be taken to a hospital. Public health officials found their lethal dope had been laced with the synthetic opioid fentanyl. In March of 2016, Seattle police began to carry naloxone, a drug that reverses effects of any opioid overdose. Conceding to the counsel of erstwhile mayor Ed Murray, the city also now is establishing safe-consumption facilities where the chemically dependent can avoid arrest. Can fire-up crack, get sterile needles and syringes, inject themselves in relatively safe conditions.

❖ ❖ ❖

Now again it is a white summer day on the city's south side. I've come back home to visit family and extract the psychic shrapnel in my wrist from long ago. It is a jagged shard that caused me pain. Lured to the surface by a now-forgotten poem, it itched within me as injuries tend to do when they begin to heal.

I escape the storming four lanes of First Avenue South; I motor down a quiet residential drive; I trace its half-circle past a dozen older homes. Here's the log home where I met Ken Magee. Outside the mossback driveway, I kill the ignition. I sit and breathe my enduring relief at having blasted through all that fast traffic.

The neighborhood looks much as it did in 1973. Pacific redcedar, *Thuja plicata*, shade the lawn. A tangle of foliage tumbles down a steep ravine. Miller Creek flows below, through thickets of vine maple and devil's club, *Oplopanax horridus*. The stuff of omens and bad dreams, its spiny canes resemble medieval battle barricades known as abbattis. A half-mile to the west, the restless Salish Sea froths, its bell buoys clanging, its kelp strands reeky in the early summer heat.

When I was a kid, a footpath skirted this same lane. It wound past purplish firs. It terminated at the saltwater's edge. Forest duff from centuries of fallen needles and leaves silenced every step. Snaking my way home one day, I heard a sound. I felt a throbbing deep within my solar plexus. A percussion much like a rototiller warming up. A ruffed grouse, I saw, was puffing chest and beating wings on a trunk beneath its feet, playing that log like a drum, transmitting sonic come-ons. The cloistered home that Ken would later rent lay a quarter-mile away.

Bearded bull of a man, emigrant New Yorker, five years older than me, he had served two tours in Vietnam. There he'd grown a tooth for high-grade Asian dope. After his discharge, he trekked abroad with an unlikely wad of cash. Found his way to the Golden Triangle, that foremost opium-producing area where Laos, Myanmar, and Thailand intersect. He sampled flights of its soothing produce and copped a primo kilo—"a key," he enunciated it, teasing out the long vowels.

It was his recipe for pleasure, his conduit to liquid bliss. Ken took a big chance. Had he gotten busted, they might have bricked him up for decades. But the fruit of the poppy transports its followers to a devil-may-care republic, a melty-swirly dream-state. There the spasms of an exhausted world evaporate like sidewalk steam. The lowly high from junk is akin to being swaddled in rose silk.

Ken leased the log house from a distance with a phone call. He packed his key inside a fire extinguisher and shipped it from Asia to the Seattle address. On the porch beside his other military mementoes he found the kilo resting. It shone like alpenglow from Mt. Rainier. It emitted tunes like a boom-box. In a show of restraint, though, Ken held off cracking the package for two weeks. He believed the DEA would have a harder time convicting him if its wrapper remained intact.

In his brassy New York laugh he shared a fantasy. He would discharge the contents out the fire extinguisher's hose on opening night. He'd atomize the sleepy stuff, fill up space. Guests would need only breathe in the atmosphere and achieve a vaporous stone. To assuage the strain of his two-week wait, he copped a couple grams of second-rate Mexican chocolate stuff out on the Pacific Highway.

Much as the Pied Piper of Hamelin lured vermin from the woodwork, Ken drew us to his home. We teenagers gravitating to suck up his dope had never seen anyone quite like him. His demands were few enough, asking only to be enabled in his tastes. His Afghani hashish, plaid-banded boater hat, white linen suit and hand-tooled Italian shoes. We bedazzled young admirers all wore rags of light.

The parties began in late May and welcomed every comer. Lawn parties, from all appearances, genteel affairs attended by well-behaved strangers. Behind the scenes, though, Ken was teaching us how to charge up Salem cigarettes like muskets. Twist out the contents, blend together the powder and dried leaf, tamp the concoction back inside the flimsy paper sheath. The craftwork demanded steady hands. And love. Like trying to put on a condom without a steady erection.

Much of the pleasure of the dope show lay in dainty preparation. Fussing with the stuff like cooks, we could dedicate hours to the groundwork of a meal. Lips smacked and lungs sucked when the suppers fired up and passed from hand to hand. We dug Ken's odd and baffling generosity, his endless fund of junk.

He served up a dreamier version of Jay Gatsby's bootleg booze. Missing out on a Daisy Buchanan to focus his devotion, he produced two cool brunettes, mirror images of one other, leggy and lethargic, sultry and remote. Their leaden eyelids, four dark moons, presided over every party. Rumors insisted they were call girls whom Ken was pimping. Twelve years later, Robert Palmer's video of the song "Addicted to Love," featuring legions of mini-skirted dancers swaying in somber lines, nailed the blunted affect of those women Ken brought to his home. Even stone-cold sober, they appeared to be nodding off. Foxy thralls to the nod.

Smoke it, snort it, shoot it, the impacts vary only in degree. First the urge to vomit leads to the nod, the nod to itching and scratching, the scratching to a down-and-out aspect straight off Skid Row. Or, in fitter comparison, straight out of poet Richard Hugo's hometown of White Center. His West Marginal Way, the seamy south side of Seattle, the district that locals called Rat City. His was a burb where biker gangs hung out, carried guns, dealt drugs flagrantly from corner lots.

The street product often had been stepped on —tainted, unlike Ken's—to plump up its volume or mimic its effects. Caffeine, laundry detergent, even rat poison sometimes adulterated it. Fearing a sickness worse than the rugged junk itself, I took a taste outside Ken's shady lane only a single time and it turned out to be PCP. Messed me up so much I forgot my name and shed my shirt in the Paramount Theater to cool the flames I believed were burning inside of me.

Our bearded Buddha was guiding us on a cooler route to illumination. A species of elitism, never spoken aloud, governed every shred of conduct on his watch. His tacit credo told us we were meant to smoke it only, push the pleasure button through the cilia of the lungs alone. Let those dirty brethren downtown sweep the streets on hands and knees. They must be forgiven. Needles terrified us anyway. We were glad to have a reason to avoid them. We could give up the stuff at any time. We would never yield to sickly addiction, not us. No, not ever.

"Come, sit, indulge," Ken sighed from lotus position on a tatami mat. Filter-first with extended hand, he proffered his loaded Salems to backlit visitors, inviting us to retire right beside him. Just give it up, become happy slumps. Ken's manner nullified the needle's threat, refuted the junkie stereotype. Salem in the Old Testament is Jerusalem, holy city and pilgrimage site for Christians, Muslims, and Jews. Before it became Jerusalem, it was named Canaan, the promised land.

Three of my friends had a father who collected science fiction and jazz. His hair shelved out like Einstein's; his utterances were owlish and few. The family home was a cornucopia of culture, a laissez-faire affair, a rambler-style all-ages experiment in communal living, where pot was smoked openly for decades before the Washington voters approved it. Music blasted from towering speakers and the parental units were absent, even when they weren't. One son became a blues musician, another a withered

junkie whose girlfriend appeared twice her calendar age. A third son kept a reefer rolled at ready by his bedside every night to set to flame when he awoke. Odd for a librarian, college-educated and liberal, the father never encouraged his offspring to attend a university. And so, they never did.

The place and time remain for me a fusion of pleasure and pain. Pleasure to have partaken in such a social endeavor, sorrow to have seen such a waste of pain. After the summer ended, Ken's shrinking supply of the white stuff divided the dabblers from the lifers. The parties shifted to other homes around the city's south side. The Salem cigarettes gave way to glossy folded paper packets passed hand to hand beside a penknife used to scoop and lift the powder to the nose. As a determined dabbler who feared and respected the sharp talons of the law, I was watching over both cold shoulders. And about that time, I began to sidle away.

One of the coterie had accused me of observing from the margins, taking notes. That true accusation made me feel salted and raw. It was like being named a narc. Some of Ken's more ardent acolytes began to buy and transport the stuff in wallet-size bindles, behaving like salesmen making kindly calls on clients, offering pinhead tasters for the first time free. Lively parties collapsed into dull and itchy standstills. Plastic circles on turntables spun silent and unattended.

My senior Guatemalan friend Omar took up the needle and it lanced me to see it. Already a published writer of fabulist fiction, he decided to indulge in what seemed to me to be a premature retirement. His ideal life began to drain away. The rain of plagues included a job on the skids and a soft sad cock. His worst grief lay not in the knowledge that he was an addict, rather in his vain efforts to get it up for his lover, a dysfunction compounded by a shameful need to twist turds the texture of basalt from inside himself, thanks to the opioid's dehydrating effects.

Omar did his best to recover heaven by backpedaling out of hell. Pledging himself to a cold-turkey routine, he sweated through a week of cramps, chills, sweats, grinding teeth. Clean for a period long enough to satisfy himself, he chose to commend his cure with one last fix, his twisted logic ambling the aisle beside his bad habituation. He wanted to reward his self-control. But his tolerance for the concoction had dropped; the stuff he bought was much stronger. He used the same imprudent proportions as before, and that last congratulation did him in.

Ken's supply ran really low. Sadder and poorer, he ventured underground and started selling remnants of his kilo. The sunny glade, the lawn parties, and snazzy threads fell away. One cloudy day a pair of would-be buyers at his house—government agents on the take, he later learned—flashed matching .45s and relieved him of an ounce. None of his hangers-on proved eager to tail them in the sports car with a shotgun, as had happened once before when a deal went south.

Ken was scared shitless to consider how close he'd come to cashing it all in. The women went to work openly as call girls at motels on Pacific Highway near the airport. Ken shed weight. The end of the spree became plain to see.

Still in high school, I saw it all as a bardo in my life. Reading the Beat poets and the Buddhist philosophy that shaped them, I understood the bardo as an in-between state, a purgatorial moment that slides on a scale between death and rebirth. The bardo also often takes the shape of growth and change and offers a chance for heightened intensity, accompanied by a sensation of uncertainty and groundlessness. The human body may no longer rely on normal reference points and habitual patterns. If my moment-in-life were a bardo, I'd better not blow it.

After I graduated from high school, I found a job at a seafood processing plant, where my graveyard shift began at 2:20 a.m. The first night on the job, after punching the drowsy clock, I zeroed in on a tall guy in hairnet and hardhat whom I knew from Ken's soirees. Staring hard at the fluorescents, he was locked and lowing like a struck steer. Suddenly he toppled, spasmed, leaked blood between clenched teeth. He was having an epileptic seizure. His love affair with speedballs—coke and junk combined, beloved of John Belushi—had delivered his affliction.

The cannery was a refuge for hard-luck cases, high-school dropouts and felons, people a lot like me. During smoke breaks on the loading dock, one former convict taught us a civilized way to practice battle. Bend the neck, lower the head, punch above the belly and below the collarbone. Stay mindful to jab only the ribs.

My job entailed spraying disinfectants on the slime lines and scrubbing them with abrasive pads once the swing shift had clocked out. Decked in rain gear from head to toe, gloves and goggles and respirator against the fumes and spray, I devised a gradual plan to get the hell out. I would go to college. Leave behind the blue-collar grind. The work was apt to kill my spirit if it did not corrode my lungs.

After a year I collected my final check and made the study-plunge. Took out loans, tightened the belt, enrolled in college classes full-time. Made myself over in that tried-and-true American way. The distance from my servitudes felt mighty fine. Not that I blamed anyone for anything. I was only turning a page.

Leaving a biology class one day, I spotted a leather jacket draped over a chair. Aiming to become a solid citizen, do the right thing, I grabbed the heavy bomber coat to tote to the lost-and-found. A fat wallet weighed one pocket down. I checked for ID to see if it was anyone I knew, anyone from the class to return it to. Tucked inside the billfold was a driver's license and a citation for violating parole. The license displayed the swarthy mug of someone I had never seen.

There were also five slim bindles, folded paper packets. They flashed me back to the silly folded love notes we had passed around in junior high. I knew right off what were. Unfolding one gram and dipping in a wet finger, I did a gummer, rubbed it on my gums. It was junk all right, even if it lacked the UPC or list of ingredients found today on products sold in state-licensed pot shops.

The stuff was doubtful in origin. Despite which, the wild idea occurred to have one last blast, a nodding bash to usher in the new age, the new me. But so many friends were chilled in prison, were sick or dead, I no longer knew where to turn for camaraderie and enablement. The desire to party also had lost a bunch of its luster. Especially when I considered going it alone. The day and night I'd piss away. The "after-dream" that Poe's Roderick Usher knew too well, "the bitter lapse into everyday life." The powder might be laced with PCP, I worried. Or worse, rat poison laid out as bait. My whiskers twitched, my instincts tingled.

I entered a toilet stall and latched the door behind me. Unfolding each of the slim packets with silence and care, I sprinkled them one by one. Flushed and watched them dizzy clockwise down the porcelain drain. The same sluice I'd found so useful to unload myself of colored yawns when the rush was coming on.

❖ ❖ ❖

The late actress and author Carrie Fisher — outspoken expert on relapse and rehab, tox and detox—never settled in Seattle. An offspring of Hollywood, a habitué of the celebrity spotlight, she survived every ordeal till she was sixty. In an interview, she owned up to the twisted cognition that drives good people mad. "I'd say, 'Oh, fuck it, I haven't done anything for a couple months, why not? Let's celebrate not doing them by doing them.'" In this belated age of social media, I spend undue energy musing whether I dare unfriend the dead. Their faces beckon me from screens. Their names still colonize my address books. They recall for me those roadside commemorations made of crosses, photos, plastic flowers, notes.

It would be easy to write off my teenage fling with heroin as a capitulation to peer pressure. To cite those days as the siren cry of a city where rock and roll became a pagan faith. Explain it away by measuring the rain, the proximity of glowering mountains, the availability of Asian imports within the Pacific Rim. Even the Greek poet Homer nodded off, though, as Horace wrote. Even Homer did not manage to keep his inner vision focused on the target all the time.

❖ ❖ ❖

Standing in front of our home on the left is Mother, Mrs. Tatini Bala Dutta; youngest sister Sayoni in the middle; and the brother who got sick and precipitated the sale of the house stands to the right. The kid in the front is a neighbor's daughter.

# Home

I had not seen my mother and my youngest sister, Sayoni, since 1968, the year I left India for Canada on a Canadian university scholarship for postgraduate studies in physics. So when I first returned to India in 1980, I took a weekend trip to visit them. They lived in Laheriasarai, my sleepy little hometown, about four hundred miles northwest of Kolkata, where I was staying.

Laheriasarai, not too far from the foothills of the Himalayas, was accessible from Kolkata by an overnight train. Soon after the train left the city, I stretched myself on my sleeper seat and slept through the night. The ride was restful and, thankfully, trouble-free. Usually these rides were known to be fraught with incidences of physical violence perpetrated by hooligans out to rob nighttime travelers.

After the train unloaded me at the Laheriasarai railway station the next morning, I stood on the platform for a few minutes and took in the ambience. The station hadn't changed since the last time I had seen it twelve years earlier: two long platforms, one on each side of the railway tracks, connected by an overhead bridge. It was still housed in the same one-story building with three waiting rooms at one end and a small room at the other for the ticket counters. The station was separated from the outside by a gate through which the arriving passengers exited. Outside the gate, three-wheeled cycle rickshaws were lined up waiting to ferry the exiting passengers to their destinations. I hired one. The driver, a scrawny, swarthy man, was clothed in a soiled *dhoti* and a shirt and had a turban on. He appeared to be in his forties.

"Bengal Lodge, please." My home was in the neighborhood of this lodge.

The sun wasn't up yet. Small-town Laheriasarai was slowly waking in the unfolding soft light of early morning. A handful of people were out on their morning walks, and a few shopkeepers had begun to raise the store shutters to get ready for the day's business. The air felt cool, fresh, and soothing. My rickshaw driver leisurely wended through the sparse streets, went halfway around a roundabout surrounding the town's only clock tower, and headed straight down toward my home, just the way I thought he would. Until the road forked, the landscape looked familiar: grocery and clothing stores, a bookstore, a gas pump, a bunch of restaurants and a pharmacy, and the road that led to the branch post office. Soon, the restaurants would be serving breakfast— *puris* and spicy peas and potato curries—and the sidewalks would be lined with noisy peddlers hawking flowers to the women headed for the temples to make offerings to the gods, the sweet fragrance of roses and *Champa* and *Rajanigandha* filling the air.

I found myself back in my youth.

The rickshaw took the right fork, and suddenly the landscape changed. The lane that used to lead to the home of Prof. Palit, my college English professor, had disappeared. New establishments—tailors, boutiques, and furniture places—had replaced the run-down small houses on the left of the road. Housing complexes had sprung up on the right. New roads and lanes had been laid to cope with the town's swelling size and population. The sleepy little hometown of my youth had taken on an urban appearance.

"Which house?" the driver asked as he reached what must have been the neighborhood of the Bengal Lodge.

Despite my earlier confidence, I was unable to point out the house. The gigantic centuries-old banyan tree that canopied our neighborhood and commanded the town, and where townspeople congregated in the evenings to socialize, was missing. In its place, there were business offices, retail stores, and restaurants. New buildings had come up near the Bengal Lodge, disrupting my line of sight to the only point of reference I was banking on to locate my home.

With my head hung low and shoulders slumped, I moped at my failure to spot the house that held so many memories of my early years. Part of the old neighborhood seemed to have been swallowed up in a gigantic earthquake, giving birth to a new neighborhood but, thankfully, my memory of my home had remained intact.

"Do you know the Duttas?" I was forced to ask a stranger, despite prickles of embarrassment.

"You mean the elderly lady who has several kids but now lives with only one of her daughters?" he said.

"Yes, do you know where they live?"

He pointed to a house behind a building near the Bengal Lodge. I recognized it, the tin-roofed house, walled in on three sides, and the tall guava tree that I could never climb in my youth. The driver led me to the house carrying my suitcase and knocked on the door.

"So glad to see you," Mother said as she opened the door, her wizened face glowing with a serene but broad smile. Since I hadn't seen any photograph of her in a dozen years, I didn't know how much her looks might have changed. She was, after all, now seventy-five. Her face was more wrinkled, but she hadn't let the years shrink her small stature; she still walked straight. My youngest sister, Sayoni, thirty years old, stood beside her wearing a faint smile. She had grown into a beautiful woman, same impish smile, bright face, and soft voice as before; her hair, which used to be shoulder-length, was still dark but much longer. I remembered her as a school girl, bookish and studious with no interest or time for girlish fashion, packing up her notebooks and lunch box and rushing to start the long walk to school so she wouldn't miss the opening bell. She was eager and determined and worked hard like all of us to be somebody in life someday. She had become a professor of Sanskrit in one of the local colleges. I wondered how long it would be before she got married and went away like my other sisters, leaving Mother to fend for herself. But I also knew when that day came, her children wouldn't let her live alone. She would live with one of us.

"How have you been?" I asked.

She smiled and said, "Good."

"So, now my little sister is a professor, eh?"

"Yes, it keeps me out of trouble," she said with a glint in her eyes.

"And she helps me with housework, too," Mother added.

As we sluggishly headed toward the steps that led to the cement veranda of the house, I saw the hut on the left where Dada, my oldest brother, now dead, used to tutor his students. On the right was a small patch of land where my sisters used to grow cauliflowers, cabbages, potatoes, and tomatoes. From the looks of the weeds, it appeared not to be used anymore.

Except for a new bathroom that had replaced the old one, the one-floor, partially thatched tin-roofed house looked very much the same as when I last saw it, sheltered from the chaos of the town noises by tall walls, banana and lemon trees on the far side of the large courtyard. The garden in the middle of the courtyard was still in its place, full of pink begonias, red peonies, golden marigolds, and white roses. The sweet fragrance of the blooms and the profusion of multi-colored petals took me back many years. I remembered flowers from this garden were the subject of one of my research projects during my sophomore year in college. I collected more than one thousand blooms over a period of a few weeks, counted the petals in each of them, and carried out a statistical modeling of the number of each type of flower having the same number of petals. This experience stood me in good stead during my graduate studies when I had to do a similar modeling for the number of alpha particles emitted by radioactive materials.

Mother was still spending much of her time puttering around in the kitchen. Cooking for the family had always been a large part of her life, and she enjoyed it. My father had owned a restaurant that didn't do well. Some days he didn't have any money for the family. Those days Mother had no food to cook, and we could see on her face she was sad, much as she tried to hide it.

"It's just the two of you now, you and Sayoni. How come you still spend so much time in the kitchen?" I teased her.

She smiled. "There's always so much to do," she said, looking at me and nodding. She always had a gentle voice. I had never seen her angry or harsh. She didn't know English, not a word. She spoke only Bengali, our mother tongue. "*Samoy kete jai*," she added, meaning "time passes."

I was happy to see Mother had found her own outlet to keep herself occupied to fill the void in her life. Once upon a time, she'd had a large family around her, six sons and four daughters, and the house was always abuzz with voices. The family kept her busy in the kitchen on those days and nights when my father had the money to buy food, but she never missed her morning and evening prayers or afternoon naps and never got involved in family squabbles. Occasionally, she would meet up with neighbors, and that was the extent of her social life. I do not remember if she ever went to a movie or a cultural show. She had a beautiful singing voice, and quite often, hummed devotional songs: *"You are my Friend, You are my Master, You are mine through Night and Day."* My father had passed away in 1961, and with the death of one son and the rest of the sons leaving home one by one in search of livelihood elsewhere, and three of the four daughters married off and gone to live with their husbands and raise their own families, the house had become quiet like the streets of the town on blistering summer afternoons. She only had Sayoni to share it with, in solitude.

This photograph was taken outside our home. Mother is on the far right. Next to Mother is youngest sister, Sayoni Bose, who became a professor. Next to Sayoni on the left is my older brother Sanjay. On the far left is a neighbor.

❖ ❖ ❖

After prolonged small talk about neighbors and my old friends, followed by a badly needed shower to recover from the night-long train journey, it was close to lunchtime. Mother had cooked an elaborate lunch for me: pale yellow sweet-smelling shrimp *biriyani*, brown-colored mutton curry with a pungent aroma, fish curry cooked with mustard, buttery-flavored vegetable *korma*, and *aloor dom*, made with small whole round potatoes and cooked in a gravy mixed with a dash of powdered cardamom, cinnamon, and other spices. Each item was served in a separate silver bowl surrounding the biriyani, which was served on a silver plat-

ter. Altogether the fare was a riot of colors and flavors. I finished off the lunch with the all-time favorite dessert of the Bengalis, *rosogollas*, made from golf-ball-shaped casein dumplings simmered in sugar syrup. Everything was just as savory as in the years long gone by. I was amazed Mother remembered my favorites. She used to cook these dishes in my youth on special occasions like *Durga Pujo* and *Saraswati Pujo*. I didn't get to eat such foods anymore, and I missed them.

"How did you remember these were my favorite dishes?" I said to Mother.

"I'm your mother, I remember everything," she said with a knowing smile.

In the midst of so much love and affection, Dada's absence didn't escape me. I couldn't avoid thinking that this was the first time I was in this house when Dada was not among us. Dada, the oldest of us ten siblings, became the head of the family after my father passed away in 1961. My father was never much of a breadwinner and had left no money for the family. Dada was still in college, an exceptionally bright student, and looked forward to a promising future with immense possibilities. He could have left home to pursue his own dreams, but he didn't, opting instead to work near Laheriasarai and support his siblings. Sadly, he suddenly passed away a month before, just about the time I'd saved up enough money and was planning to make a trip: this trip.

❖ ❖ ❖

After a short siesta, which was a common holiday practice with a lot of Bengalis, I hired a rickshaw, and Sayoni and I went out for a quick tour of the town. I was so happy Sayoni volunteered to come along. She guided the driver around and showed me the developments that

107

had taken place since my last visit: a new road that led to a redesigned marketplace, fancy buildings housing new stores and restaurants, paved roads, and the new bus station.

As we went around the town, I thought of the huge lunch Mother had cooked for me.

"She must be tired from all that cooking," I said to Sayoni.

"I don't think so; she loves cooking," she said. "Besides, she misses you and all her children who don't live with her anymore."

Sayoni's words reminded me of the hapless situation I had been trapped in for years. Living thousands of miles away across the seas from home on a paltry stipend and with a wife to support, I often found myself feeling miserable about my inability to visit Mother during my student days. Oh, how I longed to see her and my siblings! But my longing had to remain just that, a longing, until the day I landed my first job. During that long period of poor finances, I would often think back to the days just before I left India, and how I never thought it would take me twelve years before I would be able to afford a visit to see Mother. Her loneliness pained me a great deal, but my inability to salve her loneliness pained me no less.

"Do you think she's taking a nap now?" I said.

"Yea, I think so; this is her time to rest. She has to have her afternoon naps, and the morning and evening prayers."

The rickshaw driver cycled along.

We passed by Heycock Institution and M. L. Academy, my elementary and high schools, and C. M. College where I did the first two years of my undergraduate study before moving to an out-of-town college to complete my degree.

By the time we were done sightseeing, it was well past sundown, and I didn't want to stay out in the dark. The streets were not lighted well, which made me uneasy. I remembered incidents of nighttime assault and battery in this town from years ago.

On the way back, our driver pedaled through the narrow dusty streets, congested with noisy pedestrians, ubiquitous cycles and rickshaws mercilessly honking enough to annoy the most tolerant among us. We passed by Lighthouse, Metro, and National, the cinema halls of my youth, and the raucous street hawkers peddling fritters and fries cooked in the open, the air thick with their heavy pungent smells. These were some of my favorite hangouts for quick afternoon snacks during my adolescence.

"Do you want to try some of these?" Sayoni said.

"I don't think so. Western living has made me conscious of the importance of hygiene."

❖ ❖ ❖

Endless chatter with Mother and Sayoni, all innocent curiosities, filled our waking hours. Their questions were not wholly unexpected. They had hardly ever been out of Laheriasarai, let alone out of the country.

"What's it like to live in Canada?" Sayoni asked.

"Comfortable. You don't have to line up for everything like here," I said.

"Do you like it there?" Mother asked, a frown on her face.

"There're things I like, and there're things I don't, but on the whole, yes, I like it there."

"Do you get Indian food?" Mother asked looking concerned.

"Yes, I do. We've many Indian restaurants and grocery stores. Sometimes, I cook at home."

"Do you celebrate Indian festivals?" Sayoni asked.

"We do, but only a few like *Durga Pujo, Saraswati Pujo,* and *Diwali.*"

"Do you get to speak Bengali?" Mother asked.

"Yes, there's a large Bengali community in our city," I said. "When we get together, we talk mostly in Bengali."

"Do you miss India?" Mother asked.

"Yes, of course."

"When do you plan to return for good?" Mother asked.

The question made me squirm. I fumbled for a way to answer her truthfully without hurting her feelings. It had been a long time for me in Canada, and I'd grown used to the comfort and conveniences of my adopted country. I didn't know if someday I'd decide to return, but, for now, that thought didn't cross my mind.

"I've a decent job there. It'll be difficult to find a comparable job here, Mother," I said. "Maybe someday."

She became quiet for a moment, brooding, before blurting out. "You've come for a very short time after so many years!"

Sayoni chimed in to second Mother's complaint.

I did admit our conversations were far from over. There was still so much more to talk about. I realized a weekend was too short for a reunion like this, but I was stuck with my itinerary. I needed the few days left in my vacation to visit my other siblings and friends in other cities and towns. Mother's loneliness and her longing for my company cut me to the quick, but I was helpless to do anything about it. This helplessness, and the anguish that comes with it, is often the price the immigrants pay for choosing to live far from home.

"I promise I'll plan for a longer stay the next time," I told them.

Before long, the weekend was over, and it was time for me to return to Kolkata. I shuffled to the room I was using and started packing my suitcase, one item at a time. When done, I dragged it outside the room and placed it there. Sayoni shambled off to get me a rickshaw.

"Can I pack you some food for the road?" Mother asked.

"Yes, that'll be nice, thank you."

As she was giving me the food container, she looked at me and said, her voice, soft and soothing and almost halting, "Come back again soon, not after so many years like this time."

"Yes, I will. Thank you for everything," I said to Mother and Sayoni. We hugged each other for a long time. I didn't want to let loose of them while the rickshaw driver came inside the house and picked up my suitcase.

Not that I was in the mood to bid farewell, but I did, not sure when I'd see them again. I felt a lump in my throat and could hardly talk. I waved them goodbye, and, as the rickshaw started to move, I took one last look at them and the house. Mother and Sayoni were standing still, their faces somber, staring at the rickshaw as it slowly pulled away from them and the house.

❖ ❖ ❖

It was already evening, and the ensuing darkness had started to envelop the area. I boarded the Kolkata-bound train and sat by the window. By the time we started to move, my compartment was more than half filled with passengers, all local people, dressed in *dhoti*, undershirt, and turban. I was the only one in pants and shirt, which made me stand out. After fifteen minutes or so, the train stopped at the next station. Some passengers got on and

off, but the train didn't seem to be in a rush to leave. There was no announcement explaining the delay. Thanks to some enterprising passengers in the next compartment, the reason became clear: an earlier accident farther ahead had blocked the only tracks the train could travel on. Nobody seemed to know how long it would take to clear the wreck. Most passengers appeared to be from the surrounding areas. Several of them jumped off the stalled train and started walking. I guessed they left to catch a bus or something to get to wherever they were headed for. Their destinations must have been close, but Kolkata was too far, and there was no other way for me to get there.

I felt out of place among the few passengers remaining in my compartment. Situations like this wouldn't have bothered me when I was growing up in Laheriasarai and was familiar with the area and its people, but now, twelve years out of the country without ever once coming back, I felt like a stranger in my own home territory. The lights in the compartment had gone out. The faces of my fellow passengers were barely visible in the darkness. Occasionally, I caught snatches of their whispers but didn't understand what they were talking about. Could they be talking about me? I recalled from years ago the notoriety of this region as the sanctuary of violent elements. They were known to rob passengers in stalled trains. Thinking about them sent a chill down my spine. I covered myself from head to toe with the shawl I had tucked inside my suitcase and breathlessly waited for the train to move.

For nearly three hours, filled with utter tension and fear, I sat in the train thinking about the handful of times I had visited home since I moved to Kolkata for graduate studies in 1964. As if the uphill train journey, often the target of the lawless hooligans, alone wasn't enough to dampen my desire to visit my hometown, I started feeling a loosening of my attachment to the place of my birth. Laheriasarai often brought back memories of nights without food, of frayed clothes and unfulfilled needs and desires of my early years. I wanted to get out of this world of misery and indigence. I wanted a bigger world and greater opportunities to grow. I didn't see how living in the constricted environment of small-town Laheriasarai would help me become the famous physicist I aspired to become. This realization instilled in me a terrible sense of isolation and loneliness. In my thoughts and feelings, I started to drift away from my childhood friends, and the surroundings in which I grew up. A lack of a sense of belonging began to weigh heavily on me. I felt an inner urge to look for new pastures. Kolkata's bigness and modernity and its promise of endless opportunities captured my heart and imagination. I was aware of my infrequent visits to see my Mother, and I did feel a sense of guilt, but the allure of my new environment was too overwhelming for that guilt to counter. Sitting on that train, waiting in the grip of uncertainty and suspense, I wondered if I was paying the price for my past transgressions.

When the train started to move, it wasn't going in the forward direction but back to Laheriasarai. It wouldn't go forward until the next morning, it was announced. Maybe, my hometown didn't want to let go of me after all!

It was close to midnight when I arrived back home. Mother and Sayoni had already retired for the night.

"What happened?" Sayoni asked in disbelief as Mother looked on incredulously.

The journey back to Kolkata next morning was uneventful.

❖ ❖ ❖

"We're thinking about selling the house in Laheriasarai," Sanjay, my older brother, and the guardian of the family after oldest brother Dada's death, told me during one of our telephone conversations in 1995, while I was still in Canada.

"Do we have to?"

"Yes, we need the money to take care of the family expenses."

He didn't mention what those expenses were for, and I didn't ask. Asking an older brother to explain would have been disrespectful in a traditional Indian family like ours, but I was intrigued by this sudden need. How were these expenses met before? Were there new expenses he wasn't telling me about? (Years later I'd learn that my youngest brother, Probal, had been very ill, and Sanjay had been taking him to doctors and nursing homes, trying desperately to cure him. Ultimately, however, none of the treatments worked. He had a mental illness, schizophrenia, and had to be admitted to a nursing home for an indefinite period, causing an increase in family expenses.) My heart

sank. Sanjay hadn't said how much, but I had a feeling whatever the amount, as a successful nuclear safety analyst in a Toronto utility company, I could cover it.

"But I can take care of the expenses," I said.

"For how long?"

"As long as necessary," I said.

He ignored my answer, a long silence, which, in our family, had always served as the final word. Perhaps, in view of my inability to be of much help during my financially-challenged student days—what he viewed as my unwillingness—he felt more comfortable having the funds from the sale of the house readily available for years to come.

"Where are Mother and Sayoni going to stay?" I asked.

"With me in Kolkata."

❖ ❖ ❖

Until 1995, the year Sanjay told me abut his plan to sell our Laheriasarai home, I had been to Kolkata twice since my first visit in 1980, but I never went back to Laheriasarai. Even though Mother and Sayoni were very much on my mind, and I yearned to see them, our mutual love and affection couldn't win over the terrible sense of unease I felt every time I visited my hometown before I left the country in 1968.

After Sanjay's telephone call, I had a sudden longing to see our home one more time. I wanted to stand in the middle of the courtyard and take a deep breath of the ambient air. The fond memories of the monsoon seasons of my childhood came surging back like video images from a long-lost past. I remembered the times when the sky became engulfed in black clouds, slowly erasing the daylight with premature darkness, and thunder roared and lightning streaked across the sky, and wild and gusty rains came down, drenching the earth below. On such occasions, I often found myself sliding face-down, end-to-end, on the rain-slicked verandah of our tin-roofed house, letting out screams of joy amid a cacophony of laughter from my neighborhood friends. The steady music of the pitter-patter on the roof transported me to imaginary lands. When the rains ceased or subsided, I sat with my makeshift line and lure by the narrow overflowing stream that ran alongside our house, hoping to catch some fish. Success rarely came my way, but the anticipation was intoxicating.

The kite-flying festival followed soon after the monsoon season when square, circular, and rectangular kites in yellow, white, blue, and black dappled the sky like random flicks of paintbrushes and swooped and pounced on one another, cut-ting some loose in the airborne skirmishes. The unraveled kites surged forward in the gusts of wind, gradually losing height. I ran after them from the court-yard of our house with the neighborhood children, some older than me, sometimes suc-ceeding in catch-ing one, failing most of the time, but always pant-ing with the excitement of the wild chase.

Sayoni is seated on the left; next to Sayoni is Mother, and next to Mother is our oldest brother, Dada, who supported all of us siblings.

❖ ❖ ❖

Our home, the center stage of our shared laughter, sorrows, and struggles for decades, passed to someone else within a matter of days, bringing to a quiet end our family's checkered history amid a great deal of unspoken grief and sadness.

With the sale of our house, and Mother's and Sayoni's subsequent move to Kolkata, our home lost whatever appeal it had for me. I was afraid the new owners might have reshaped the house to suit their own needs and predilec-tions, transforming the look I grew up with. I wanted to cling to my memory, sheltered from the ravages of unwelcome interferences, and so, I never visited the house again. Despite the many ups and downs in life brought on by the pitiless march of fate and time, even now, more than thirty-five years after my only return to Laheriasarai in 1980, the memory of the house where I was born and spent all my adolescent years fleets by in my mind's eye like the crawls on a silver screen. I see the burst of white and gold and red and blue of spring blooms in our garden, waving gently in the westerly wind; I hear the pitter-patter of the lusty rains on the tin roof of the house as I slide end-to-end on its rain-slicked veranda; I see multicolored and multi-shaped kites criss-crossing the sky with the ad-vent of the kite-flying season. These were our small joys on an island of stark poverty and deprivations. On this island, I also see Dada quietly return-ing home late at night after toiling away at multiple jobs to take care of his fatherless siblings; I see my mother moiling away alone in the kitchen, cooking for her family of twelve. I see the glum patina of masked sadness on her face when she didn't have any food to cook and sent her family to bed hungry. I see my siblings and me, despite our daily challenges, clustered around the yellow light of dim kerosene lamps every evening, working on homework for school the next day, striving and competing for academic excellence and building castles of lofty dreams. Little did I know at the time that life in that house, with all its pain and pleasure, was en-dowing me with a character that would serve me well as I grew older. A few years later, when I left India with eight dollars in my pocket and the promise of a student scholarship, and sub-sequently decided to settle in Canada, alone in the midst of an alien culture and far from family and friends, I knew all would be alright because I carried with me the image of Dada's selfless sacrifice for his siblings' future, his strict discipline and guidance so we didn't go astray, and his inspiration that led to our single-minded determination to succeed despite our adversities.

❖ ❖ ❖

## Marc Frazier

# All about Us

*NOAA Fisheries Pacific Islands' dolphin viewing guidelines threaten a large tourist industry, especially in Hawaii.*
*– http://www.fpir.noaa.gov/PRD/prd_swim_with_wild_dolphins.html*

We are tired of us
the constant glare
of screens
with conflicting data

brain patterns fracture
attention spans shrink

The dolphins are tired of us
our need to be soothed
swarms of us who
invade their pods

throw off their
echolocation
their speech to one another

they want rest after feeding all night

their sleep cycles disrupted
they swim to places
where predators wait

but what delight to see them break water
and spin
such joy

starved for
the spiritual
our need for play
staying fifty feet away
is a tease

when we leave
everything everywhere
will be with us again

as we aim to integrate split
screens split lives

# Maintenance

*—from Old French, maintenir: to hold in the hand*

I know what's expected. Seriously. I'm on duty here.
Watchful, yes.

"Maintain: 1. To keep in good condition by making repairs,
correcting problems."

Don't worry.
Seriously. I've taken care of it.
Filled the prescription
Adjusted the thermostat burped the baby
The heater cover's on back order
I tried to match the old one.

(Are you sure you're okay?)

It's all kept running by invisible hands—
Hands that hold. Touch.

It's said
Maintenance can be preventive
Or corrective
Calibrating's often complicated
You can spend all day on the fine-tuning.

Review the manual one more time. Then
Wait by the window.
It's known that true maintenance includes
Repair
and sometimes even overhaul.
"Maintain: 2. To cause something to exist or to continue without changing."

Look, stupid, you know that's not even possible.
Yes. But hold my hand.

Lissa Hatcher. *The Promise* (detail). 2017. Illuminated photographic print on panel with hand embellishments. 30 x 60 inches. Courtesy of ARTicles Art Gallery.

*Halvor Aakhus*

# Two Women, One Gay Viking

*July 2013. A birthday.*

"Can I braid your hair today?" she asked me.

*Hell no*, she knew I'd say.

Granted: In six weeks I would be marrying this woman on a beach. On horseback. And yes, this bride-to-be loved doing hair—of horses, that is—loved to tie her horsies' manes into a sequence of dressage-y grape-sized knobs along the arch of their bay veiny necks, loved brushing smooth the dirt from their corundum rumps, loved picking rain rot from their scabby hocks and combing knots out of their feces-caked horse tails.

But me, I am a man. Not a pony. So yah, no way would I let my fiancée braid my hair. And oh, oh how she wanted to. Hell no, I'd tell her. No way would I permit the future wife to lay a finger on the ponytail. Yep. Though a man, I did have this long girly ponytail. Down to my ass. And oh would I please let her braid my hair for our beach/horseback wedding, she kept begging me. Hell no. What about your eyebrows? Can I just pluck your eyebrows for the wedding, those hairs there in between at least, just right above your nose? Hell no. Not even by the morning of, with but an hour to go before our horseback ceremony on a beach of Seabrook Island off the coast of Charleston, South Carolina, would my bride last-minute be deterred, as she inveigled, plotted, and conspired to guilt my ponytail into a dainty nuptial braid.

But marriage came later. *Back to braiding hair in July of 2013*: It was the (future) wife's birthday. Mid-July, about two months before our beach wedding. And the wife and I were backpacking some five hundred miles from France to Spain: south from Dordogne, through the mountains of Basque Pyrenees, then west across the north of Spain to Santiago de Compostela. By my wife's birthday we were a couple days' hike from St Jean Pied de Port on the Pyrenees's French side.

Her birthday morning I woke first inside our tent, which we had pitched onto a steep hillside, our bodies so inclined that through the "skylight" screen atop our tent I could now see the east's horizon and its long slow dawn, how this medieval castle at the hillcrest of some nearby village (with a French name I cannot recall) grew red then golden in the rising light, the Gothic spires of its cathedral spiking up from amber foothills, stained glass windows glittering, the sky aflame—sunrise's slow strip-tease between the dark of night and day. It was magical and new. New to me, the Viking raised in USA's Midwest, between its flatnesses, its gray slate sky above you, and below an earth long logged and razed, the rippling terrain of its forgotten virgin forests flattened into fields of crops to plump the livestock, level cornstalk seas to fat the calves.

And so this morning, waking first inside our tent beside my future wife somewhere in France, I felt a happiness more pure than my sarcastic jaded ego ever would admit. And it is this moment, as the woman in my arms, her head yet resting on my chest, our bodies interwoven in the coolest hours before the dawn, it's as my bride-to-be began to rouse, she asked me drowsily:

"Can I braid your hair today?"

"Hell no," I answered. Me, I was a man. Not girly. Not a pony.

"But it's my birthday," she protested sweetly, and kept on at it, stubbornly ignoring my insistent iterations of *hell no*, as she bombarded me with arguments: how hot today will be, throughout our twenty-mile hike, a forty/fifty-pound pack at my back, and how each day all my shirts, my identical black Walmart Hanes wife-beaters, were completely soaked with sweat, but how the braiding of my hair would be less hot, would take the heat off of my neck, and how it wasn't girly, how men braid their hair too—Native Americans, for example—how indigenous Americans are strong and masculine and love to braid their hair, and blah blah bl' on she went, much as did I, Hell no Hell no Hell

115

no, until our argument, as arguments so often did, came to a sudden end with both the wife's hands down my pants and—*whoopsie*, there she goes—the wife goes down on me and, just like that, I am distracted by the phases of our whole "routine," as then inside her I hold back to make sure that the birthday wife comes before I do, until at last we are both done, our mouths full of each other's hair, our manes both tending to escape mid-coitus from hairbands, and also, in the process, somewhere, at some point, somehow, driven mad and mindless with desire, I have let go, slipped up, erupted with a series of humiliating "Minnesota Nice" affirmatives—*yah, uffdah! okeydokey! oh yabetcha!*—and the wife has got just what she wanted: The wife has made me promise mid-routine to let her braid my hair. Damn that sexy woman getting everything she wants. But fuck it. It's her birthday. And once I'd packed away the tent, I did it, I submitted, kneeled, I let her braid my silly hair.

This was a big mistake. We'd fight harder and more bitterly this day than any other, married or unmarried. Shit flew down the hillsides, hurtled at each other's heads. Backpacks of projectiles, emptied. Our shouts and screams rang violently, echoing throughout the foothills and the ranges of the Pyrenees beyond. Worst birthday of all time, she'd dub it ever after.

One year later, we'd get horseback-married on a white sand beach of Seabrook Island. The wedding was successful: In particular, I did not fall off my big horse. This giant horse, his name was Reign Cloud. I can't ride horses worth a damn. But buzzed on Everclear and benzos and whatnot, I managed not to fall off my colossal Iliadic horse into the beach's hot white sand. There were Bloody Marys too, there at the beach, in mason jars, I think. But frankly, I do not remember much. Throughout the horseback ceremony, I was elsewhere, stuck inside my head, remembering another white beach.

❖ ❖ ❖

*January 2012. The other white beach.*

Each day, a little farther from the shore I swam into the ocean, against the waves, away from those white beaches where my mother lay behind, dying.

My mother wanted to die. It was New Year's 2012. She was fifty-nine. Lying on the beach, she gobbled potent opiates, as I swam slowly from the shore against the tide. She was taking

two weeks off the chemo, celebrating winter break on white sand beaches in the Virgin Islands with her family. She had pancreatic cancer. In five months, she would be dead.

Mother and I were not close. But I the son did not want her to die. Later on that spring, for Mother's final months, I would desert my first job out of grad school, a full-time teaching post at Pittsburgh, and return to Indiana to help nurse her. But it was back at New Year's when my mother first told us—my father, sister, and myself—that she was ready to die. She lay upon the beach and took her fentanyl and morphine, as she discussed her death to come in writerly detail. It was tough to listen to. We preferred it when she was hallucinating, when wolves would creep across the ceiling, or when snakes would slither in her belly, or when once again the naughty tongue of Saint Louis the IX's decapitated head would lick her earlobes.

At first, before this New Year's on the beach, the mother hadn't wished to die. She'd had things to do. She taught magic, alchemy, and Dante at the college level. She was busy writing this new book, a historical novel set in Venice, about a werewolf. In Ireland, back in the nineties, she'd published three books, novels based on Celtic myths. But now things were different. Now she had stopped doing things. On New Year's, Mother would not swim. She, her body but a tipsy skeleton of who she'd been, no longer wished to live.

Throughout the holidays, my father swam in silence, grim and distant, and reorganized his seashell piles. Silent was his mode, nonverbal Norge Viking that he was. "Fine" was the Viking's universal adjective. Everything was *fine*. But five months later, when my mother'd gasped her final breath and, suddenly, he wailed and drooled onto her deathbed, I would learn that Viking Daddy didn't want his wife to die. My sister and I would be shocked by all his tears and drool: We'd not thought that our icy Viking father loved our fiery Irish mother.

After New Year's in the Virgin Islands, my mother resumed the chemo in Indiana, while I resumed the teaching job in Pennsylvania. But back at U-Pitt, things were different. Things no longer mattered. Each night I sat on my apartment's empty floor—I had not bothered to get furniture—and stared up at the bare white walls as I just drank and drank, and could not cry. This was new, the drinking. For two-plus years, I hadn't drunk a drop. But then, in January, with my death-wishing mom eight hundred miles away in Indiana, I began with Scotch. I chugged a pint of it, not in one gulp, but in two. Out of practice. Had to take a breath.

After that I switched to fifths of Everclear, and time slipped faster. Weeks passed by—bottles everywhere. I wished that I could cry, but I could not. Not until the birds. Not until, one day on my drive home from work, a half-full fifth of Everclear clamped tight between my thighs, when suddenly, through my windshield, I saw a flock of blackbirds, rising from a snowy field, take flight: Rising all around me, this dark cloud of wings aligned into a perfect V above me and, at last, I cried.

After those blackbirds, I stayed drunk five years. My heart stopped just the once, on my birthday: When I came to at the hospital, I was yellow and handcuffed. It was my thirty-fifth birthday, they told me.

Happy birthday! the nurses said.

Good luck making it to forty, the doctors added.

Uffdah, what a bummer, I thought. But I was thirty-something still. So I had time.

❖ ❖ ❖

*May 2012. Another birthday.*

My mother died the night before her sixtieth birthday. Although six years have passed, I can still see her dropped jaw clearly. Her mouth that hangs wide open in a silent howl. I see it in my dreams. The night she died, it was I who shut her eyes—so cold and glossy like a pair of polished stones—and it was I who kept on trying, even as the undertakers took her corpse away, to shut her mouth, that dropped jaw, hanging. But gravity kept snatching it.

It was not quick and easy, Mother's death, but slow and violent: such panic, fear, such brutal grunts of pain. After that last rattle of her breath, the Viking father, who'd until then been so still, so stern, so stubborn in his silence, suddenly let out a battle cry and just began to howl and drool. His sobs did not sound human, more like bulls at slaughter. My sister and I watched the tears and drool stream down his chin onto his dead wife's lap. I'd never seen a man wail on and on like that, much less our father. Me, I could not drool. Without chugged Everclear and blackbirds rising from a snowy field, I could not cry. I could only stare at walls.

Mother's body was a bare white wall now. And I just stared. Stared at the body that was not she. *Here, let me show you . . .*

*Look—there it is*: your mother's body in that bed, her bald, jaundiced head, her cancer-eaten body, just the bones left, starved, her legs like poles, like broomstick handles, and her arms like twigs, her face just a skull, her body just a branchy scarecrow with a skull as head—it is not she. Is not. Your mother's not the scarecrow in that bed. That body's not your mom. Is not, is not not NOT.

*All that is is NOT*: Your mother's NOT the thing that dies so brutally, so violent: She does NOT gasp. Does NOT convulse. You do NOT hold her down, to drip the liquid morphine underneath her tongue, these jaws you must pry open as they groan and grit in pain, gnashing at your fingers, as she fights death, fights for breath: She is NOT drowning in her tumored lungs. Despite a bottle full of morphine down her throat, she is NOT conscious. For hours, awake, she does NOT aspirate. Her gasps and grunts, so deep and guttural, so resonant for such a wasted cage of ribs. In the years to come, you will NOT hear your mother's grunted moaning in the night, in dreams. You do NOT hear it now. Now sitting in her bed, you do NOT hold her head upon your lap, her bald skull doesn't hammer in your stomach with each metronomic groan, your mother's yellow face so full of panic, pain, as if you were attacking her, as if it's you that tortures her, that beats her, drowns her, kills her, as if your embracing her, her skull caressed here gently in your arms, is itself the cause of this, is causing all her pain. In her final minutes, she does NOT decay: Her groaning doesn't slow. The moaning doesn't dampen. Doesn't lessen. Until, at last, it does NOT stop. And you do NOT hold your breath then, waiting for another groan. Just one last groan, just one last gasp. Minutes full of silence do NOT pass. You do NOT sit here, Mother's head now growing cold upon your lap, and think: It's better now. No more pain. No more hallucinations. No more wolves that creep and crawl across the ceiling, no more snakes that slither in her belly, no tornadoes in her head. No more screams. Just that dropped jaw, your mother's open mouth, the lolling of its cancer-eaten tongue, her mouth that will not shut. Her chin that hangs, her mouth that silent howls. You are NOT sad. You do NOT care. Do NOT. Cannot. Are NOT. Is NOT. Ain't.

❖ ❖ ❖

*Some other things that ain't.*

My Viking father is not gay. My parents marry in their twenties, they never get divorced. After her slow death, the Viking will proclaim to all that Mother was the one true love—the only—of his life. My sister and I know better. Throughout our childhood, our parents rarely speak, they do not kiss or hug, they never ever touch. Indeed, if you attempt to touch my father, he will jump and twitch. Friendly pats on Papa Viking's back, regarded as attacks. Once, as newlyweds, when Mother tried to tickle him, my dad lashed out and nearly broke her arm. Since then, for thirty married years, my father has a separate bedroom. And it's here, while he's away at work, that I, as ten-year-old, sneak into Dad's private bedroom to steal Valium—oh yabetcha, Vikings love their Valium—but also find his porn. Underneath his bed are stacks of magazines that showcase naked college boys with crooked penises, their penises erect but bending sharply ninety-ish degrees. Such geometries of giant circumcised right-angle penises are a bit confusing, even frightening, to Viking offspring yet in Mrs Knutson's fourth-grade math class.

Less confusing is puberty, when as teenager I am bored and all alone, deposited in Father's office at the university, while he goes off to teach art history with soporific slide projectors, and so, I decide to use his work desktop, a fancy Packard Bell with speedy dial-up, to surf the web and check my AOL email, but nope, I quickly change my mind because of all the gay porn *popup* ads on Daddy's screen.

In my twenties, things are clearer. I'm strictly just an Everclear man at this point and suddenly observe how Dad loves jewelry, and how he's always been a flashy dresser, when he isn't walking nude about the house, that is. Or how, when he's had a glass of wine or two, he will erupt in high-pitched squeals just like a stereotype queen. Or how when you browse his television, everything his Netflix recommends is gay, gay, gay, his video downloads all X, X, X. And these days, now that he's retired, employed no longer as flamboyant Dean of Liberal Arts, the Viking paints nude men. And fruit. Recent paintings of nude men with fruit look like this:

Even so, no. Uffdah no, the Viking is not gay. For five long years (2012-17), my father will remain alone, and medicated, ever since the one love of his life, my mother, died.

Me, I wish I were a gay Viking. Shit would be easier. Perhaps. Women can be scary. As a daughter of an alcoholic Anglican priest who daily beat the wife and kids, my mother would return the favor on her own. Unlike the Viking, I could never love her, not my mother. Nor any woman. Not until her death would I seek out a first relationship. First ever. One month after Mother's death, I moved down South, into the house of this horse chick, and yep, within a year, we would be married.

It's not until late 2017, at the age of sixty-six, that the Viking dates a man at last.

❖ ❖ ❖

*Xmas, 2017.*
*A poem I wrote to Mommy's dropped jaw.*

To me, her mouth that hangs wide open sings.
With shaky hands, I close her agate eyes.
I'm wrapped in black, ascending clouds of wings.

Mom's body fixed by wires and their machines,
the bloodstained catheter between her thighs—
to me, her mouth that hangs wide open sings.

From her cold hands, I must pull off her rings,
while in her lap, my dad just drools and cries:
I'm wrapped in black, ascending clouds of wings.

I'm full of rage and don't know what it means,
I go outdoors beneath the winter skies:
To me, her mouth that hangs wide open sings.

Outside, from snowy fields, a dark flock springs,
as all around me blackbirds squawk and rise:
I'm wrapped in black, ascending clouds of wings.

Hate's hallowing is all her dropped jaw brings:
Reductions like "abused abuse" are lies.
To me, her mouth that hangs wide open sings.
I'm wrapped in black, ascending clouds of wings.

❖ ❖ ❖

*Today, 2018. As I sit here, writing these words.*
I've been dry for ten months now. It's slowly, slowly that the shakes should fade.
I found some photos of the wife on horseback, galloping across a white beach in her wedding dress, the fabric of its long train thickly layered like the overlapping petals of a bleach-white rose, opening, much like her auburn hair that billows back behind her, flapping back like flags in ocean's strong headwind. It was her idea, the wife's. Nonnegotiable. A horseback wedding on a beach of Seabrook Island, off the coast of Charleston, S.C., was absolutely necessary, even though I don't ride horses. Cannot. Won't. And never did, even though my Brit wife trained them, broke them, owned like twenty-something of them.

I have not seen her in four years, albeit our beach wedding was just five years back. Our wedding was, perhaps, our end. We should probably get divorced. As the years go by, I miss her less and less. The photographs I found look like this:

Married, I was a man. Not a pony. Not gay. But as a man, I did not ride. Hated riding, couldn't ride, wouldn't. Even though it was her life. The wife's life. She rode and stubbornly I did not: *Hell no*, I'd say. I would not ride her horses, I would not let her braid my hair. She tried not to show it, how sad this made her. My wife was strong and hard, she did not like to cry. She was brave, I made her sad. I said Hell no, while she was brave and sad. And I did not care. I did not care about what she loved. And never did. Despite the miles we walked together.

*July 2013.* The summer of our wedding, it's the Pyrenees that I remember most of all. Especially that first steep climb. That first mountain we would conquer. I remember how, a forty/fifty-pound pack at my back, with walking stick in hand, my wife and I raced up that mountain, up that first one. Nearly sprinting up its slope. Because we had to, had to run. Because my bride was being bitten, stung, being eaten by these insects. The feet of this green mountain, swarming with these biting insects. They were not biting me. Just my wife. But I raced on after her, on up and up, my sides both burning, gasping, chest jackhammered. I was fit and younger then, not the fat-ass fart I would become, but it took like all I had, like sprinting at a marathon's end—thousands of feet seemingly straight up I clambered after her, our walking sticks stabbed hard into the rocky path, as up and up and up I chased my wife who kept on shrieking, swatting both her arms, groaning angrily at these mad bugs that bit her. The bugs that left me be, the bugs I could not see. Invisible flesh-eating bugs. At last, hours later, two-thirds up this mountain number one, the biting bugs would disappear (apparently) and we collapsed upon a ledge, an outcropping along the path that zigzagged steeply up the mountainside. We both heaved. We sucked warm water desperately from our three-liter Platypi pinned to our packs. We sat there eating plums and oranges and more plums and breathed. After half an hour, we climbed the rest of this first mountain. But now more slowly. At a steady pace,

but no more side-split gasping. At the top, at mountain's peak, is where it happens, my most precious memory, how at the summit I beheld the endless verdant ranges of the Pyrenees—how at the top, I would be shocked. For behold, here from this mountain's peak, upon the slopes descending from my feet: ponies. Wild mountain ponies. Hundreds and hundreds of them. A vast wild herd. I'd reached the mountain's summit first, my wife some fifty yards behind me, yet climbing that last steep slope. From the top I hollered down to her ecstatically, incomprehensibly. Gleeful, joyous, smiling like an idiot. I remember how my bride-to-be below just frowned and raised this one snide eyebrow at my silliness. But at last she reached the top, to stand beside me, and she saw them too: hundreds of wild ponies. I remember then the joy. How happy she was. I remember how she had no halters, ropes, or bridles. All she could find inside her backpack was a phone cord. This electric cord to charge her cellphone. With this phone charger, though, she spent the day's remainder catching wild ponies. Taming them. Cautiously approaching them, as she horse-whispered secret words to calm them and avoid their bucking hooves, their kicks, their rears, their rising up upon their hind legs and box-kicking like the wild stallions they were, and no—hell no—the wife was not afraid. The wife was brave, she caught them giddily, she noosed her phone cord past their snorting heads and lassoed them. Unafraid she leapt in single bounds upon their backs and, with her charger's cord around their thick rippling necks, around their wild matted manes, the ends of her white plastic phone cord tightly clutched in both her fists, she charged and leapt and raced across the mountaintops, her long brown hair flag-flying back behind her in the wind, until at last, just as the sun began to dip into the mountain shade, behind the rolling shadows of the soft green peaks, we pitched our tent and slept, my chest against her back, embracing tight my gently breathing wife deep into the dark cold night.

## Notes

Page 118: Oil paintings are by Michael Aakhus. [Top, nude with grapes] *Roswell #6: Nature Morte, The Celestial Tree,* 48 x 72 inches, 2017. [Bottom, nude with squash] *Roswell #1: Nature Morte, the Meat of the Squash and the Flesh of Man,* 36 x 48 inches, 2016.

Page 119: My wedding photos are by Ben Gately Williams.

*Levi Andalou*

# Untitled Poem from State of the Wards

Impulse buying is not confined to the checkout line, to the one-click purchase. This house, for example, where the doorways are large enough to enter, but too narrow to leave through. Where each door opens into a slightly smaller room. My parents, for example, whom I chose based on a gross misconstrual of the facts. I took the lack of regional accent to denote lack of region. I conflated chronic bad credit with a dependable incredulity. I saw the patrilineal lack of eyeteeth as a categorical dismissal of biblical notions of jurisprudence. I took the absence of a second story as a dare, I took it one night, scaling a ladder to sleep out on the tar paper, wondering whether I, like the universe, was the result of a decision that never reached consciousness, wondering what was wrong with everyone. What I missed was that the missing second story was just their little way of repudiating the equation of verticality with the sacred. At the sight of the morning star, I found a way off that roof that would forever erase my impulses.

Jaclyn Dwyer

# Job's wife brings store-bought cookies

to the school bake sale, hard plastic
nesting inside softer plastic.
First, a rustle and then
the incoherent snap of shame
as a better mom plops
lemon drops and thumbprints marked
with actual thumbs. They all
have KitchenAids, apple red
and stainless. Job's wife has a whisk
and aches from sliding a safety
pin into sores to open pustules
all night. She feeds her children
frozen waffles every morning
and listens to the moms
rattle off reading lists and swimming
feats when all she has taught
her children is how to want.
In a rented room lit by a milk jug
flush against a flashlight she stuffs
her pillows with wadded tissues
and grieves over everyone else's
grief, wet and unending. Job's wife knows
how a shadow can stretch, how water
and light and sand can take
the shape of almost anything,
even a small hand tugging
at a body gone dry.

*Carol Guess*

# First a Decision, Not a Feeling

The moment before the moment before the moment you knew. The moment before the moment you knew. The moment you knew. The moment you stood in the knowing. The moment after the moment you knew. The moment after the moment you knew before you knew what you know now. The moment you erased the knowing. The moment you stood in not knowing again. The moment after erasing the knowing when you stood in the room and opened the door. The moment you saw the person you knew. The moment erasing became what you knew. The moment you laughed and had dinner, not knowing. The moment erasing not knowing stopped working. The moment before the moment you knew again the thing you'd stopped knowing before. The moment you walked through the door in your knowing. The moment your knowing became what you knew. The moment of facing the person who knew the knowing you knew, but not your knowing. The moment of naming. The person erasing. The moment of knowing erasing was naming. The moment you shut the door on not knowing. The moment a stranger knocked on your door.

# Emarginate (adj.)

The leaf in the margin
              of the dictionary is a child's
shaky outline of a leaf,

              with a notch at its tip.
I close the book. And now I can't think
              of one other thing in the world

that's emarginate.  And when I ask my glow screen
              it smoothly unscrolls meaning: wings,
and photographs of a feather

              with jagged edges, then an eagle in air:
"Like a boat that floats?" "No," my friend types,
              "It's more like how spread fingers pull

water as you swim forward": a fish's fin
              has a notched fan: and now I'm learning
such a jewel-box of shapes: thank you,

              fish-loving indexers of the world:
pointed, forked, double-emarginate,
              truncate, lunate: these fins are drawn

like cycling moons: different-sized scoops
              of emptiness that propel bodies on:
(v.) to take the edge off, to remove

              the margin, as, in the glow we see
margins gone:  ourselves pinned down
              to our coordinates: and missiles have such

smooth surfaces: may their flight be slowed
              by the friction of anything: fish or leaf or bird:
by these notches that count, with a blade

              what's ours: a day, and a day, and another day.

# The YMCA

In Bloomfield, New Jersey, there was a YMCA. I lived there for two years. New Jersey is an expensive place, and the Y was the only place I could afford.

It was a nice YMCA. There was a front desk with a receptionist. A lobby with several red and brown leather chairs. Also, they did not let in too many black people in those days—a few, but not many. There was another YMCA three miles away—they let in black people there, but not Bloomfield.

There was even a professor there from Harvard. He was a thin man, about five feet six inches. He used to teach economics, but now he was retired. He wore a tweed jacket with a patch on the sleeve, and he always wore a bow tie.

There was a TV room. The people at the YMCA liked to watch TV. They especially liked to watch the New York Yankees. The Yankees had been bad for many years, but now they were again getting better.

The professor lectured to the people. He raised his voice. "You should not watch TV," he said. "Baseball," he said, "is that all you care for? There is news in the world: the Middle East, a war, a President who is corrupt, who lies." He meant Richard Nixon. "Don't you care about any of this?"

Most people in the TV room would ignore the professor. Some would not even turn around to look at him. Others would look at him briefly and then return to their game.

Some would try to be polite—or would try to humor him. "You are right, Professor, of course you are right. But this is a good game. Join us just for one inning—just one."

The Professor would snarl, curling his lips in disdain. Then he would turn on his heels and walk away.

The Professor did not like these people; he looked down at them. Perhaps he was the same way with me. And yet, for some reason, he treated me a little differently. Perhaps it was because I was from another country (and therefore "exotic"). Perhaps it was because I spoke better English ("grammatically proper," as the Professor called it). Perhaps it was because I had a beard: "a sable-silvered beard," the Professor called it. "Just the way Horatio describes the beard of Hamlet's father—or better, the beard of the *ghost* of Hamlet's father."

But whatever the reason, the Professor treated me a little differently. When he saw me in the hallway or in the lobby, he would greet me. When he saw me in the diner or the cafeteria (a half-block away, where many of us ate), he would often call out to me. More than once, he asked me to join him.

When we ate he did most of the talking. And, who knows, perhaps this was the greatest attraction. The Professor liked to talk. And in me the Professor had a good listener, a captive audience.

One day the Professor and I went out for dinner. Then we went to a French movie. After the movie, we walked, and we walked. When we came back, it was well after midnight.

The Professor lectured to me throughout the walk. He told me about interest rates, about Adam Smith, the federal funds rate. Most of it—ninety percent? ninety-five?—was over my head. But I tried to listen. Wasn't that the reason, the main reason, that the Professor liked me—or at least that he tolerated me?

The Professor spoke to me about some of the other professors that he had worked with. He spoke about someone named James Tobin, about someone named John Galbraith. He said that Keynes (of England) was a genius. He said that Milton Friedman (of Chicago) was a reactionary. "No breeding," he said. "He is a grocer, nothing more, the son of a grocer. It shows in his ideas: money, money, money. It shows in his prose (have you read it?). It is labored, all labored."

Most of this was above me, beyond me. But so it was.

❖ ❖ ❖

The YMCA was not the best of places, but it was not the most terrible either. There were shared toilets; we used the shared toilets. In a separate room, with a separate door, were shared showers. We used the shared showers.

There were no bathtubs, but that would have been too much to expect. How many bathtubs would they have had? Who would have cleaned them?

Men walked around naked. A few were young, most were middle-aged or old. Some walked around bashfully, the towels around their waists; others walked around less bashful, their penises erect.

Some stood at the small enamel sinks brushing their teeth. There was paste on the rims, paste on the glass mirrors in front of them. One man brushed his teeth and said that his name was Eddie Shea. He had been a boxer for over twenty years, a feather lightweight. The man was short, but he had big strong shoulders and big callused hands. I had no reason to question his words.

Another man boasted that he went to New York every weekend. It was only forty-five minutes by bus.

"You get nice pussy there," he said. And then he told us of his latest trip. "She was a fine woman. I gave her twenty dollars. When we were done, she even cooked me a nice meal."

"In Manhattan?" someone said. "You found her in Manhattan?"

"Not downtown. Around 110th Street. She has her own place there, I've been to her before. She's got nice tits, she smells good. And when we were done, she even cooked me a nice meal."

He seemed proud of the meal, especially that. Perhaps he was telling the truth, perhaps not. But at the YMCA there were no kitchens. You always had to go and eat outside at the diners or the cafeterias. So a home-cooked meal was indeed a reason to be proud.

The man was one of the few black people there, and his name was Luther. He was about six feet tall with big broad shoulders. One time we were in the bathroom, both shaving, and he told me the same story. Then he asked me if I wanted to go to New York with him.

I was surprised at the invitation but flattered as well. Having nothing better to do that weekend, I agreed.

We took the bus to Manhattan. We changed two more buses and then walked a few blocks. It was a run-down area; we walked up dirty steps to the third floor of an old brick building. It was the middle of summer, the windows were open. Children played in the stairwell, more than a few people had the TV or radio running.

A tall black woman received us. She was in her bare feet and wearing a thin fawn-colored dress that came two or three inches above her knees.

The woman knew Luther by name. She held out her hand, taking his and walked him inside.

I hesitated, then entered after him.

"My friend," Luther said when we were inside. Then he mentioned my name.

"Pleased to meet you, honey," said the woman simply.

It was a small place. A kitchenette to the side, a sink overflowing with dishes. An oven covered with grease marks that had not been cleaned in months. A green plastic trash can overflowing with paper plates and scraps of food.

Is this where Luther had received his home-cooked meal?

Luther and the woman went to the room in the back and closed the door behind them. I was left standing by myself.

The front door was slightly open and I did not know what I was supposed to do with it. I hesitated. At last I went to it and closed it shut. But I did not lock it from inside.

I waited in the living room. There was a sofa there stained in several places, with two or three pieces of cloth on top. A small dining table with three aluminum chairs. An open bag of Fritos, half-eaten and jumbo-sized, lay on top of the table. There was a *TV Guide* and a *Reader's Digest* as well. The *Reader's Digest* is what caught my eye. I was afraid of touching anything or sitting anywhere. But some reading was done there. And, so, maybe it was not all bad.

I heard some sounds from inside the closed room. But why go into all that? Some forty minutes passed, perhaps forty-five. The door opened, my friend emerged from inside in his white undershirt and black pants, the shiny black belt with the silver buckle dangling to one side. He was trying to put it through the last two hoops.

The tall woman followed him. She was still in her fawn-colored dress, still in her bare feet.

My friend came and stood beside me. "Wanna stay for some dinner?" he said.

"No no, I'm not really hungry," I said.

"Are you sure?" he said.

"I'm sure."

A few seconds passed. "I'm starved," he said.

"I'll wait for you outside," I said. "Why don't I wait for you outside?"

"Suit yourself."

It was a hot day and it was a strange neighborhood. I had no idea what waited outside. But I also knew that I could not stay in that place. The smallness of the place, the dirt. I needed to get outside and breathe.

I said goodbye to the hostess and stepped outside to the landing. I saw children on the stairwell, two or three black men: tall, menacing. I bowed to them slightly and smiled; they looked straight through me.

I came to the landing at the bottom, pushed the glass door and stepped outside. How searingly hot it still was.

But at least it was air, God's air. At least it was that.

Maybe because of the heat, few people were outside. Few people to see me, to bother me. I stood at the glass door and then I walked around a bit.

There was graffiti on the walls, broken glass all around. I did not want to venture too far— my friend might emerge at any time and I did not want to miss him.

Luther took his time. An hour passed, then an hour and twenty minutes. At last he did emerge.

"I told you," he said.

"Yes," I said.

"The best pussy. The best home-cooked meal."

"Yes," I said.

"I'm a lucky man. Sometimes I think I'm the damn luckiest man in the whole world."

I was surprised at his words, but impressed as well. He spoke with sincerity, absolute sincerity. Was I a little jealous as well?

❖ ❖ ❖

When we arrived back at the YMCA, it was almost midnight. I had not eaten in hours and was starving. My friend went to his room; I went to the bathroom and washed my hands. Then my face. And my feet—how I wanted to wash them as well.

But I would have to put that off till later. For now I needed something to eat. I went down the tiny elevator and through the lobby.

The night air of Bloomfield felt good against my face. After New York and all the noise and congestion, the town seemed almost pastoral. There was still a deep haze and through the reflection of the town lights it was difficult to see more than two or three stars. But after the City, not so bad. Not bad at all.

I ate at the nearby diner (it was open all night) and came back to the building. I again washed my face. And this time, yes, my feet as well.

Over the next few days, I did not tell anyone about my "excursion." Certainly I did not tell the Professor. He would never have understood.

Many days passed. I had a small job at an accounting company—I went to my small job. Other people in the building had their small jobs—they went to these.

Some people did not go anywhere. The Professor was retired and he went for walks or he stayed back at the building. When people watched the Yankees in the TV room, he lectured to them.

In the evenings or on weekends, the Professor and I went out for walks. We did it two or three times a week. There was a long street called Bloomfield Avenue which went right through the middle of the town. There were shops on either side: gas stations, a church, a restaurant, a diner. In the distance you could see the older buildings, or at least you could see the roofs of the old buildings. The buildings were a drab brown, the roofs made of slate or asphalt.

They said there was a park in the distance. One day the Professor and I went to the park. It was a nice park with even a lake nearby. We passed a big tree with leaves that had begun to turn orange, another tree with leaves that had begun to turn copper and gold. The grass was nicely manicured, the pathway clean and paved (and then painted white).

It was all clean and nice. But it left me empty as well. All this cleanliness, even all this beauty. But to what did it add up? Did it make me warm? Did it make me feel *whole*?

One time I mentioned my feelings to the Professor. I do not think that he was impressed or interested. His mind was on other things.

The Professor asked me where I had been that evening a few nights ago. He had been looking for me.

I certainly could not tell him about Luther, about my trip to New York. He would be angry and would not understand.

I said that I had gone to a movie.

"Which movie?" said the Professor.

*The Last Detail*," I said. It was the first movie that came to mind. It was a movie I *had* seen, but some three months earlier.

"What is it about?"

"There are three men in the Navy. They're on shore patrol. One of the men is innocent, inexperienced. The other two decide to show him around. They decide . . ."

But the Professor had already lost interest. "Fluff," he said. "All fluff. Why do you waste your time with such things?"

❖ ❖ ❖

More weeks passed. I had my small job at the accounting company—I went to my job. Other people had their small jobs—they went to these.

There was a blind man at the YMCA called Tom Sawyer. He wore dark glasses and walked with a thin cane. He held the cane at an angle in front of him and tapped it on the ground. Slowly, slowly, he tapped it on the ground.

"I know Huck Finn," he would sometimes say.

But no one believed him. They knew it was just a joke.

"When is a door not a door?" he would say.

The other would pause in thought. "I do not know," he would say at last.

"When it is ajar. Get it? *A jar*. A door is not a door when it is a jar."

This time the other would be impressed and would laugh. "A good one," he would say. "I gotta use that myself." Or else: "Mind if I use it myself some day?"

"Go right ahead. It's a free country."

One day Tom Sawyer heard Luther walking through the lobby.

"How are the women?" he said.

"Fine, just fine," said Luther in a loud voice, and not without pride.

"Been to New York lately?"

"I try to go as often as I can."

"The women are pretty?"

"The best."

They both spoke in a loud voice. After a while Tom Sawyer invited Luther to come and sit next to him.

Tom Sawyer was sitting on a red armchair. A nearby sofa was empty, but if Luther sat on it he would be some seven feet away.

"Let me pull up a chair," he said.

There was a wooden desk in the distance, a simple wooden chair beside it. Sometimes people sat there, writing a brief note or putting a stamp on some envelope. Luther got the chair and sat next to Tom Sawyer, less than two feet away.

Tom Sawyer sensed him there, leaned forward and put his hand on the other's knee.

They both continued to talk out loud. The conversation was New York, women, the pretty women of New York.

"I'm old now," said Tom Sawyer, "but it wasn't always this way."

"I bet you were something in your time. A Romeo, a real Romeo."

"*Casanova*, that's what they used to call me."

*Casanova*. Luther spoke the word slowly, felt the sound—or was it the smell?—of the word as he spoke it.

The Professor was going by, overheard some of the conversation.

"Is that you, Professor?" This was Tom Sawyer now.

The Professor was surprised and stopped in his tracks. A blind man, a perfectly blind man, and yet he could tell who was passing by.

"Yes, Mister Sawyer, it is me."

"*Mister* Sawyer. See how polite he is."

Tom Sawyer spoke the words simply, directly. If there was irony in his words, it was not easy to see it.

The Professor stood there, waiting for the other to go on.

"Going for your walk, Professor?"

Again the Professor was surprised. How did the blind man know all these things?

"In a few minutes, Mister Sawyer. I was just headed to the front desk."

"Seen any good movies lately?"

"A few."

"Seen *The Godfather*?"

"No, I haven't."

"*Love Story*?"

"No, I haven't."

"It's set at Harvard, you know. The Harvard campus."

The Professor cringed. A sentimental and low-class movie. It was a few years old. A Harvard student falls in love, marries; his wife gets sick and dies. It was terrible when it came out, still terrible. Why would anyone want to remember it?

"Haven't seen it either," said Tom Sawyer. "Too blind, you see—blind as a bat. But I've *heard* about it."

And suddenly Tom Sawyer stopped. The Professor was left there, dangling. Were these idle words? Were they words with a purpose? Were more words to follow?

Tom Sawyer was a blind man and perhaps he was alone. He needed someone to talk to. Was that all? Or had the words about the movies been directed at the Professor, specifically at him?

"Go to the movies, Professor, don't put them down." There was a pause. "We can all learn something. Never too late to learn."

*Never too late to learn.* Was Tom Sawyer lecturing to the Professor? Was he making fun?

But the Professor was a polite man. He prided himself on his composure. "I'll remember that," he said with some flatness of voice and some restraint. "I'll keep that in mind."

❖ ❖ ❖

More months passed. We lived at the YMCA and we went about our routine. A few of us went to our jobs. Luther was in and out—whether he worked or not, I still did not know. The professor and Tom Sawyer—and so many others—were there all the time.

Yes, we went about our routine. Things were going on in the world: trouble in the Middle East; the Vietnam War; the Watergate hearings. The Professor said that these were the important things. But our own lives, were they really so small? So insignificant?

The Professor spoke up about these other "big" things. Sometimes the others answered the Professor. Mostly they ignored him.

One day the Professor was lecturing on the evils of President Nixon.

"Let it go, Professor; they're all crooks."

One day the Professor was lecturing on the Middle East when Luther happened to overhear him.

"Pussy, Professor, that's what we all need."

The Professor stopped in his tracks and glared at the other. But the other would not be deterred.

"Pussy, Professor, don't knock it. It's a good thing. It's what we all need."

Some of the people in the TV room laughed openly. I took a peek at the Professor from the corner of the room: his face had turned a deep red.

The Professor lectured to me—lectured about the others in the building, lectured about the "decline in American society." He was a smart man; he should know best.

One day I was shaving in the bathroom and I ran across Luther again. He said he was going to New York and asked me if I wanted to come.

I had already been there with him, perhaps I had had my fill. I thanked him for the offer, but said the upcoming weekend was not a good time.

Luther asked me if I wanted to bring the Professor along.

"The Professor!" I said. "Are you kidding?"

"It would do the old man some good. Loosen him up."

Again I asked him if he was joking.

"The man's too tight, too stuck up—and too phony. He needs to loosen up."

One day the Professor found out about my original trip to New York with Luther. How he found out, I still don't know. Perhaps Luther told him himself. Perhaps Luther was boasting to someone about his trip, as he often did, and my name came up. One person told another, somehow it got all the way to the Professor.

"To New York?" he said to me.

I did not answer.

"With *Luther*?" he said. There was obvious disdain in his voice. "And I thought you were different. You, of all people."

Clearly he was disappointed in me. Or was he even jealous? Was that possible as well?

I had gone to New York—perhaps he wanted to go along too. I had gone with Luther—with someone else, not *him*. Perhaps he was jealous of that.

Or perhaps it was all just my imagination. Human beings are complicated. Not so easy to figure out.

❖ ❖ ❖

The Professor avoided me for some time. He saw me in the hallway, he nodded slightly. He saw me in the lobby—he ignored me.

But this could not last. He needed me, and perhaps I needed him. Soon we were back to our ways: eating at the diner, going out once in a while for a walk.

He spoke about Watergate, he spoke about interest rates. He spoke about the wage and price controls that Richard Nixon had put in place.

He spoke, I listened. He spoke, I listened. This is the way it had always been. Why should things change now?

But things do change; they do not always stay the same. One time, through the company I worked for, I was sent on an auditing assignment. Three weeks in Philadelphia, two weeks in Wilmington, Delaware. When I returned I learned that the Professor was no longer at the YMCA.

"Where did he go?"

"You think he would tell any of us?"

"You have no idea?"

"The Professor is a private man."

The Professor *was* a private man. All those walks, all those lectures, and I still knew so little about him. Where he was from originally, why he was even staying at the Y.

One day I saw Luther in the bathroom, shaving in front of the long mirror.

"Want to go to New York?" he said.

"You and me?"

"The Professor isn't here," he laughed. "You and me, baby, you and me."

A few seconds passed. And then: "The best pussy in the world. The best."

I was tempted. I said to Luther that I would think about it. I said that I would get back to him.

"Don't wait forever," he said. "Don't be like the Professor."

"The Professor?"

"Don't miss out on life. *Real* life."

Luther was a smart man—or so he thought. He may not have gone to Harvard, but he knew a few things about the world. He may not be a Professor, but he knew a few things. He did.

❖   ❖   ❖

# Could Be Worse

It's just a little bit flat, nicked but
at the back, torn at a seam,
not the only water ring
on the tabletop. It could be worse,
my mother told me forever after
I got old enough to stub my toe

in a house rigged to trip, confounded
with petrified furniture and dimness.
Her voice a stone-wet hush,
much like the basement
echoing radon. She confessed
the fates of my sisters before me,
each death worse than the last.

I was born to doubt her but still
I pictured them all so clearly.

*

One sister ran out into the road, too shy
to look both ways. Her favorite color

went dark, the summer heat rolling back
like an eye then closing. She had no name

but she wanted as I wanted
to be a dancer. I'd never be a dancer.

*

Another sister, ugly by twelve,
hid among grape hyacinth

with sleeping pills. I spy her dress
too white to exist. One black shoe

a bird's shadow, the other a pothole.
Long division came easy to her, remainders

beyond the frozen
dot. For me, thankfully, smart was enough.

*

The armless sister could be no little teapot
nor catch herself falling down stairs.

*

I might've liked the bad sister most
had she been real and survived her comeuppance.

Dwarfed by hindsight, she's a tiny abstraction on stilts.
Brat decocted, she's the whole cake in one crumb.

Pitching soluble fits, prying open the nursery
to rattle a shrill window, jabbing

nostalgia blind while my cradle
tilled a furrow. Her locket unhinged—

she told on Mother by not resembling Father
who fled to Timbuktu. Mother insisted I

could never be that bad yet someday
I may, as well, find myself devoured by wolves.

*

Mother let the sickly sister rule. Perched
in her castellated disease, she wanted

bedrails to fall
and a Jesus-shaped nightlight. Bravery

—she reeked from it. I know
I would've hated her. Just what

flutter in the history of our mother's suffering
began the cellular-level whisper campaign

to saint her? She took her medicine so
over time I took mine.

*

I've kept the house, Mother upstairs
watching our crocodilian yard

from her window; the river,
in earshot, drops to rise again—faint
the tune. Why tell my name
like clockwork if the shadow
fits? I enter her room: "It's me."
I could neglect her;
she wouldn't remember.

A few songs on the radio away
is a brunch-prone town
where I take my dog to meet other dogs
around the park each Sunday. Granted,
some big dogs are more man than men
and my dog's a sniffling teacup. We
come home to turn on the news,
hoping for disaster.

The Summit Diner in downtown Summit, New Jersey.

# Gordon Thompson

# Greasy Spoon

In the midst of offices and clothing boutiques in downtown Summit, New Jersey, a wealthier-than-average town in a dense and affluent state, squats the classic train-car-style building. Compared to some of the garish chrome replicas that have sprung up all the way from New York City to San Francisco, this original is almost nondescript. A lot of people drive right by. Others dismiss it as dirty, ugly, old: "*That* place? You *go* there?!" You have to squint to read the faded lettering that boasts "WE DO OUR OWN BAKING" and "BOOTH SERVICE" on its white-paneled side. Opening the heavy steel door, with its ovular window and three horizontal bars reminiscent of a streamlined locomotive, you're greeted with soothing warmth and smells, and, almost as palpably, a sense of equality, a sense of ease. Investment bankers in tailored suits sit on stools next to telephone repairmen in grimy canvas jumpers. Over by the windows, a young family nests in a booth.

Everything down to the seat upholstery, a lumpy burgundy vinyl, is a throwback, made the way they don't make things anymore. Even the toast is industrial-strength—thick, perfectly square slices from long loaves in plain wax-paper wrappers. The coffee cups and saucers, and the soup bowls, are somehow larger than life to match the portions, as if waiting for Paul Bunyan to stomp in. Oblong plates, made of heavy off-white porcelain, are carved deep to allow plenty of room to pile on grub. A lot of things are broken or jury-rigged: a styrofoam cup for a coffee spigot, a bare bulb where a glass cover should be, raw plywood in place of paneling in one of the booths, the butcher block that could be flooded to form a small reservoir. The ramshackleness is endearing, as if the original craftsmanship is at once too good to let die and too masterful to match. The men's room door closes with a quarter-inch dead bolt. It's tiny and none too clean, yet the cooks wear surgical-white scrubs. Conventional wisdom holds that you can judge the cleanliness of a restaurant's kitchen by the cleanliness of its bathroom, but I have my doubts: the cooks here are too busy working the grill and dishwasher to waste time on the bathroom. They won't win any awards for hygiene, but hardly anything sits still long enough to gather germs.

There are no menus, and familiar customers don't look at the letter-board overhead, which hasn't changed in years. It seems that the urge to raise prices is trumped by the annoyance of having to get on a stepladder and shift all those little white numbers around. An erasable whiteboard lists a handful of daily specials that rotate reluctantly. While many "family restaurants" seem in competition to produce the world's thickest menu, they understand here that less is more. I dream of the day when I can walk in and ask for "the usual," the way the regulars do, or expect the cook to recognize me and have my eggs half-ready before I've got my coat off, without even asking for my order, as he does for the real old-timers. Being an occasional patron, I must articulate my order: "Ham and Eggs over easy, wheat toast, and a large grapefruit juice." Coffee is something you have to decline. Sitting at the counter, I make my request directly to the man filling cups, laying out silverware, and stuffing the toaster. The man at the grill listens and starts shuffling piles of potatoes around. Nobody writes anything down; when I finish I'll move to the huge mechanical cash register and tell the man what to ring up. Three people can walk away stuffed on a twenty; they don't take American Express. Whenever I take a friend here, she'll ask "How's the French toast?" or "How's the soup?" and I'm forced to confess that I don't know; the only thing I've ever ordered is ham and eggs. "How boring!" my companion typically replies. But there are a finite number of breakfasts in a lifetime, and I don't want to waste any. I've seen others eating off the specials board: pot roast, turkey with stuffing, fried chicken, split pea soup . . . it all looks delightfully coarse. At the far end of the counter, under glass, there's always a plate of two or three doughnuts, each half again as big as anything from Dunkin' Donuts. I'm not sure anyone's ever eaten them; they just sit there as a kind of taunt: "*This* is a doughnut!" Up behind the register lurks the unavoidable kaleidoscope of mini cereal boxes—for children, presumably, these are the only modern, commercial items on the place; they do have Heinz ketchup, but you have to ask for it.

This is the only place I know that still uses cups and saucers, rather than mugs, and eschews pitchers, instead filling each cup individually from the brewing spigot. The double-barrel gas-fired coffeemaker runs constantly; one barrel stands watch whenever the other needs its cloth filter re-armed. Because of this, and because there's only one waitress, you sometimes have to get a little pushy for refills. They'll come eventually, but it's not one of those places where you never see the bottom of the cup. The brew is dark, rich, uncomplicated, always piping hot, and strong as a good handshake. Decaf is Sanka, with a capital "S," though it may be an empty threat—a companion tried to order it once, and the waitress talked her out of it. Sugar comes in a big shaker next to the napkin dispenser at every couple places, and cream lives in beat-up stainless steel pitchers—no ultra-pasteurized cupettes or paper packets. Jelly does come in sealed plastic mini-tubs (rather than a jam pot); you can have any flavor you want so long as it's grape. The quality of a diner is inversely proportional to its jelly selection.

The customers tend to be quiet—maybe in reverence for the food, maybe because they're afraid to interrupt the orders barked back and forth between the waitress and cook. This is all for the benefit of those who choose to sit away from the counter at one of the six booths located across such a narrow passage that the waitress will bump into you if you don't sit up straight. For years I'd only ever seen one waitress, a stone-faced black woman who never skips a beat, keeping the food bustling from grill to table no matter how relentlessly the customers pour in. She is the only black person on the premises, save the occasional customer, and she is also the only woman working here, surrounded by Greek men cooking and washing. Efficiency experts would do well to watch her work. She reminds me of a jazz player, her basic moves pre-choreographed from years of practice but every specific variation improvised anew for each order. She almost dares the customers to eat faster—just try to get ahead of her, crowd her spotlight. She hassles the customers and the cook to make sure everyone understands the order exactly; she wastes no time on sweet-talk, and she never makes a mistake. After years of anonymous breakfasts I nearly fainted when she suddenly greeted me with: "Eggs over with ham, right?"

"Yes," I stammered, "and—"

"And a grapefruit juice—I got it."

The big day had come: I was getting "the usual." I was elated, but from now on I wouldn't dare order anything else.

❖ ❖ ❖

The weekday waitress, a chain-smoking white woman, is almost cloyingly sweet, but so frenetic it seems a miracle she hasn't broken every dish in the place. She all but shreds the napkins and stabs herself with the forks laying them out. "What can I get youse, honeys?" she greets me and my companions, her voice almost screechy with eagerness. She always forgets part of the order, and then apologizes so guiltily I wish I hadn't asked for whatever was missing. I can never project enough patience to staunch her redundant reassurances: "I'll be right back with your toast, sweetie, just hold on there for a second," she lilts, as if narrating her actions will somehow quicken them, or calm her. "I'm so sorry about the wait—I just can't believe how busy it is in here today," she sighs. I get the feeling she'd make the same complaint even if I were the only customer. I tip lavishly, hoping she'll buy herself a long vacation to one of those places where you do nothing but lie on the beach and raise a little flag whenever you're thirsty so the attendants know to scurry back with your drink. She's not a bad waitress, but it seems she missed her calling as something else: receptionist, maybe, or nursery school teacher—some job where all her nervous energy would do more than bring sloshing coffee cups to hurried diners, some place where haste isn't a virtue.

When I sit at the counter, the toast-and-napkin-man slides my order in front of me nonchalantly, as if such a gargantuan heap of food can be found anywhere. The idea of this meal is a cliché, but most attempts actually to cook it are a feeble imitation of what stands before me. The home fries are without rival: quarter-sized chips of potatoes boiled whole, sliced, and grilled crusty brown; never shredded, and never dry. Some argue that they're "hash browns," but it's hard to reconcile these with the standard rehydrated frozen shreds or patties. Even I, a ketchup junkie, wouldn't dream of adding any here. Graduates of the Cordon Bleu would be unable to duplicate them, and would not dream of piling such an obscene mound of anything onto a plate. (I once asked the owner of an extraordinary nearby bakery, a punctilious Austrian woman, where she liked to eat on her days off: "The Summit Diner is the only place that makes a proper breakfast," she replied.) Two perfectly cooked eggs (white on both sides, yolk still runny) stand proud atop the mountain of potatoes. And then there's the ham. No Oscar Meyer preprocessed stuff here; sliced thick for emphasis, this meat was baked a few feet away and hand-carved into wonderful misshapen slices. I've seen them carry a whole haunch out from the kitchen and lay into it with a carving knife as recklessly as you'd shuck an ear of corn. This is not food for the faint of heart, and given the grease quotient, it's not exactly health food. But it's remarkable by today's standards for all the things it lacks— preservatives, flavoring agents, fillers, conditioners, packaging. . . breakfast here has essentially three ingredients: potatoes, eggs, and ham. Even as an eighteen-year-old, with a nuclear reactor metabolism, I was almost defeated by my order. A friend joked about wiping our plates clean with toast, licking our chops, and barking, "Another round!"

There's a narrow window between 10 a.m. and 11 or so, after the breakfast crowd has thinned out and before the lunch crowd has begun, when the grill-man gets to lay down his spatula, mop his brow, and eat an all-whites omelette. And the customers get to linger over their coffee and chat with him, or the waitress, who's busy replenishing her nicotine reserve, or each other. At any other time, there's a constant ingress and egress of customers, and all you see of the cook is his back. If you go on Saturday or Sunday morning, you stand a good chance of waiting. Once a companion and I were asked if we wouldn't mind giving up our table to incoming customers. This is fast food without the trademarks (or mania-inducing de-

cor, mechanistic behavior, pictogram menus): if you need nourishment, come here; if you need to brood, go someplace else.

I'd been going here for years before I heard any of the staff say more than "two on three with ham," or "two French, three over with Taylor, Western on a kaiser, no onion." Then one morning I overheard the cook talking to a customer in rapid-fire Spanish. "*¿Hablas español?*" I asked sheepishly as he set down my plate. "*Si, si,*" he replied, so I kept up the Spanish, telling him I'd just been living in Chile for a year, and he smiled and asked if everything was all right and shook my hand, and every time I've gone in since he's saluted me with a broad grin and holler of "*¡Mi amigo!*" Living out of state, I only get there two or three times a year anymore, and I've grown a beard and lost my glasses, but he always remembers me. "Mel," they call him. He's from Puerto Rico, I think he told me. Like a good bartender, he listens more than he talks—and he hustles more than either. One or two of the busboys is Mexican now, and there's a cranky old Irishman on toaster duty sometimes, but by and large the workers are Greek, from the middle-aged man with the godfather voice at the register to the tall, gangly young guy at the dishwasher to the amiable, chisel-featured fellow with the sculpted moustache who seems to own the place. Before Mel there was a grill-man who looked like Adonis from the chest up, with a belt-busting gut swelling his half-apron. No worries about thin cooks.

❖ ❖ ❖

Diners are peculiarly American, the way jazz and highways and pumpkins are American— and the way urban sprawl and big business and TV are American. The same free-market capitalism that allows the little guy a shot at making it big allows the guys that do make it big to squash the little guy into oblivion. As a result, the Great American Diner finds itself crowded out by McDonald's and Wal-Mart and Rite Aid. Places like the Summit Diner, not long ago as common along the thoroughfares of America as tumbleweed in an old Western, have become rarities. Two towns over, another classic, "Louie's Excellent Diner," literally disappeared. Gone are its gleaming, sculpted steel panels, its corned-beef hash flecked with green pepper, its family photos of loyal customers plastering the walls. Having lost their land lease, the owners of the building and business sold the sleek stainless steel monument to a German entrepreneur who plans to make it the first in a chain of "American" restaurants in Germany. (Ironically, living within walking distance was Rita Mahoney, niece of O. Mahoney, the most famous builder of steel diners.) So the Germans will be luxuriating at a classic American diner while we natives fight the line at McDonald's. That's America—the richest culture on earth, with the poorest sense of heritage.

God only knows what they'll call the German diner; in the U.S. the replicas tend to have much more outlandish names than the originals: "Fog City Diner" or "Johnny Rockets" versus simply a town or a person's name. In La Línea de la Concepcion, Spain, just across the border from Gibraltar, is a chrome gem called "Rock Diner." The macaronic pun almost redeems the oddity of the placement. I didn't have time to eat there, but a glance at the menu suggested that the food might not be any more off-the-wall than what you get at some American monuments these days, some of the prettiest of which have been converted (and in some cases moved) into anything from cheap Thai joints to upscale seafood restaurants. Outside the Northeast you tend to find great food in awful buildings, whereas in New Jersey and environs, where architecture has outlasted cooks, the opposite is often true. For many Americans, diners are no more than museum-pieces: the Henry Ford museum in Dearborn, Michigan, features an entire fifties diner reassembled inside the museum, right down to the Coke-emblazoned napkin dispensers and neon-ringed clock. Unfortunately, they're not serving. On Woodward Avenue, "Michigan's Main Street," an eye-poppingly shiny replica, "Athens Coney Island," serves glorified White Castle, operating under the common but fallacious idea that hamburgers spell classic fifties cuisine. I'm not sure they even serve burgers at the Summit, and I know they don't make milkshakes—such finger-food was the purview of drive-ups, not diners.

There were five original manufacturers of the classic train-car-style diner, and three of them were in New Jersey. Moving a manufactured eatery was an expensive process, which is why

authentic diners sputter away as you move North or South or West, with only a few scattered examples as far as Maine and Maryland, and essentially none past Buffalo. Suburban sprawl—and the strangulation of Western rivers to make California arable, and thus able to wrest truck farming from the East—has made New Jersey a shadow of its former Garden State self and scattered the population from the old villages and crossroads. But even though it has lost a lot of landmarks, New Jersey is, and always was, diner central. All those highways out-of-staters love to mock carry a lot of hungry truckers. And all those ugly industrial sites everyone sneers at are filled with hungry workers, too tired and poor to want anything other than basic food, and, in many cases, too recently immigrated to understand anything else. A young Colombian guy I tutored told me he stopped off at a diner on his way to work in the chemical plant and every day for three years he ordered "homaneggs" because that was the only thing he knew how to say. "That's what I always get too," I smiled. "Yes," he said. "Eez good. I no mind." Diners don't serve "ethnic food," yet they rely on ethnic people to prepare it and still more ethnic people to eat it. The more blondes, the fewer diners—and New Jersey, with its wealth of Italians and Jews, not to mention blacks, Greeks, Vietnamese, Indians, Jamaicans, Colombians, Portuguese, Brazilians, West Africans . . . is possibly the most un-Aryan state.

Sandwiched between New York and Philadelphia, New Jersey has always been a state on the move, and eating a matter of recovering from the last drive, or preparing for the next one. Consequently, diners are best measured in miles: Summit Diner breakfasts have kept me going as far as North Carolina, Maine, and Ohio. The rich food sits heavy and unforgettable in my belly like an old friend all through the morning, and, if I'm lucky, most of the afternoon, so that I don't have to eat again until dinner. By then I'm usually ready for a nice salad and a glass of skim milk, to counterbalance the grease and protein overload for the day and rest fat and happy all night until the next morning, when hunger pangs and cold make the lure of a Summit Diner breakfast pull irresistibly again.

❖ ❖ ❖

*Sabatino Smith*

# Tunnel of Cheap Breakfast (or Love)

Aroma tumbles down up-escalator steps
And lifts skirts with wafts of fried eggs,
Sinai of home fries,
Two stone tablets of sausage patties,
And corned beef hash (from the can, specifically).

Bacon grease chars the tile walls of indistinguishable color.
Grimy, grout cross-sections, to the eye (before 9 a.m.),
Are the perfect sear of a poorly selected cut of steak.
Hungry me peers through legs of muffin-topped commuters,
Scanning for the waiting eyes of my tired waitress.

The subway intercom dings, "order up."
Young love or sexual anticipation is facilitated by two-for-one specials.
Eyelids hang heavy over coffee-black pupils.
Fingers claw, sleepily, at phantom mug handles.
The escalator concludes and takes a bite out of my shoe.

*Rob Stephens*

# After Hearing the News

After hearing the news, I'm giving myself the day off—
    I'll wrap up in an electric blanket, sip cold Sprite,

and binge on *Happy Days* so I can pretend I'm the Fonz
    —*Eyyyy*, he says, and then everything's apple pie.

After hearing the news, I have to call my parents to make
    sure their estate is in order and call my psychiatrist

to cancel our next session because all I'll do is ask
    for stronger pills and email my students so they know

that I'm a hermit now and they'll have to figure out
    how to punctuate sentences on their own. After hearing

the news, I have a newfound addiction to Pepto Bismol—
    the pink tube-stopping magic is the only substance

that will stay in my stomach. I've just noticed that when
    snow packs into the ground tightly, I can press my face

into it and become frozen like Hans Solo so maybe one day
    I'll wake up not feeling like Jabba the Hut's slave

after hearing the news. I'm finally going digital—no more
    listening to records or grandfather clocks. I'm a new man

after hearing the news, but I'm sorry to say there's no way
    to explain the news we've all received, but if you're like me,

you'll be relieved only when you realize that we're fucked, yes,
    but we should have seen this coming a long way back.

# Television

After removing the cathode ray tube, I hollowed out the wooden floor cabinet and installed a crude steering system. Powered by a lawnmower engine, now I putter around the neighborhood and provide free entertainment to families. I wave and the adults stop watering their square hedgerows or sipping their tall glasses of lemonade, just long enough to acknowledge me with thin smiles. Children are often confused, sprinting across the glistening yards and twisting the metal knobs in futile attempts to increase the volume or flip to a different station. At twilight, I reverse up my driveway into a single-car garage and sit there alone with both hands on the wheel. The sky above the rooftops darkens, each streetlamp clicking on and beginning to hum.

# John Davis Jr.

# Statue Boys

*For Todd and Michael, convicted of trespassing*

We knew our names were already deader
than confederate generals erected
in gray cement at Dunson Park.
But nobody would care about curs
like us that summer of seedless
melons and faulty bike chains.
So we posed atop the platformed
columns in front of the Old Marsh Place,
raising sleeveless arms to point
long invisible sabers at some
butternut horizon we'd never see.
Protruding our pretend-medaled chests,
we awaited some darker enemy—economy,
phosphate mine labor or its blue-collar cancers—
to end seasons, break cycles,
fell us from small-town pedestals.

Adam Tavel

# My Father's Truck

His rear view mirror dangles like a claw
that tore on prey that was no prey at all
but mouse-round stone. A stack of circulars
addressed to neighbors yellow on the floor.
A moldy liquor box slashed down its side
spills clothes (some tagged) he never wore. Behind
that, farther still, shadows read the cast
of bills where every notice was the last.
A hundred Miller cans, crushed and lusterless
as broken stars, poke through bags. *Hiss hiss*
is what escapes when I crank up the heat.
Inside, a landlord disinfects the seat
where my father clutched the dark and fell.
Come back, O ghost, and drive us from your hell.

Jack Barrett. *Cascading Figures.* 2007. Oil on canvas. 20 x 24 inches. Courtesy of ARTicles Art Gallery.

# My Only Hunting Story

We were at the bar, though she had not told me to meet her. I knew she was coming to town because it was a Thursday and she had class on Thursday, but she didn't call so I checked one of the parking lots for her jeep then went over to the Lion's Head and she was there talking to the bartender Seth. She was very drunk and smiling when I came in. From how drunk she was I knew she had been there a while, but I didn't care when I saw how she looked at me. She put her arms around me and kissed me on the cheek and did not ask how I found her or why I was there but only what kind of whisky I wanted as she patted the stool next to her. I laughed and she laughed and we drank. It was later, after Seth had gone, that she said, "My father has a hunting lodge. You should come down. I'll bring you there. I always wanted to go, but there's no women. When I was little I could kind of poke around and sometimes go out there, but after I was like ten he wouldn't let me. Even now. Even though I drink with his friends." And I said, "You drink with your father's friends?" And she said, "Yeah. Some of them. They love me. We hang out. But he won't let me go on the hunting trips. But you should go. You should. Have you ever been hunting?" "No," I said. "So you've never fired a gun?" "No," I said. "It doesn't matter," she said. "He'll teach you," she said. "They're a great bunch of guys." She ordered us two more and I wondered if I could kill anything bigger than a bug and finally decided that, yeah, I could. It wouldn't be easy, but I could do it. The experience perhaps was something I needed. Something that might finish off the childish way I sometimes thought about things. "You should go," she said. "It'd be great," she said. Then she was swaying around the street and I took her keys and walked her to my place to sober her up. "I have to go home," she kept saying. "I have class in the morning and I don't have anything with me," she said. She fell asleep while I was kissing her on the couch. When she woke, she jumped up saying she had to leave and gathered her coat and shoes and bag while I told her to calm down. "My grandmother's going to be up," she said, "waiting," she said and she was out the door before I could get her keys away from her again. There were times after this, when we were naked, a few times, that she told me why her grandmother waited for her. This girl/woman who seemed mostly like the rest of us until the stories came out about drunkenly putting her car through a tree and the engine going through the passenger seat, about failing and quitting different colleges for no reason other than she didn't feel like getting up, about being brought back to life on your parents's bed by a team of EMTs with your family standing around and it's obvious to everyone you're not wearing underwear, about being in the ER again with tubes coming out of you, another car, another storefront smashed to pieces. She said her grandmother was always giving her second chances. She said she had no idea why. She didn't deserve them, she said, but now she said she was tired, that she was getting it right or at least too tired to get things so wrong. At twenty-three. Once when she stayed at my place she called her grandmother and told her she was sleeping at her friend Elizabeth's. I didn't care much for being some kind of secret, but if I had to be a secret at least I was an Elizabeth. The name Elizabeth somehow made things okay. It was only about a week after this that the texts slowed, then stopped, and I spent more time with Seth looking for her than with her. No word. No reason. Just gone. In February I found out from someone she'd quit going to class and basically failed out of what was her fourth school. Then I was walking back home where there was ice, and I still missed how quietly she ate eggs, and I hoped that she quit maybe to give herself some space to get out of her own way and gets things clear as the same sort of drunk fuck-filled nights of her past had obviously started to repeat themselves with me. Sometimes you just need your feet to stop falling under your own feet. This was how I made things better for myself, until my head started to even out without any prompting. The job I had at this bakery wasn't doing much, but it wasn't killing me so I coasted. My birthday passed, and my friend Tim told me he would teach me how to fix cars by helping him work on an engine he had in a shed when the weather got warm enough to only be in short sleeves. Once in a while, I would let myself wonder what would've happened if it had lasted and I had made it to her father's hunting cabin. Drinking with armed old men who wanted to fuck their friend's daughter. Shooting guns in the twilight sunrise. Maybe knowing she was waiting for me at the end of the trip to ask how it went would've gotten me to actually pull the trigger. Someone who believed in me as I went into the woods to see if breaking off a piece of life like a lit shard from a cracked mirror would usher in a wisdom that would let me know none of us would ever have to act out the terrible versions of who we were anymore. That we could finally go beyond those shit-filled days that were supposed to so obviously teach us but never did. And maybe me and her in those cool November beds with nothing more than our skin and smiles and what we had put together in our thoughts in the afternoon got her thinking about how it wasn't about second chances, that it was something more about just going and going and that at our best times we could keep going forward to find the places where things did not perhaps have to end so bitterly or perhaps even so quickly. When I thought about her, I thought that maybe that was what she knew now. That maybe the time she spent fighting herself and giving up and pissing around with me and giving that up, too, I guess, until it was all gone, all of it, gone, gone, from the both of us somehow made this true.

❖ ❖ ❖

*Kostas Anagnopoulos*

# Highlight

It's fine to have an idea
But first make the bed
Learn the routine
The Plaza reopens next month
Make sure to put in an appearance
Meet and greet the shades
Plots waiting to be filled
Wanting more of you than you can manage
When you're alone you're beautiful
There's more breathing room
Enough for a nap in the solarium
Your heels so close to me
We unearth plaster borders, frame cumulus
Changing the constituents of the florid but skinny event
Mexico City is the capital of Mexico
This you know is true

# Weeding

Weeding the carnations, you cry.
You say you feel you're vanishing,
that you really do want to vanish before
your gums pull away from your teeth,
and you forget to turn off the stove.
Your mother gave you marked-down bananas
and a washcloth for your birthday,
weeps reading TV Guide aloud,
deploys random nouns—
Burger King, grandchild, teacup, giraffe—as adjectives,
roosts in assisted living
on her bed in a posture of conversation,
lips parted, leaning in, but looking away.
"What's it like to be ninety-six, Louise?" I ask.,
"Not everything is like something else, dear," she says.
"Don't be Walmart."

*John Schneider*

# Bottomless Water

The boat has almost tipped over, its keel
reaching for air. We're sunburned but white
with fear, leaning as far over the upper rail
as we can without falling, hoping our weight

can save us. What if it can't?
We make every effort
to re-center
our greatest fear: being exposed to something

we have no control over.
We work to persuade ourselves
we can prevent *it* by doing the right thing--
assuming we are on solid ground

but not certain.
We do all this,
but still fear that
apprehension is all that lies on the other side.

We do not know how the story will end.
At the moment it has lost its shape
and taken ours.
The water that was

to hold us up did not.
As we move through it
we realize we are more like the water
than in it.

# Noah Gave Us the Ark

There may come a time when there is no water at the kitchen sink.
But there will still be water in a puddle, or a pond, or the ocean.
It might seem undrinkable. But just take an empty Coke or beer can,
and an empty plastic water bottle, the tall quart size. Cut the bottom
off the plastic water bottle. Here is the only tricky part: You know
the cuff on pants? Fold a one-inch cuff inward at the bottom of the
water bottle. It folds, just fiddle. Fill the beer can with ocean water,
or toxin-laced farm run-off, or your pee. Place the cuffed plastic bottle
over the beer can, and place the lovely apocalypse rig in a sunny spot.
Sit in the shade, or scavenge for ants, or write a poem in your journal.
Evaporation will suck clean water out of the beer can, and it will dribble
down and into the cuff. You can pour a shot of pure water. You might
want to scavenge for beer cans and plastic bottles, which isn't hard.
Remember all the times you went to a restaurant and the waiter poured
ice water in a crystal glass, and you forgot to bow your brilliant head?

Christine Poreba

# Gaps in the Sky

*There are gaps in the sky the sky fills in with sky.*
                                    —Suzanne Buffam

"Final Boarding Call for Kirby,"
    calls the agent from the gate
beside mine. Kirby, who is where
    now? Running down this corridor,
his suitcase tilting on its wheels
    behind him? Or in a car, not budging,
or a bed, not leaving someone's arms,
    intentionally? "Kirby," the agent
repeats, "last call." She means it because
    now his name is replaced with that
of a stand-by passenger. No figure of Kirby
    arrives out of breath, but what if it did?
After which announcement of "final"
    does the seat really cease to be his?
His seat that is just another empty space
    for the agents to fill as they guard the planes
parked in pointed rows like opportunities
    ready to carry off whoever catches them.
Did someone call my name like this when
    I missed the single flight to Montpellier
after landing in Heathrow instead of Stansted,
    my boyfriend's thrifty arrangements made
knowing I didn't like to fly? A fresh coating
    of tar blocked the bus I rode between
the airports; when I finally made it, I stood
    at a bank of payphones, light streaming,
and tried to tell the stranger whose house
    my boyfriend had just left for the airport
the essential phrase, "J'ai manqué mon avion."
    I remember the clicking of his tongue,
as though I'd disappointed him. But what are
    we to do when the space we want to fill
goes on without us, the way, later, that boyfriend
    would? I remember changing into my
purple-flowered dress after twenty-two hours,
    compressed in time to a glass of sherry
in the airport bar, strangers in motion, all
    of us missing somewhere else. I cut a scrap
of that dress to save, sitting by the window
    while birds flew into the opening made
by an oak tree's branches. What a painter
    might call *negative space* the birds know as *doorway.*

Boats anchored near the Catalina Casino on Santa Catalina Island.  Photo by David Lee.

Dan Lundin

# A Narcissist's Guide to Catalina

You can swim to Catalina Island from the coast of Southern California. If it's been a few years since your last full-body shave down, however, some preparation may be in order before you snap on your cap and dive in, and when I say preparation, I mostly mean swimming, a twelve-month calendar full of endurance swims, timed sprints, and all the colors in between. This isn't an easy commitment. As the demands of work, inclement weather, and/or a genetic predisposition to laziness can derail your best intentions, a bonafide twenty-one-mile motivator may be in order. My nominee: the great white shark, a familiar Pacific Ocean inhabitant more likely to attack a struggling dog-paddler than a speedy, untroubled freestyler. Paste his image to your refrigerator. Watch *Jaws*. Feel the energy surge commonly known as fear.

Of course, you don't have to go it alone. Employing a kayaking escort to convoy you across the channel makes sense, though this individual will need a few skills to be of any value. Along with a certain amount of boating proficiency, the escort should be trained in basic water safety and have a deep understanding of hypothermia, as the classic terrestrial signs— the inability to walk and terminal burrowing, i.e. the unquenchable desire to tunnel into composting piles and/or homestead under tents of fallen trees—will be less than apparent in the unwooded ocean waters.

Alternatively, if you can get ahold of an outrigger canoe and half a dozen acquaintances with good upper-body strength, you can paddle across the channel, Polynesian style. You would still get wet and hopelessly sore, but the trip would be shorter, relatively speaking, and as part of a team, there might even be opportunity for you to occasionally slack off, to lower your paddle and admire your hands' ability to rapidly blister. A less physical course is to simply buy a ferryboat ticket. It's easy, but far from original. Of the million or so tourists

that visit Catalina every year, most shuffle off a ferryboat or cruise ship. But, again, these are only suggestions. No one will stop you if you decide to jump right in and start kicking. That is to say, no one is going to arrest you. It's still a free country in that respect.

I have yet another option for you. It includes more variables, sure, but it would be criminal not to include it on the list. Make a friend who owns a boat, or, better yet, make a friend who is a member of a boat-owning family, ideally the youngest of three brothers, with parents worn out and uninterested in properly monitoring their eighteen-year-old son's activities. A sailboat would suffice, a small keelboat, something in the twenty-two- to twenty-seven-foot range, one that could be equipped with a modest motor. A boat this size is easy to manage and roomy enough to accommodate guests, plenty of gear, and the basic creature comforts—a head, an icebox, and simple cooking facilities. You and your boat-owning friend and another, non-boat-owning friend could go to a mainland harbor the night before your trip and sleep on board for a few hours to wake in the wee, octopus-ink morning and loose the ties and maneuver out of the harbor and beyond the breakwater and adjust the autopilot and revisit sleep while slowly motoring out on the calm, breeze-free ocean, and wake up again hours later with the sun newly risen and there she blows, Avalon Harbor, where you find an available buoy and tie up your boat and jump in the water and climb back on board and remove the inflatable dinghy from its storage space and hook it up to its pump and crack open a Tecate and laugh a giddy, early-morning beer-buzzed laugh because it was so, so much easier than swimming, and who likes to suck oily boat fumes on a rusting ferry for an hour anyway?

❖ ❖ ❖

I was disoriented as I swam to the surface. I'd misjudged the size of the submerged tube

153

in the reef, and as I kicked through the other side, I scraped the back of my leg along a rock crusted with barnacles. Bobbing on the water, I pulled my mask up to better examine my stinging limb. A carpet-bombed pattern of shallow pink divots ran from the fat part of my calf to my ankle, bringing new and grotesque life to the scales of my mermaid tattoo.

With one arm spastically slapping at the water, Steven kicked his way back to the dinghy, his curly helmet of hair moving stubbornly forward, splitting the choppy waves with all the efficiency of a face-shaped cattle prod. As he neared the boat, he barked inaudibly at Ian.

"What happened?" Ian shouted at me from the boat.

"I cut up my leg," I yelled in reply.

"You cut Steven!"

Circumstantial evidence suggested he was right. From a deli-thin slice across the top of his shoulder, blood cascaded down Steven's boney back, a smear of crimson watercolor fanning out to connect freckle-dot after freckle-dot. I pulled my pole spear close, and with knife end jutting out of the water like a tiny dorsal fin, I examined it for bits of flesh.

Spear, certainly, was a generous term. We had only one professionally manufactured fishing device in our possession, a capable Hawaiian sling, and Steven had laid claim to it earlier in the day, a property grab that had left me no choice but to cobble together an alternative weapon from a corroded kitchen knife, a yard of duct tape and a wood pole, one previously employed as the non-business end of a deck mop. Viewed from the proper distance, it may have looked the part, but my crude spear proved ineffective. Because the water deepened to forty feet in places, I was reluctant to attempt a throw and had instead resigned myself to diving and stabbing, succeeding in finding nothing but the occasional Garibaldi for my dull blade to bounce off. Protected and illegal to hunt, the cocky orange fish was the only one that would swim within striking distance. And apparently Steven. Steven would swim within striking distance.

The three of us were alone in the alcove. Ian had stayed in the boat, content to sit and read. Collar up, glasses on, hairs in their appropriate places, Ian was incessantly put together, often exceedingly so, the prototype for the modern dandy. Finding my blade clean of incriminat-

ing material, I swam to the dinghy and pulled myself inside. My calf throbbed. Blood and salt water wept down my ankle and pooled around my heel.

"Sorry, man," I offered. "Do you think it'll need stitches?"

Holding a towel to his shoulder, Steven ignored my question.

"It's a long cut, but I don't think it's that deep," Ian answered.

"At least I didn't stick you in the eye."

Steven dug his sunglasses out of the bottom of his duffel, which either meant he did not want to talk or the light was bothering him. As the sun was burning overhead, reflecting off the water and the shear rocks of a nearby cliff face, I wagered on the light.

"You're up to date on your tetanus shots, right?" I asked, looking into his scratched lenses. "Maybe beers and spears aren't the best combination after all."

"Maybe not," agreed Ian.

"That is a shame," I said. "They sound so perfect together."

"Because they rhyme," added Steven, annoyed to the point of participation.

"Well, sure, I won't deny that that's part of it."

The goodwill I had acquired earlier in the day by swiping a barbeque from a neighboring boat had apparently been spent. But we had three days on the island. There was time enough to make amends, and fortunately for me, opportunities were everywhere.

❖ ❖ ❖

Catalina Island is a quaint twenty-two miles long by eight miles wide of not all that much to see. Avalon, its provincial headquarters, is a Starbuck's-free, two-car town where most people get around by way of pimped-out golf cart or bicycle. As far as landmarks go, there is the quote, un-quote famous casino, but in recent times most of the monkeyshine has happened in the water. (For cases in point, search the web for "Natalie Wood fails to stay afloat long enough for either husband Robert Wagner or actor Christopher Walken to take notice" and/ or "Lisa Marie Presley proves that women can throw as well as boys when she chucks Nicolas Cage's $65,000 engagement ring overboard.")

On shore later that day, we shopped for dinner, planning to test the abilities of our newly acquired grill. Two blocks inland from the boardwalk we found a market, its turquoise paint sunburned and peeling from the façade. Hanging inside the entrance door, a hulking fan greeted us with a swirling gust of air. I gathered its aim was to discourage feral flies from plotting a course inside, and perhaps it did accomplish that goal, but however hard and continuously it might have blown, it was incapable of transporting the hatched-in-the-rotting-produce insects out. Nor could it defeat the smells, the most attention-getting among them being a fermenting, locker-room tang that more than hinted at some long-lost dairy item. Though the old man stationed at the register didn't look the type to stay up on a Sunday night to take inventory, the store proved to be stocked for our needs: briquettes, lighter fluid, case of Coors (just weeks away from my first year of college and my stomach lining had precociously rebelled against any association with Lucky Lager and its ilk), ice, barbeque sauce.

The chicken threatened to bust our thirty-dollar budget, but as it was stored in a refrigerator in the back and as the store's only surveillance camera was aimed at the wine and spirits aisle and as the shelf between the chicken cooler and the register was stacked with a motley crew of plastic beach equipment that nested on top of a dozen or so yellowing, styrofoam coolers, I slipped a pack of breasts with rib meat down the front of my shorts. The four pounds of raw poultry sent a chill pulsing down my legs, but I was undeterred. I shuffled to the counter like an orange-jumpsuit-wearing convict, presented my fake identification, and paid the bill.

❖ ❖ ❖

On our first night in town, we headed for a bar over the boardwalk. A bad bar. A sticky-stooled dive from six a.m. until lunchtime, a feeble, two-television sports bar by afternoon, and an unapologetically dreadful dance club by night. The only redeeming qualities to the place were a skinny balcony that boasted an unobstructed view of the harbor and cheap drinks.

At the top of the stairs a fat-lipped man-child negligently checked our identifications. Once inside, we grabbed a cocktail and a basket of stale popcorn at the bar and made our way to the balcony, optimistic that good fortune would somehow find us there. The patrons were a mix of leathery, liver-stressed locals and overly energetic, first-night-of-vacation cruise-ship passengers, their commonality being tone-deafness and pitiable coordination. I watched them through the tinted window and sipped at my Captain and Coke. Flat and over-syruped, it didn't taste very optimistic.

Two drinks later, darting between un-timeable hip spasms as I crossed the dance floor, a loosely defined space that included everything outside of the restrooms, I bounced into one of them (cruise-ship girl, not swarthy, cirrhosis candidate). The impact toppled her drink onto her shoes and between her toes and the toes of her friends. Being nothing if not an opportunist, I stole her away from her sticky-footed girlfriends and rushed her to the bar.

"So, what can I replace?"

"Is this how you pick up girls?"

"To be determined. It's a completely new technique."

"Somehow I doubt that."

Her name was Carma, spelled, she quickly pointed out, with a "C." Why I needed to know this, I wasn't exactly sure, but it did help me remember her name, a facility that typically eludes me in the presence of alcohol. Carma was immediately likeable, witty and flippant, with exotic, wide-set eyes and a riot of hair dyed a supernatural plum. When I couldn't find Ian or Steven in the bar, eh, dance club, I immediately jumped to several conclusions and invited her to the boat to party with my friends.

We boarded the water taxi from the pier. It was a short trip. Ian's sailboat was the second stop. As we neared it, the taxi captain hit the abandoned shell with his floodlight, and the wild shadows created an atmosphere worthy of a B horror film.

"Come on," I called over the revving engine, my hand extended.

"There's no party here. Where are your friends?"

"On their way, no doubt."

"I'm not getting on."

She was serious, but I was beyond caring. Withdrawing my hand, I stepped onto the sailboat without her.

A few words in my defense. After a long day of continuous drinking, my motivations had been compromised, and even if I could have mustered the strength to override my sedated libido, there was exactly nowhere for the two of us to go. Late-night visitors were forbidden aboard cruise ships, and if we messed around on the beach, I feared I'd be stuck there. On the beach. All night. So, just like that and quite unexpectedly, judging from the look on her face, I let her go. The taxi motored off with Carma scowling from the stern.

The cabin of the boat was locked. I tried to sleep on the bench outside, but Ian had put the cushions away to spare them from the damp, and the remorseless plastic took advantage of me, separating my soft tissue and grinding its way into the back of my skull, shoulder blades, tailbone, heels. Frustrated, I returned to the cabin door, and after some exploration, I found a kink in the armor: a length of the wood frame wiggled. Tugging at it with my fingertips, I created a pinky width of separation, wide enough to slide in a leveraging tool, or, in my case, a cooking utensil. I snatched the spatula off the barbeque and worked it down into the gap, blackened chicken bits scraping off along the way. I tried to remove a single piece of the frame to allow for reattachment at some later, daylight-filled time, but alcohol births poor burglars. The wood snapped, splintering in two. Leaving the collateral damage, I stepped inside, unearthed a pillow from the bowels of our emergent laundry pile, and fell asleep.

I didn't sleep long.

"What! The! Fuck!" screamed Ian, his voice twisted by the cabin acoustics.

I had worked out my list of excuses before the break-in: I could not find the dingy, the water taxi abandoned me, my throat felt sore on a level that registered as contagious or on the verge of possibly being contagious if not immediately treated with hot tea, warm blanket, etc. But with Ian leaning over me—knee on my chest, one hand pressing down on my trachea, the other hand balled into a tight fist—I failed to properly state my case.

"I'll get it fixed," I muttered. "I promise. I'll fix it."

❖ ❖ ❖

Morning arrived, the proper morning, and I faced it first. After peeling a bruised banana, I smeared it with peanut butter and wrapped it with a slice of bread. I poured some juice into a chipped coffee cup I found head first in the sink. Between bites of my breakfast, I slipped off my sweatpants, wound a beach towel around my waist, and stepped outside.

The beach stretched in front of me. The channel waters swept in from behind. Because the island acted the part of a mammoth breakwater, there were no swells. We were tied to a buoy north of the pier in the next-to-last row. It was all sailboats, floating in a parking lot for the neurotically ding-averse in roomy harmony. My swimsuit hung from a cord, which skirted the edge of the boat like a handrail for someone that doesn't really need a handrail, only the suggestion of one. I slipped into the damp suit, dropped the towel and jumped overboard. Then I swam. I swam between the outermost row of boats and into the open ocean. I pulled and kicked until my body grew warm and turned cold again, until my eyes swelled with salt water, until my fingers felt numb. Only when the fear came, the creeping belief that I might not make it back, did I finally turn around.

❖ ❖ ❖

I napped in the sun that afternoon. Distorted seaside noises flew elastically overhead, as if projected by a short-circuiting amplifier. The boat rose and fell, drawing rhythmically on its tie, slacking back, drawing again. Waking into a post-siesta daze, my thoughts bobbed along too: a novel idea for a tattoo, reasons not to eat horsemeat, my mother's birthday.

"Steven, what day is it?" I asked.

"Saturday?"

"No, what's the number?"

Ian replied from inside the boat. "The fifteenth."

"Shit."

My cell phone was out of order, or so I assumed. Even if I had the diving equipment required to locate it, few electronic devices recover from an overnight soak. Steven had tossed it overboard at Ian's request. At the time, I hadn't protested. Its sacrifice trumped a punch to the jaw. Ian's phone lounged in the cabin, fully charged and water-free, but even if it could be argued that he owed me a call, I wasn't up to soliciting the favor. Instead, I loaded my pant pocket with change and boarded the dinghy.

A lone pay phone stood at the end of the pier. With its melted plastic receiver, swastika-riddled metal face and sticker-barricaded change return, I almost felt sorry for the endangered machine as I lobbed in my coins.

"Hello."

"Hi, Mom."

"Oh, baby! Hello! How's the trip going?"

"Great. Thanks. Happy birthday."

"Happy . . . oh, yes! My goodness, I'm amazed you remembered."

"How could I forget?"

"I suppose you're right. It was a big day for us all."

"Yes?"

"I mean, for everyone at the intervention. I can't believe it's been six years."

Wrong month, right day? Right day, wrong month? Wrong mom? Fears of dementia tape-wormed into my head.

"I can't believe it either," I spat.

"How's the weather?"

"The weather, ah, is . . . good," I said, looking around to confirm my report. "The weather is good."

"I'm glad. The island can get so fogged-in."

"Yeah. We lucked out."

"Okay, well, I'd love to chat, but George and I are heading out the door. Call me when you get home, okay? Love you, baby."

"Love you, too," I echoed.

The trance I had been enjoying had evaporated, swapped out for another symptomatic spell, one that blended the split of sky and sea and lifted a docked cruise ship out of the water and onto the rocks.

Taking a break from his plastic-bag lunch, a neighboring seagull rose up to mock me. He knew. I knew he knew, because it takes one to know one, and he had one too, a mad-making worm whipping about behind the Jurassic, unblinking marble lodged in the side of his head.

❖ ❖ ❖

With no restaurants willing to deliver a pizza to the boat, we dined out. A few words on the island's culinary scene. While there are no chain restaurants on Catalina, nothing prevents the mom-n'-pops from modeling themselves after them. Indeed, the place we chose to dine that evening could have passed for the TGI Friday's in your favorite airport terminal, but with slightly less fresh, less interesting food.

Kangaroo-bouncy Michelle scribbled down our drink and binge-suggestive food order, six entrees in total, without a flinch. When she walked off, I took an overdue wallet accounting—real I.D., fake I.D., AAA card, three fives, and a one. (To prevent myself from "going Vegas," I had left my ATM card at home.)

"In the spirit of full disclosure, I only have sixteen bucks on me."

"I don't have much more than that," Steven added.

Ian pulled a twenty out of his pocket and laid it on the table. We all knew he had more, but he was done underwriting our trip.

"We should cancel the food," Steven urged.

"Easy now. Let's think this through," I said. "The restaurant is providing us with beer from a keg and meat from a freezer. We came in without a reservation, so it's not as if our presence is preventing them from making money with another party. We are dirtying some dishes, true, and getting the hopes of our waitress up a bit, perhaps."

"A cute waitress," added Ian.

I continued. "She may indeed, categorically speaking, fall somewhere between above average and hot, but we cannot confirm or deny that she has any feelings for any of us. What she does have feelings for, and has reasonable expectations to receive, is a tip. That being said, here's my suggestion. We eat our food. We drink our drinks. We leave what we have and walk out. It'll be short, but it'll cover their costs, so it is not a dine-and-ditch, technically speaking."

"It isn't?" questioned Steven.

"Or, if you guys want, we can cancel our food order."

In the time it takes to pour three large beers and walk a twenty-foot distance twice, our drinks arrived. And soon after that, oversized plates of oversized food crowded onto our table. I sliced a burger in half, dunked it in ketchup, and stuffed it into my mouth. Steven poured hot sauce over a glimmering heap of nachos. Ian said nothing, just kept sending text messages on his phone. Appearances suggesting my line of reasoning had won out, I ordered us another round of drinks.

Later that night, we hooked up with some like-minded teens on their way to a house party. As I tripped along the boardwalk with the group, my inner moth was summoned by the flickering candlelight of a Mexican restaurant. Perched on the sills of open, street-side windows, the candles screamed "Take me!" and so I did. Bulbous in shape and a smoky ginger in color, the glass cupped a steady, dancing flame that gripped me a moment too long.

"Hey! Hey, you!" boomed a block-lettered voice from inside the restaurant.

I blew out the candle and placed it on the sidewalk, under the window and right at my feet. By the time I returned to an upright position, silhouettes were weaving their way around stools and tables in my direction. I darted around the corner, crossed the street, and hid behind a parked delivery truck, crouching down in the dark. I didn't hide for long. After all, I thought, it was a cheap candle, and I had barely even removed it from the restaurant. So when the fat-lipped man-child panted my way, I stepped out of the shadows with my arms raised in a mock surrender.

"It's still there," I tried. "It's under the window."

But the narrative had already been written. No one cared to hear my side of the story. And unfortunately for me, the previous night's doorman/bouncer, the one I was surrendering to, was a recently laid-off island cop, at that moment a fairly intoxicated one. He spun me around and artfully pinned me to the pavement, face first, craning my arm in the air behind me. A police car pulled up and cuffs were unnecessarily applied. Into the car, into the station, into a lonely cell went I, thereby ending my forty-two-hour crime spree.

Too drunk to be uncomfortable, I fell asleep on the metal bench. I woke up curled on the floor in the fetal position, the tip of a steel-toed shoe tap-tap-tapping at my ribcage.

"We found a driver's license for a Maximilian T. Saturday in your wallet," the officer said, holding the I.D. in front of my face. "The picture looks an awfully lot like you."

"Mr. Saturday is my alter ego of a drinking age."

"Let's go, kid."

The officer escorted me to the front office where I exchanged my signature for my wallet and an unrequested receipt of the crimes charged against me.

"I'm afraid to ask what the 'T' stands for," said the officer.

"Tweedledum."

"Funny."

"You think?"

Sandwiched between two fictional names, I would have agreed. Tweedledum is funny, if only modestly so. Sadly, it was the only real part of my fake I.D. No, I wasn't one half of a semantically handicapped pair of twins. No, neither of my parents was a devoted fan of Lewis Carroll or, more improbably, of John Byrom. (Trust me when I say I have done a lot of research on the subject.) My Tweedledum had been applied much more thoughtlessly. After a protracted labor, I had leapt out, bald, chubby, and, according to my father, void of any visible genitalia.

"Humpty Dumpty!" my father had barked upon seeing me. And then, recanting "No, no, I got it. Tweedle-fucking-dum!"

Cooler heads would, sort of, prevail. "Fucking" never appeared on my birth certificate.

❖ ❖ ❖

It was early. The sun had yet to come up. I was, as they say, a free man. I headed to the shore and walked the beach. A backpack, faded and worn, slacked out of a garbage can. I pulled it out, dumped out the empty energy drink cans and drained pint of vodka inside it, and filled it with sand—main pouch, exterior pocket, still smaller far exterior pocket. A few holes revealed themselves, but they were too small to drain much away. Guessing the ballast to weight thirty pounds, I swung it onto my back. For my prescribed purposes, it would work just fine.

❖ ❖ ❖

A mile out from the island, Ian shut off the motor. We would sail the rest of the way home.

"Anyone swimming?" he asked. "Last chance before mainland."

"I am," I said from the bow.

I slipped on my fins, mask, and newly acquired backpack, then swung my legs over the side. Forcefully inhaling and exhaling, I counted backward from twenty, checking my watch at five, filling my lungs at one, plunging feet first into the water at zero. With the added weight urging me downward, I watched as the bubble cloud above me widened into a loose ring and disappeared at the surface. I watched as the boat hull, little by little, melted away. Through the liquid prism of the ocean, I watched as colors shifted to deeper and deeper shades in steady waves.

❖ ❖ ❖

Until recently, I spent a month out of every summer in the high desert of Scottsdale with my father and stepmother and their three dogs. Summers in Arizona are, naturally, miserable.

(Not that the springs or falls are all that much better.) Thankfully, they had a pool.

When I started holding my breath underwater, I kept myself down by fluttering my arms. Along with hours of practice, increasing my submersion time required an alternative, less energy-consuming way to stay sunken, and so I began anchoring myself with boulders from the pool's adjacent desert landscape. The first time my father saw me motionless and pinned under a rock, he dived in after me, polyester sweat suit, designer sunglasses, and all. The second time he saw me, he waited at the water's edge, leaning over so that I could see him as he worked to remove his belt. I stayed under for nearly a minute and a half that morning, besting my previous time by eighteen seconds. As my father liked to say, we are all born capable. Some of us just lack the proper encouragement.

❖ ❖ ❖

My descent continued. The ocean collapsed upon me. Carbon dioxide burned my lungs; heartbeats sledge-hammered my head. My brain, clogged as it was with nagging images, both real and imagined, took the low-oxygen opportunity to sort and catalog: the casual stabbing, the destruction of property, the shoplifting, the poaching of protected aquatic species, the unrequited meal, the petty theft, the

shadows of sharks and sea monsters circling the outskirts of my vision.

The ache in my head grew to hemisphere-splitting proportions, and I welcomed it, greeting it like a chemotherapy, a self-inflicted mutilation for the greater good. I pushed into the center of it, a sluggish, timeless space free of worms and pain. But as much as this eye was my goal, it was also my warning. I had gone far enough without the ship.

Each deep dive was a baptism of sorts, a chance to roll the dial back to zero. It wasn't the water that reset things, not in the obvious way. It was the flirtation with death. My watch read two minutes, twenty-five seconds. I slipped off the backpack, and as it vanished into the cavernous obscurity, I kicked myself up. The dive would be another personal best. Once again, fate had taken a pass.

❖ ❖ ❖

As an added bonus, this last travel option guarantees a return visit to the island for your arraignment. If this seems too convoluted, you might consider getting to Catalina via helicopter. Fifteen minutes from takeoff to landing. A bit on the pricey side, but if you can handle the noise, it makes for a memorable trip.

Have fun, and whatever you do, take lots of pictures.

❖ ❖ ❖

# Pit

Stevie, Phil, Eddie, and I drove up to The Electric Factory to see Dropkick Murphys.
"You better go into the fucking pit," Stevie kept saying, "You better go into the fucking pit."
"I'm going into the pit.  I already said I'm going into the pit!"
After whiskey at the bar,
outdoor smoke, while Chuck Ragan screamed his lungs and played his guitar,
a young soldier, call him David, bummed a cigarette off Stevie.
This soldier reminded me of someone who during those days I considered a little brother,
who was fighting in Afghanistan: shaved head, scrawny paste bones and skin,
trying to impress us with the tough cuss words he recently learned in the Army.
David was leaving for Afghanistan in a few months, he was alone in the city,
he asked if he could stay with us,
I wanted to keep him around, keep him safe, I wasn't sure from what.
Bagpipes started playing, "Cadence to Arms," I think.
We ran back inside and formed a line,
grabbing each other's shirts,
to pull in the one behind us as we forced our way to the forming pit.
I took hold of David's.
As a moving hole developed in the people, hands without bodies pulled David to the ground;
many others fell with him.
I dug the limbs out of the way, searching for the young soldier,
thrashing in the darkness, my hands making their way to the bottom of the bodies pile,
he was gone, vanished.
Pushing through the fists and elbows of the pit and around the venue,
I hoped to find David somewhere in the crowd.
I never saw him.
Where was he? Hospital? Driving alone back home, hurt?
Maybe he was absolutely fine, I had no idea.
After the concert, at a truck stop, the first time we were in light in hours,
Phil pointed out a sizable stain on my shirt: someone else's blood.
When I made it back to my dark, small, dorm,
I threw off the shirt, took a shower,
and laid awake in bed thinking of David and my little brother.

*Cammy Thomas*

# A Constant

It accumulates gradually and provides
nothing except a covering. Despite
your constant labor on it, the wetting,
the drying, the smoothing, it will not
redeem you. You are merely
maintaining something required
but not strongly desired. In the wind
it flaps and folds on itself, sometimes
lands on sand, stiffens. Inevitably,
it spins sopping, then circles hotly
and slowly fades and softens until
it disintegrates. The only pleasure
you can take in it, is the way it rubs
against you, maybe the way the wind
stirs it against you, or maybe
the way it gives when you give.
Never will it hold you, never
embrace, just enfold you.

# Measures of

I have already passed the age of counsel,
not that anyone ever came for it, only my son
who once asked me *How do you know you're
in love?* which made everything in the kitchen
shine with my wisdom. He went on to marry
a girl who has her own opinions about mothers
-in-law. There was a mouse slipping across
the kitchen last night. *Let it be a gecko,* I said
to its shadow, *let it be a lizard*, but this morning
there were droppings by the door where
it waited for the glass to open or disappear,
while my Labrador, who can smell a crust of bread
from a thousand meters away, wagged his tail.
And since women keep their girlfriends, I made
a pact with mine: we'll live together when
our husbands die and save one bottle of morphine
each, because at one hundred it's as if you were
already dead, and at ninety my mother claps
her hands as I turn on the lights, and says, *Oh, lights!*
Her apartment heated to a sauna, steam on all
the windows, her helper barefoot even though
it's February. I put my hand on her shoulder and say,
*It's just a job*, another piece of time to box up
and label: the age of commandments, the age of
discernment, and I wonder how a mouse can slip
beneath the baseboard; is its body an illusion,
only tiny bones under all that fluff? I try to think
of famous mice so I can give it a name, but I am
in the age of forgetfulness, left out by the sages,
the age of crying at inappropriate, and also appropriate
times, the age of sunscreen and my own particular
pillow case, and I notice that the age of *Gevurah*
is translated as *power*, when actually it's *restraint*,
as in *Who is a hero? He who controls himself.*
And it is one crumb of comfort that the wise men
also turned to dust and blew away, but left me
these clues, so that I can enter the age of listening
to words that keep changing, but also stay the same,
till I know them by heart, which is like a refrain,
the continual repetition of myself, into the slippery now.

Michael Malan

# Despite What They Say

I broke up with Salma in the summer of 2004 while I was working at the Army Navy Store in Dayton, Ohio. When I told her I wanted to date someone else, she punched me so hard my glasses flew across the room and hit the wall. I can't see a thing without them, so I felt around on the floor like a blind man—by the time I found my corrective lenses she was gone. I thought maybe she had cast a spell and what followed was seven years of bad luck. My signature Tarot card was The Hanged Man and the *I Ching* advised me, "Do not marry the maiden." One good thing happened during those seven years: I gave up smoking. Except for one or two gaspers every now and then. In 2012 I went down to Mexico and did a sweat ceremony with a Mayan shaman. He told me that the Mayan calendar is circular—there is no end of the world, even though the American news media had been forecasting the end for years. Despite what they say, creation keeps on going, one little bang after another. Trees fall, are reborn as houses and tables. Once the mojo gets going, it's hard to stop. After two hours in the sweat lodge I imagined a white jaguar was sitting across from me. Just last Sunday, at church, a woman in the first pew turned and looked me in the eye. When I see a tree I step outside myself.

Robin Perry Dana. *Why I Wake Early,* from the *Watershed* series. 2018. Still from video. Dimensions variable. Courtesy of ARTicles Art Gallery.

# Seeing Green

*I bring you branches green with dew.*

–Edith Sitwell

I'm going into the garden, green with fern. It's my parklet, my oasis, my corner of the green world. I breathe the oxygen exhaled by the trees—cascara, incense cedar, shore pine in its big pot. I commune with the Steller's Jays flashing neon blue, fluttering and perching high on my neighbor's western red cedar. But commune is not the right word—for what do these loud intelligent corvids think of me? For sure, they know I am here. How do I know they know? When I'm in the garden they stay high away; when I'm indoors looking out they will come down to peck at the moss paths. We don't commune, really, but let's say I am witness to their busy rasping and clucking . . .

❖ ❖ ❖

My birthstone is green—aquamarine. I live near Green Lake in the Emerald City in the Evergreen State.

❖ ❖ ❖

You could go green with envy. Or, you could get the green light. Or you could build green or vote green or go green about the gills (look sick).

❖ ❖ ❖

You could be spooked by the curse of green. The curse of green spooked American race-car drivers between 1911 and about 1955. On September 17, 1911, a green Knox driven by Lee Oldfield in a fifty-mile race at the Syracuse Fairgrounds went out of control, through a fence, into the crowd. Eleven fans died, including a ten-year-old boy, who had the top of his head taken off. It was one of the worst accidents in racing history. About ten years later, on November 25, 1920, during the Thanksgiving Day race at the Los Angeles Speedway, race-car driver Gaston Chevrolet crashed into driver

Eddie O'Donnell. Both drivers were killed, along with O'Donnell's mechanic, Lyall Jolls. And no wonder, since Chevrolet's racecar was painted green. From then until a very long time later, race-car drivers shunned the color green. According to William Lidwell, in his "Green Lecture" published by The Great Courses, some still do.

❖ ❖ ❖

In about 1400, an unknown poet composed *Sir Gawain and the Green Knight*. Its Middle English script was likely that of a scribe. Nothing is known about the Gawain poet. Nothing.

In the poem, King Arthur and his knights are sitting convivially down to a Yuletide feast at the round table. Enter the green knight, a handsome, fearsome giant, with green skin, green hair, and green horse. The revelries skid to a halt in shocked silence. The man, if he is a man, has wondrous vestments embroidered in birds and butterflies. He carries a green sword "al bigraven with grene in gracios werkes." The story is set reeling when the green giant mockingly throws down an impossible challenge to these supposedly most courageous and honorable knights in the land. Sir Gawain, King Arthur's nephew, takes up the terrible challenge. (The tale, too complicated to relate, involves the decapitation of the green knight, whose head, unfortunately, fails to stay off.)

And what might this scary green apparition stand for? Nature itself—cruel, chaotic, enigmatic. Out there, in the forests of England, where Sir Gawain must venture for a full year, were "wermes" (serpents), wolves, "bulles," "beres" and "bores" and wodwos (these were hairy scary wildmen or wildwomen alleged to hide out in the forests). Nature could be nasty. An iconic figure of that period, according to Bruce R. Smith's book *The Key of Green*, was "the green man," of which there are more than two thousand carvings on Medieval-era buildings in England. The Medieval green man leers out from stone-carved leaves. He is not your friend.

And what has "the green man" morphed into, six centuries later? Consider the Jolly Green Giant, the advertising icon displayed on a Minnesota firm's can of peas. He smiles, avuncular. Let's say the Jolly Green Giant is Sir Gawain's green knight—tamed. Wild and fearsome nature turned into fields and roads and cities and towns and cans of green peas. Not so fearsome now.

Or so we hope.

❖ ❖ ❖

Nature, though, is good for you. Time outdoors is good for you. Nature is therapeutic and calming and cheering. Time spent in nature increases self-confidence and self-discipline. So studies report. And here's what Henry David Thoreau reports: "To anticipate, not the sunrise and the dawn merely, but, if possible, Nature herself! How many mornings, summer and winter, before yet any neighbor was stirring about his business, have I been about mine! (*Walden*, 59-60). Thoreau's business was, as we know, to walk in the woods. I don't walk much in the woods but I do walk in our emerald city almost everywhere I go. And I do work in my garden and go there almost daily, even in winter. I find it therapeutic and calming and cheering.

❖ ❖ ❖

For painters of the past, green was trouble. In his book *Bright Earth*, Philip Ball illuminates what has been largely ignored in art history—chemistry.

Verdigris is the green crust that forms on copper. Soak copper in winemarc—the stems, seeds, and skins remaining after pressing grapes—and the crust forms faster. Winemarc provides acetic acid and acetic acid plus copper gives you verdigris (copper acetate). Used since antiquity, verdigris was pretty much the only decent green available until the 1800s, but its acid content eats parchment and certain chemical conditions turn it black or dark brown. It's a *fugitive* color.

Another ancient pigment is Green Earth, a mineral combination of celadonite and glauconite, which is mined from rock deposits of ancient seabeds. It's a permanent green. Dull. Olive-green looking. Unexciting.

In 1775 a Swedish apothecarist, Carl Wilhelm Scheele, working among his mixtures, invented Scheele's Green. This was copper mixed with arsenic. Do we need to mention that Scheele's Green was a deadly poison? It became a cheap and popular color for wallpapers and dresses and paints. It may have killed Napoleon, who had Scheele's Green painted on his walls in his elegant house on Saint Helena, the island to which he was exiled. It's carcinogenic, especially prone to cause stomach cancer. Napoleon died of stomach cancer. Also, arsenic mummifies. Napoleon's body, transferred to France nineteen years later, had not decomposed.

For painters, Scheele's Green was soon replaced by the same formula modified into the beautiful Emerald Green, invented in 1814. Copper, acetic acid, arsenic. Winsor & Newton, purveyors of artists' pigments, began selling Emerald Green in 1832, and the painter Frederic Turner began using it about then. Later in the century the Impressionists adored Emerald Green. Monet painted his exquisite "The Japanese Footbridge" (1899) using it. Like Scheele's Green before it, it went to tremendous industrial use for dresses and wallpapers. It likely killed many children in their beds in their beautiful green-wallpapered nurseries.

Eventually better greens were invented. Viridian (chromium green). Cobalt Green, invented 1790. Artists have shied from Cobalt Green, due to its expense and low tinting power, but scientists have discovered the pigment's magnetic properties. One day Cobalt Green will enable computers to load software in a flick.

Phthalo Green (pronounced thalo, rhymes with follow), invented in 1938, a synthetic organic green made from copper phthalocyanine. Before the introduction of Phthalo Green, reports the website of Winsor & Newton, "the only greens capable of equal brilliance were the original Emerald Greens." Winsor & Newton calls Phthalo Green *Winsor Green*.

❖ ❖ ❖

But is any object, any painting, any leaf or green bug actually green? Are the green gemstones—bloodstone or green tourmaline or turquoise or serpentine—actually green? No. They are not. "The much-cherished sense of color," writes neuroscientist Christof Koch, "is a construct of the nervous system." And that goes for all colors, not just green.

Green happens in the following way. Lightwaves about 510 nanometers long (a nanometer is one billionth of a meter) hit our green leaf. The leaf absorbs lightwaves of other lengths but refuses our 510nm lightwave, which bounces back to our eye, enters the cornea, passes through the lens, travels through the vitreous fluid that fills the eyeball, and hits the cones, the photoreceptors in the retina at the back of the eye. So far we don't see green.

The cones convert optical to electrical. They send the pulse through the optic nerve to a part of the thalamus called the lateral geniculate nucleus. (In neuroscientific terms a nucleus is a collection of brain cells working together to perform a function.) On each side, the lateral geniculate nucleus relays the pulse farther back, to its opposite visual cortex. The visual field is projected like a map onto the visual cortex, with neighboring locations in the visual field projected onto neighboring locations in the opposite visual cortex.

Still we have not seen green.

The visual cortex projects this visual information forward to the prefrontal cortex along two pathways. The ventral path (the low road) carries information relating to color, form, contour, and identifying objects. Involved in the ventral path is the fusiform gyrus, a long narrow structure, fat in the middle, connected to both the occipital (visual cortex) and temporal lobes. Persons with damage to the fusiform gyrus cannot see colors.

The dorsal path (the high road) runs through the parietal lobe, and is concerned with space, motion, and depth. The two streams run separately but remain in close communication.

They reunite in the prefrontal cortex, the forward-most part of the cortex, that big part of the human brain that plans, discerns, ascertains, makes decisions.

Only now do we see the color green.

Out there, there are no green objects. Without biology, without eyes, without the brain, without the retina, without cones, without the visual cortex, without the fusiform gyrus, green would not exist.

Lightwaves would exist, certainly. But not the colors, not green. It's *seeing* green that makes the color green.

❖ ❖ ❖

But we do see green. And, weirdly, the color green sparks creativity, or so it seems.

In the following limited sense. Psychologists give three identical creativity tests, assigning tasks such as finding as many uses for a square as possible within a two-minute time frame. The tests, which by now have been administered numerous times to numerous subjects, are identical, except that the covers of the folders that contain the task are black, white, or green. (There are other permutations such as administering the test in rooms painted different colors or on computer screens of different colored backgrounds.) The results are consistent and rather dramatic. The three color groups score the same in terms of quantity of answers. But the solutions of the green group, scored blind, are noticeably more creative, more interesting.

Why should this be? I have no idea. Nevertheless, I've changed my screen saver to the color green. I will hereafter work out of green folders. I'm deciding what shade of green to paint my study wall. For I want art. I want the creative life. I want the color green. I, for one, am going green.

❖ ❖ ❖

# Lithia Springs, Three Times

1
What do we call it, eternal? The springwater, domestic
as a swimming pool at 72 degrees,
always about as blue        as a child's eye
or the sky when all they promised        was rain.

We drive home with sand collected to our feet
reminds us        this is your dead brother's car
this is a long summer        the mouth of a firework
before the sound


2
There is a young boy trying to drown
his sister        making water
laughter. She cries
for a mother I cannot        see I cannot see

any alligators        just egrets engaging
ibis; summer in a chorus of green around us, watching
to see what becomes of us all after
falling        asleep with the oven on


3
What if it's true this springwater is colder
in your throat?        The Alafia river is generous
with its mistakes, its illusions
of felicity, Arcadia, Wonder-
        land.

But where are they        the alligators

*Alex Quinlan*

# Near Mint

Your second paradise, brother—the first one lost or locked up
    years ago—is a record shop where you haunt the back room,
flick through crates of new arrivals in search of
    first-press singles from before our parents were born,

sonic miracles made in the shadow cast by
    the statue of Nathan Bedford Forrest astride his war horse,
standing guard over the klansman's dissolving
    bones sealed inside the marble pedestal

across the street from Sun Studio where Ike Turner
    committed to an acetate plate the strutting ode
to the Rocket 88 that carried him and the Kings of Rhythm
    from the amnesiac mud of Clarksdale, Mississippi,

up Highway 61 to Memphis, and thereby invented rock and roll
    while Elvis was still learning how to drive, how to steal
the sound you're searching for, sealed in the groove's coiled ribbon,
    decades unplayed, sound so sound you can see

the sweat pearling on Jackie Brenston's upper lip
    when Ike leans back from his out-of-tune
barrelhouse piano and shouts, *Blow your horn, boy,*
    *blow!*; can feel the walking guitar line buzzing

because the road up was cracked and torn,
    and the amplifier got busted on a bump, but they couldn't
afford a replacement, so they stuffed the housing
    with wads of newspaper to hold the cone in place,

and because they only had one shot
    at the recording, and because it almost worked
but didn't, because you do the best you can
    until you can do better, the flaw, the fingerprint of current

driving the sound downhill like a river of magnetic light,
    became—in its buzzy rawness, in the distortion
that perfects the pure—beautiful, and if you can find
    just one copy that isn't bottomed out and crackling,

even if it isn't dustless and shining under unbroken shrink wrap
    you know how to clean it up well enough to taste
the sound shot from the needle, let it lick your skin raw
    like a mother-cat's rough tongue. When they put your first love

away for what happened to her mother, for what she did
    or didn't do that night with that knife, you learned to live with
not knowing, with knowing and not knowing why
    our mother still went to visit her every month, why she

still sent money, why she wrote and read those acres
    of letters the story carried across, echoed back
until the signal half-drowned in fuzz, lungful of static
    the suggestion of a tune breaks through, last gasp

from a far radio tower. Down here, when the women say
    *la otra*, they're talking about the kind of woman
you're always looking for, the kind who knows
    music is locked in all our bones and it has to come out somehow

no matter who gets hurt by the sound. When I see you again,
    I'll know it's you by your scent—oiled leather, the char
inside whisky barrels—at once exotic and familiar,
    like a postcard from next door or a new group

covering an old song. You can forget the second
    love who left you; if you let the memory play out
enough times, you won't be able to hear the signal
    over the noise, and sure it's lying but it's the way

to teach yourself the truth you don't know
    you know. When the summer rains come hard
it puts me back in that room in Chattanooga again,
    down the street from Bessie Smith Hall, where you played

Anne Peebles for me that first time, the liquid pizzicato
    backbeat of "I Can't Stand the Rain" intruded upon midmeasure
by the nighthawk of her voice rising a sudden updraft
    to a falsetto fragile enough we know she isn't singing

about the weather. You have five copies.
    You save and store, but you never
keep track of any of it; you've got a hundred more
    keys than locks, and half the time you can't

open the door in front of you, but I'm just as guilty
    and we both know when the passenger door
pops open on a late-night ride I slide in
    every time because I want everyone

to love me, so I tomcat and holler and shake em
    on down, hang in there till dawn like a hair
in a biscuit, though I always wind up
    like the grandmother of loneliness

running a finger over the dial on her rotary phone
    but never letting it sink into the numbers
even after the dial tone has given way to silence.
    Any good singer can tell you the key

isn't sound but silence, just like
    any good lockpick knows there's no sound
like the last cylinder sliding home.
    Every lock lets you in if you listen.

## Gabrielle Frahm Claffey

# Grade-B

I'm supposed to live off one egg a day
like my teacher Beruty.
On the bus, in cabs, soon she says
I'll be ready for the big city.
But the adagio begins
its dreamy trill and I lose the rigor
of the spin, my center, that pole I'm supposed to imagine
running through me, behind the eyes, head to toe,
(always the carousel animal)
and I'm caught in the mirror and my teacher Beruty
looks right through me as if she doesn't even know my name—
must be the green bruises of those hard-boiled eggs.
And the mirror's thin silence, what is it?
Cellophane for second thoughts, or the sticky membranes of eggs?
Here's a glittering confession: I hate ballet.
But I'm going to the big city anyway, to get my point shoes wet.

Candles, I read on the bus, in a magazine, were once used
to reveal the grade without breaking the egg.
It's simple. I'm spotted. I want to be clear, I want to
have that one white air bubble. But I'm ruptured with dialogue—
bubbles and bubbles and bubbles
and ballerinas don't use words, they're supposed to be
wordless and mystical.

It's simple. I fall out of the spin
and feel the singe of her estimation in my head,
and bear the dark in me that made
the glitter so promising.

*Gabrielle Frahm Claffey*

# The Impression Room

It was a hot day, overcast and chalky,
and those were my crooked teeth,
and those were my cliffy pink gums,
scored with reptilian striations
on the rickety aluminum shelves
in the Hyde Park Bank Building—
quiet always, no matter when;
quiet as this crooked slip of a room
with all the crooked teeth in the neighborhood
next to the examining chair.
Never a sound on the fifth floor;
halls and doors rolled out gray
and spare with arrows pointing
and sign-in. Soft hush though everyone's running late
and the dim waiting room's packed,
the small sconce lights fanning yellow.
Open your mouth, hold still, don't bite down, wait,
and the tongue gets tucked away
and they ask but you can't answer.
So hard to be a self.

The door was left ajar so I stole my impression—
tagged and numbered, sunk in my raincoat pocket
before Dr. Block returned with cement
for the braces. The sky went black,
cracked with rain, and I, still-life with wires spitting
light, could hear, through drill and polish and thunder
and through the dry wall, the buoyant chattering and laughter
of the plasters on the shelves in their dismal ark.
The same way I always heard my mother's
out-at-sea whistle long after she picked me up,
dropped me at school; whistle for the fog that came to
surround me, my tightened smile saying I'm on my way,
and I'm here, I'm here.

*Chris Green*

# Reading for Ms. Doyle's First Grade Class

My daughter looks painfully proud, whispering
to her friends. Among the low smells and scrawls
of elementary school, the kids sit
in odd angles at my feet, look up

with much nose-picking and tittering.
Today, I don't read the greaved poems underlined
with suffering, but one set on the bright side
of the moon, another with undead birds

flocking over a tire store, a rant about the pain
in my shoulder, a Big Bang pantoum,
and my hopeful ode to folding a napkin.
Question-and-answer time. A long silence

hovers over the packed classroom.
I start to panic . . . I lean forward and ask,
"What is poetry?" Instantly, I see the truth
in their faces. They ponder

the arcana of another adult.
I look over to see Lydie's worried face.
She teaches me about difficulty. A poem
is a classroom that contains my daughter,

the molding world map, math games with X times
and repeated Y's, hand-made
planets, and the nearness
of the alphabet. On a good day, poetry's

dry silence surprises.
So it is that finally, Caleb,
the bad boy with an unpained face asks,
"Can you tie my shoe?" And I do.

# Bonnie Naradzay

# They Workshop My Poem

The time has come for their comments
on my poem; I'm the last of four.
"We don't know what the father does
for a living," says Fran. How *odd*,
I think. Why should she even care?
*Her* poem had a whale in her bed;
I never asked how it got there.
Joan asks me something, but I look
down and don't respond. It's the rule:
when your poem's being scrutinized,
just listen. For this, I'm grateful.
"What does 'sort of' mean," someone asks.
"Like he didn't mean to, but it
happened anyway?" They argue.
I take a drink from my latte.
"We don't know if he ever came
back. Did he simply disappear?
Unsatisfying," Fran concludes.
"A mystery!" Joyce nods her head.
I want to reply that the poem
means something else. Stella comments,
"These folks are viable, but odd.
The intensity," she goes on,
"dims towards the end. Is that what needs
to happen here?" Responding to
her own rhetorical question,
she says she's not quite sure yet but
it may not be the way to end.
Now it's my turn to speak. I say
"My poem's in eight-syllable lines."
Nobody noticed. Joan tells me,
"Now I know why your poem looks odd."

Gustave Doré. *It Was Wondrous Cold.* Wood engraving from *The Rime of the Ancient Mariner* by Samuel Taylor Coleridge (New York: Harper and Brothers, 1877).

# FedEx

Melo put me on the Newark Airport shuttle, and my alarm startled me at 3:15 a.m. I pulled the coffee close so that the steam melted my face, and I peered through the rusty fire escape and down upon the frozen street illuminated by the menacing florescent signs in the window of the beauty salon. I tried doing pushups, but lay upon the floor without purpose.

I stared at the postcards on the refrigerator that my ex-girlfriend had been sending me from around the country. The first was of the St. Louis Arch, the Iowa Corn Palace followed, and a week later I received one from the Badlands of South Dakota. She simply signed her name, inviting me to guess the details of her journey. Every week, I'd find a new one inside my mailbox, and I picked up magnets at the nearby hardware store and arranged them as if somebody were going to swing by my apartment and view them as evidence of a life that no one had fathomed. Seattle, Portland, Crater Lake, Redwood National Park, Yosemite.

I knotted my steel-toe shoes, and in the mirror I psyched myself up for potential confrontation. I double-checked that my keys were in my pocket and exited my apartment, and I was swallowed by the night. *I will bite your fucking face off if you block my path.* My need to believe in the ability to perform violence felt futile.

It was fifteen degrees, and I caught myself as I slid on patches of ice. I encountered no people on the way to the train. I descended into the earth, and I was the sole human on the platform other than the homeless man mummified in blankets and propped against the tile wall. Two people were knocked out on my subway car. My legs were spread and my elbows stabbed into my knees in a posture I'd learned exhibited the fatigued confidence of a man who belongs in the city, and I looked up from "The Rhyme of the Ancient Mariner" with annoyed disinterest and held eye contact with the guy in a hooded sweatshirt who stepped onto the train at Atlantic Avenue. Thankfully, he walked to the other end of the car and dropped into the plastic seat. The previous week, Roland showed up on the conveyor belt and said that on the way to work he opened his eyes and some guy was smiling at him and masturbating.

"What did you do?"

"I beat his ass—what do you think? Little bitch was trying to crawl away with his pants falling off. 'I'm sorry. I'm sorry.' You goddamn right you're sorry, motherfucker."

We all burst into laughter. Roland's forearms were monstrous. He was younger than I was, had three kids and said he was waiting to be called back by the MTA for a job as a bus driver.

"I need to get the fuck up out of here."

We all lived it. And beating a subway pervert half to death would have felt like a gratifying counterbalance to the demoralization of working at FedEx. I attempted to stretch out my back, and I returned to Coleridge. At Dekalb Avenue, the doors of the Q train opened, and I swept the platform, and thankfully nobody entered the car. The train crawled over the Manhattan Bridge, and through the window I saw the skyscrapers against the clouds and thought of Fritz Lang's *Metropolis*, and there was a boat upon the East River and the Statue of Liberty in the distance, and then we were pulled down into the bowels of the city. We were dragged through the darkness and jerked to stops where the doors bonged open at the desolate platforms.

By 4:45, I was walking with a handful of keys to select a small Grumman from 33rd Street. You had to be careful because sometimes prostitutes broke into the trucks, and you'd find food wrappers and condoms on the floor. One day, I started up the engine and was just about to drive off when I realized that there was a rattlesnake of feces coiled upon the passenger's seat, and I had to sprint back upstairs and grab another set of keys to switch trucks.

"Can't you just wipe it off?"

"Somebody took a massive dump in the truck, Melo."

"Well, hurry up then. You've got to make that shuttle."

By 5:15, I was through the tunnel and rocking across the landscape with sports-talk radio blaring above the sound of the engine vibrating off the metal interior. I didn't have a television to know the sporting events about which Doris from Rego Park, Jerome from the Bronx, Bruce from Flushing were voicing opinions, and imagining these people's lives magnified the fact that I myself had no justifiable reason to be living the life I was living, that while everybody my age was racing across the stage of the city, establishing themselves, I was just standing around, writhing in some sort of performative meltdown.

By 6:30, I was back at the station and in the cans with Jamaal and Mike, heaving boxes onto the conveyor belt.

"Get your bitch-ass over here and help me with this box before my balls fall off."

❖ ❖ ❖

The "cans" were fiberglass containers as large as medium-sized gorilla cages, and we wrapped our arms in the nylon ropes and grunted them out of the tractor trailers and dragged them across the rollers to the other side of the basement where we lined them along the conveyor belt. Filled with packages, each can must have weighed five thousand pounds. It was fifteen degrees outside, and sweat was rolling down my stomach and streaking my uniform.

Mike was eating a blueberry Pop Tart from the upstairs vending machine with pull knobs, and Jamaal called him a little bitch and grabbed him by the neck and pretended to assault him against the conveyor belt while Mike protested that he was going to drop his food. "Get off me, bitch." "Just let me bust a nut, Unh, Unh." Jamaal squeezed Mike's breasts as he pushed into him one last time in quivering orgasm. Jamaal asked me what I was laughing at, and he discarded Mike upon the floor and lunged towards me, and I attempted to escape by leaping onto a computer box and vaulting inside the can, but Jamaal grabbed my calf and tugged and I rode an avalanche of packages to the deck. Before he had time to finish molesting me, however, the horn sounded, and the conveyor belt came alive.

"Get your white ass over here and lift some boxes," Jamaal said.

Every day started just about the same, getting play-raped on the conveyor belt before sunrise. I'd work until 11:30, take the train home for a two-hour nap, and wake up to try to trick my brain into believing that I had some sort of future beyond my current existence.

❖ ❖ ❖

The Dominican barber on my block wore a thick chain outside his oversized t-shirt, and his cologne was strong. He placed me into the chair and draped the cloth over my body. "You like working at FedEx?"

"You can get by on the pay, but your body breaks down. And they give the station bonuses when nobody gets hurt, so it creates peer pressure not to report injuries."

On the bathroom door was a poster of a woman sliding her hand beneath a wet bikini.

"No disrespect," the guy said. "You make decent money though, right? Because I need to look to do something else. I got bills."

I closed my eyes and fell asleep. I awoke intermittently as the barber adjusted my head with the tips of his fingers and thumbs.

"See what you think," he said, unsnapping the cape from my neck.

I stood before the mirror, dazed from sleep, and my stomach sank when I made sense of the haircut.

"Your head has a good shape for a Caesar."

I gave the barber a large tip and scurried up the block to my apartment. Inside, I stared into the mirror. He'd cut my hair short along the sides and back and left about an inch of bangs straight across my forehead. It was mortifying. The fact that I'd found it impossible to ask him just to shave it added to the shame. Maybe I'll grow into it and become a different person, I thought. I stared at the window, open on the fire escape, and imagined somebody creeping inside to kill me. I didn't have the energy to pretend that I might resist. I told myself I'd have to play the haircut off as a decision.

The next morning, Jamaal grabbed me around the waist and said, "Look at how my pretty little bitch got all dolled up for me."

"You look like Frankenstein, motherfucker," Mike said.

At every stop on the route, the receptionists commented on my hair, and it was deeply mortifying, as if I had given them some kernel by which to judge my true self.

For a week, I walked around like this. Then, I bought clippers and shaved my head.

"Skinhead, skinhead, skinhead," Mike said.

"Get over here and give me a kiss, racist bitch," said Jamaal

❖ ❖ ❖

Amanda slid her hands down my chest, and I lay with my fingers at my sides. I closed my eyes, but I had spent too many panicked nights upon that bed and I was too aware of myself against those sheets, and I opened my eyes and stared at her hair falling over my stomach, at Amanda's hair falling over my stomach, and I looked at the ceiling and at those walls which were now merely walls with her here, and I gently brushed aside her hair draped over my chest, and I closed my eyes again and I tried to lose myself in it, to shut my mind off, to tap into the eroticism of our doom, but the potential "hope" of a reunion yet to be killed dominated my mind and I opened my eyes and I looked at that tattoo, the black and white tattoo of pinup model Betty Page upon her bicep, which she had gotten in Austin on her cross-country trip as an Expression of Self, I assumed, that tattoo she asked me if I liked almost as soon as she arrived, showing up wholly unannounced, a Sunday afternoon in the second week of January, and Amanda inched back up my chest with eyes meant to be seductive, and I slid my hand over her breast, and she stretched her thigh over my hip and pushed my shoulders back, and she locked eyes with me and said in that voice, "Do you want to get a condom?" And the question, the suggestion that I might not have stopped for protection if she hadn't asked, that she was asking if that was what I wanted, or might we just embrace whimsy and become some blue-collar couple from *All in the Family*, and I unrolled the crinkling latex carefully down the length of my penis, so aware, so petrified of that condom breaking or slipping off.

❖ ❖ ❖

"I fly out of my apartment in the middle of the night and race to the Q train and invariably I encounter people my age, swaying arm in arm, returning home to mount one another in self-congratulation at how perfectly their lives are working out, and here I am, bursting out of the darkness, nine hundred miles an hour with my arms flailing against an unbelievable undertow dragging me into an abyss, and they freeze, like I'm there expressly to machete them into a billion pieces and drag them into a black cargo van I have idling around the corner, and I want to beg, 'You've got me all wrong. Wait, wait, it's the purple uniform,' but they've hurried off in their trendy shoes, and I have to hustle so as not to miss the subway, where I will sit next to some fast-food manager splattered with French fry-induced acne, crouched and scribbling out the weekly work schedule on graph paper, and wonder what gives me the right to see myself as anything more than this atrocity."

I was trying to make her laugh, but as the words erupted from me, I felt the tears in my eyes.

Amanda tilted her head and pressed her lips. "There's something sexy about you working at FedEx. Do the receptionists ever try to pick you up?"

"It feels like most of the receptionists on my route are women who escaped blue-collar upbringings on Long Island and talking down to me helps distance them from their high school boyfriends who are now plumbers. And then in half the elevators I step into some guy claps me on the shoulder and tells me to hang in there, that he too had a soul-crushing job in college."

"At least you're getting big muscles."

"They're the wrong muscles. We grunt and heave and slam and roll boxes onto the conveyor belt, which runs through the warehouse like a polluted river. We have to wear back harnesses, and you try to bend your knees so you don't fuck your spine like the old-timers, but usually there are ten thousand boxes around your feet, so you just cross your fingers and hope the tightness and pain aren't permanent. Just as you manage to get a grip on the seventy-five-pound box of lobsters, which are packaged in waxed cardboard beading with water, Jamaal slides in behind you, throws his gargantuan hand over your face and pulls back on your eye sockets with his fingers as he thrusts into your contorted body with a series of howls and groans."

"Well, smile because I have a surprise for you," she said, walking over to my closet. "I bought us a sled today while you were at work, and we're going to walk over to the park and find a big hill. I want to go sled riding. Don't you? For tonight, we can just let go and be like kids again."

My head spun. For the last seven months, the floor dropped out of the world every day, and I staggered forth, petrified at losing my mind and becoming a metropolitan absurdity, and now that Amanda was here, I was in the presence of somebody who actually knew me, and it felt so warm, so safe, and everything fell into place and I was no longer being eaten alive by self-consciousness. But it was absolutely impossible.

At Prospect Park, people plunged down the hill, dodging trees and benches. They spread across the winter landscape in their bulky snowsuits and they laughed and screamed. Amanda scooted up in the sled, and I wrapped myself around her achingly. I planted my fists in the snow and pushed us off as the people before us reached the bottom of the hill. We were slow to start, but we quickly gathered speed and spun past the tree and then past the bench, and we hit the iced-over sidewalk and launched into the air and rolled into the snow. Ice crystals were sharp and burned my face and neck in prickles, but I sprang to my feet, and I smiled and blew the snow from Amanda's cheeks and forehead. I started to laugh, and she laughed, and I turned to locate our sled, and a young boy screamed, "Watch out," at the last minute and cut my legs from under me and flipped me over onto my back with Amanda landing on top of me. There was a pause, but when she met my eyes, we both laughed harder and harder, and then she was laughing so hard that tears ran down her flushed cheeks, and for a minute it was as if we got it, the doom of it all, and for that moment we owned that doom, and I pulled her up the hill by her gloved hand, and we again waited in line and we again flew down the hill, but we were each noticeably let down not to crash. That night I attempted to find a rhythm during sex, but what we had before was gone and its vacancy was apparent as we both closed our eyes and avoided one another's mouths.

The thought of how we'd dipped back into it devoured my brain. I lay awake anticipating the suffering that awaited. The dull light from Washington Avenue caught the tattoo on her arm, and I glanced out across the fire escape at the snow coming down and burying the parked cars and the blurry color of the florescent signs from the window of the beauty salon bleeding through.

At 3:15, I slid out of bed and stepped quietly to the closet and pulled on my uniform and laced up my steel-toe shoes and walked out into the frozen landscape. Snow danced silver and dark through the shadows and blotted out my face. A car fishtailed slowly in acceleration, its taillights exploding in small pops of fire that hung in the falling snow, before the tires gained traction, pulling forward and disappearing into the darkness ahead. Snow was swirling in gusts. A sanitation truck thundered up Vanderbilt Avenue, its caution light whipping out against the chaos towards me, its mammoth snowplow drilling into the earth and heaving slush atop parked cars before it too disintegrated into shadows. I bent forward, taking careful steps as the blindness closed in around me. I was engulfed and extinguished in the sheets of snow that began as showers of sparks in the halo of the streetlights and whirlpooled down between the blackness of the buildings' ominous loom. I hovered at the intersection in the partial mute of the city as flakes began to collect upon my eyelids. The crunch of wet snow packed beneath my step. My cheeks stung, and I gulped for air. The world dissolved and popped and dissolved once again feet from my face. A harrowing solitude and isolation devoured my mind. As I approached Flatbush Avenue, the train beneath the street like a rumbling conveyor belt shook the buildings, and the shadows teetered, and I lowered my head and shouldered forward, inhaled into the chaos and sent spinning, six-headed Scylla nested upon some blackened rooftop high in the heavens, ready to swoop down and pulverize.

❖ ❖ ❖

# Notes on Contributors

**Halvor Aakhus** graduated from the University of Florida with an MFA in Creative Writing. His chief mentor was Padgett Powell, and his graduate thesis won the $10,000 Henfield Prize. Halvor has since taught writing at the universities of Pittsburgh and Louisiana, and is currently the G. Ellsworth Huggins Fellow at the University of Missouri, where he also works at *The Missouri Review*.

**Kostas Anagnopoulos** is the founder and editor of Insurance Editions. His book *Moving Blanket* was published in 2010. His newest book is *Seven Books*. He lives in Queens.

**Levi Andalou**'s work has appeared or is forthcoming in *Mid-American Review, The Minnesota Review, Lake Effect, Spillway, BOMB, Virga Magazine, The South Carolina Review, Sugar House Review, DIAGRAM, F(r)iction, Cleaver Magazine, Sonora Review, Phoebe, Ruminate*, and *Pembroke Magazine*. A reading of his work was featured on the literary podcast "On the Edge." He graduated from Brown University, where he studied with C. D. Wright, Michael S. Harper, and Ange Mlinko. He lives in the San Francisco Bay Area. Read more of his work or contact him at LeviAndalou.com.

**Bipin Aurora** has worked as an economist, an energy analyst, and a systems analyst. A collection of his stories, *Notes of a Mediocre Man: Stories of India and America*, was recently published by Guernica Editions (Canada). Individual stories have appeared in *Glimmer Train, Michigan Quarterly Review, Southwest Review, Nimrod International Journal, Witness, The Chattahoochee Review, Western Humanities Review, Southern Humanities Review, The Texas Review, New Orleans Review, Confrontation, Grain*, and numerous other publications, and are forthcoming in *The Fiddlehead, The Literary Review*, and *Boulevard*.

**Jack Barrett** was a prominent illustrator for the *St. Petersburg Times* and the *Evening Independent* for over twenty years. He studied at the Carnegie Institute and the Art Institute of Pittsburgh and taught figure drawing at St. Petersburg College and the Morean Arts Center. His work has been published extensively, and he is the recipient of many awards and honors including recognition for his remarkable newspaper illustration. He was a prolific artist, exhibited his work throughout the U.S., and is included in many prestigious art collections including Raymond James Financial, St. Petersburg College, Museum of Fine Arts St. Petersburg, and the Leepa-Rattner Museum of Art.

**Nathan Beard** earned a Bachelor of Fine Arts from Colorado State University in 2001 and then worked in galleries and as an art consultant in Denver for seven years. He grew up on a dairy farm in western New York. Prior to his university studies, Nathan lived in Egypt for one year as an exchange student and worked as a cowboy in Wyoming for two years. He currently maintains a studio in St. Petersburg, Florida, where he lives with his wife and six-year-old daughter. He also serves as Curatorial Assistant at Dunedin Fine Art Center, Preparator at Scarfone/Hartley Gallery (University of Tampa), and as preferred installer for ARTicles Art Gallery.

**Taylor Bostick** is from Alexandria, Virginia, and is a graduate of Virginia Tech, where he studied engineering and writing. His fiction has appeared in *The Rappahannock Review, CHEAP POP, Hobart*, and *Natural Bridge*. He's

currently working on a biography of a world-class athlete you've never heard of.

**Stephen Brook** was born in London's east end. Following school, he worked as a commercial artist and graphic artist in Fleet Street, London. After his work was shown in an exhibition in the Whitechapple Gallery in London, he began painting full time. He has had two one-man shows in Munich, Germany, and has shown and sold paintings in many galleries in London, Europe, and the U.S.

**Dorothy Chan** is the author of *Revenge of the Asian Woman* (Diode Editions, 2019), *Attack of the Fifty-Foot Centerfold* (Spork Press, 2018), and the chapbook *Chinatown Sonnets* (New Delta Review, 2017). Chan is the Editor of *The Southeast Review* and Poetry Editor of *Hobart*. Beginning in Fall 2019, she will be Assistant Professor of Creative Writing at the University of Wisconsin-Eau Claire. Visit her website at dorothypoetry.com.

**Marianne Chan** grew up in Stuttgart, Germany, and Lansing, Michigan. Her collection of poetry *All Heathens* will be published by Sarabande Books in 2020. Her poems have appeared or are forthcoming in *The Journal, Poetry Northwest, Cincinnati Review, Indiana Review, West Branch*, and others. She is the poetry editor at *Split Lip Magazine*.

**Gabrielle Frahm Claffey** holds an MFA from Columbia University. Her poems have appeared or are forthcoming in *Alaska Quarterly Review, Poet Lore, New American Writing, River Styx, Paterson Literary Review*, and *Mudfish*. She lives in the Hyde Park neighborhood of Chicago.

**Marsha Truman Cooper**'s most recent chapbook is *A Knot of Worms* (Finishing Line Press). She won the *New Letters* Literary Award for poetry and received the Bernice Stole award from *Prairie Schooner*. Her father's work as an ornithologist resides in the Santa Barbara Museum of Natural History; her work with him long ago points her to parallel behaviors . . . birds and people both with admirable, even lovely, survival mechanisms.

**Robin Perry Dana**, a native of Georgia, resides in St Petersburg, Florida where she serves as Gallery Director of Articles Art Gallery and Curator of its satellite gallery devoted to special exhibition projects, The Leslie Curran Gallery. She earned a BA in Studio Art from Agnes Scott College in Atlanta and an MFA in Photography from the University of Connecticut. She has exhibited her work up and down the east coast, taught photography in the U.S. and abroad, curated art exhibitions, written on contemporary artists, and worked in book and magazine publishing.

**John Davis Jr.** is the author of *Hard Inheritance* (Five Oaks Press, 2016), *Middle Class American Proverb* (Negative Capability Press, 2014), and two other collections of poetry. His work has appeared in *Nashville Review, The American Journal of Poetry, The Common online*, and other international venues. He holds an MFA from University of Tampa. His poem in this issue is from a project that chronicles and commemorates the victims of The Arthur Dozier School for Boys in Florida's panhandle.

**Shiv Dutta**'s personal essays have appeared in *Compose Journal, Under the Sun, Tin House, Connotation Press, The Grief Diaries, South85 Journal, River & South Review, The Evansville*

*Review, Green Hills Literary Lantern, Hippocampus Magazine, Eclectica Magazine, Epiphany, The Evergreen Review, Silk Road Review, Pilgrimage, Front Porch*, and other journals. He has also produced forty-five technical papers and two technical books. One of his personal essays was nominated for a Pushcart Prize. Links to some of his essays can be found on his website at shivdutta.com. He is currently working on a memoir.

**Jaclyn Dwyer** has published stories, essays, and poems in a number of literary magazines, including *Ploughshares, Pleiades, Witness, Indiana Review, Electric Literature*, and *Salon*. She received a Tennessee Williams Scholarship in Fiction to attend the Sewanee Writers' Conference. She earned a PhD in Creative Writing from Florida State University, where she received a Kingsbury Fellowship. Her full-length poetry collection, *The Bride Aflame*, will be published by Black Lawrence Press in April 2019. She lives in Ohio with her husband and daughters where she is at work on a novel.

**Liza Flum** grew up in California. She holds an MFA in poetry from Cornell, and her poems appear in journals including *Narrative, The Southeast Review, Lambda Literary, H_NGM_N, The Collagist*, and *PRISM international*. Her work has recently been supported by fellowships from the Saltonstall Foundation, the Vermont Studio Center, and the Yiddish Book Center. She is currently a PhD student in Literature and Creative Writing at the University of Utah, and she works as a poetry editor for *Omnidawn*.

**Marc Frazier**'s poetry has been widely published in journals including *The Spoon River Poetry Review, ACM, Good Men Project, f(r)iction, The Gay and Lesbian Review, Slant, Permafrost, Plainsongs*, and *Poet Lore*. He has had selections from his book *Without: A Memoir* published in *Gravel, The Good Men Project, decomP, Autre, Cobalt Magazine, Evening Street Review*, and *Punctuate*. He is the recipient of an Illinois Arts Council Award for poetry, has been featured on *Verse Daily*, and has been nominated for a Pushcart Prize and a "best of the net." His two books, *The Way Here* (Aldrich Press) and *Each Thing Touches* (Glass Lyre Press), and his two chapbooks are available on Amazon. www.marcfrazier.org.

**J. Malcolm Garcia** is a frequent contributor to *Tampa Review*. His writing has appeared in the *Virginia Quarterly Review, McSweeney's, Mother Jones, West Branch, Alaska Quarterly Review*, and various other publications. He's written about the drug war in Mexico, race relations in Jena, Louisiana, and the poor of Buenos Aires, among other topics. His books include *What Wars Leave Behind: the Faceless and Forgotten* (University of Missouri, 2014), *Riding through Katrina with the Red Baron's Ghost* (Arcade, 2018), and a memoir about his work in Afghanistan, *The Khaarijee: A Chronicle of Friendship and War in Kabul* (Beacon Press, 2009).

**Chris Green** is the author of *The Sky Over Walgreens, Epiphany School*, and *Résumé*. His poetry has appeared in such publications as *Poetry, The New York Times, New Letters*, and *Prairie Schooner*. He has edited four anthologies, including *I Remember: Chicago Veterans of War*. He teaches in the English Department at DePaul University. www.chrisgreenpoetry.com

**Jan C. Grossman**'s poems have appeared or are forthcoming in *Poet Lore, Salmagundi, Think Journal, Potomac Review, Poetry East, The Midwest Quarterly, Atlanta Review, Plainsongs, American Arts Quarterly*, and other journals.

**Carol Guess** is the author of twenty books of poetry and prose, including *Darling Endangered, Doll Studies:*

*Forensics,*and *Tinderbox Lawn*. A frequent collaborator, she writes across genres and illuminates historically marginalized material. In 2014 she was awarded the Philolexian Award for Distinguished Literary Achievement by Columbia University. She teaches at Western Washington University and lives in Seattle.

**Carolyn Guinzio**'s most recent book is *Ozark Crows* (Spuyten-Duyvil, 2018), a sequence of visual poems. She lives in Fayetteville, Arkansas. carolynguinzio.tumblr.com

**Lissa Hatcher** is an award-winning photographer, painter, and writer specializing in surrealistic fairytales. She has received awards from Kodak, Fuji, and other industry leaders, with features in *American Photo Magazine* and Kodak.com, and a variety of other publications. Primarily self-taught, she received certification as a Master in Photography from the Professional Photographers of America in 2011. After traveling the globe with her military husband, she has returned home to her native Florida native and currently resides in Tampa.

**Christopher Heffernan** has had poetry and fiction published in magazines and journals around the country such as *The Believer, The Writer's Journal, Pacific Coast Journal, Cottonwood, Talking River, Toasted Cheese, The Broadkill Review, Midway Journal, The South Dakota Review, Louisiana Literature*, and the *Sierra Nevada Review*. He has published a book of poetry and flash fiction titled *Rag Water*.

**Liana Jahan Imam** was raised in Southeast Michigan and finished in Brooklyn. Her stories, essays, and reviews have appeared in *Whiskey Island, Devil's Lake, Electric Literature, Fiction Writers Review*, and more. She holds an MFA in fiction from the University of Montana.

**Joshua Eversfield Jenkins** lives in Edinburgh, Scotland. He has a BA in English with double minors in Art History and History, an MA in History from George Mason University, and is currently earning a PhD in the History of Art at the University of Edinburgh. Prior to his doctoral research, he worked at George Mason's Gunston Hall and the Hirshhorn Museum and Sculpture Garden.

**Jennifer Key** is the author of *The Old Dominion* (University of Tampa). She currently holds a John and Renée Grisham Fellowship at the University of Mississippi. Her work has appeared in *Callaloo, The Cincinnati Review, The Antioch Review*, and *Poetry Daily*. Her honors include a Diane Middlebrook Fellowship at the University of Wisconsin and a Henry Hoyns Fellowship at the University of Virginia.

**Virginia Konchan** is the author of two poetry collections, *Any God Will Do* (Carnegie Mellon, 2020) and *The End of Spectacle* (Carnegie Mellon, 2018); a collection of short stories, *Anatomical Gift* (Noctuary Press, 2017); and three chapbooks, including *Empire of Dirt* (above/ground press, 2019). Her poetry has appeared in *The New Yorker, The New Republic, Boston Review,* and elsewhere.

**Michael Lavers** is the most recent winner of the Tampa Review Prize for Poetry. His poems have appeared in *Best New Poets 2015, Crazyhorse, 32 Poems, The Hudson Review, Hayden's Ferry Review, Georgia Review,* and elsewhere. He is the winner of the 2016 University of Canberra Vice-Chancellor's International Poetry Prize. He teaches poetry at Brigham Young University.

**Eleanore Lee** has been writing fiction and poetry for many years in addition to her regular job as a legislative analyst for the University of California system. Her work has appeared or is forthcoming in several journals, including *Alabama Literary Review, Atlanta Review, CQ (California Quarterly), Crack the Spine, Meridian Anthology of Contemporary Poetry, Penmen Review,* and *The Portland Review.* She was selected as an International Merit Award Winner in *Atlanta Review's* 2008 International Poetry Competition. She also won first place in the November 2009 California State Poetry Society contest.

**Paul Lindholdt** is a professor at Eastern Washington University who has been recognized by the Academy of American Poets, the Society of Professional Journalists, and the Washington Center for the Book. His 2018 volume of original poems set on American frontiers is titled *Making Landfall.*

 **Priscilla Long** is a Seattle-based writer of poetry, creative nonfiction, science, fiction, and history, and an independent teacher of writing. Her five books include *Fire and Stone: Where Do We Come From? What Are We? Where Are We Going?* (University of Georgia Press), *Minding the Muse: A Handbook for Painters, Poets, and Other Creators* (Coffeetown Press), *Crossing Over: Poems* (University of New Mexico Press), and a how-to-write guide, *The Writer's Portable Mentor: A Guide to Art, Craft, and the Writing Life.* Her awards include a National Magazine Award. Her science column, *Science Frictions,* ran for ninety-two weeks in The American Scholar. She earned an MFA from the University of Washington and serves as Founding and Consulting Editor of www.historylink.org

**A. Loudermilk**'s poems can be found in *Tin House, Smartish Pace, Cream City Review, Gargoyle, Mississippi Review,* and his collection *Strange Valentine.* A recent *Writer's Chronicle* featured his essay on neglected Ohio poet Alberta Turner. He has taught creative writing at Hampshire College in Amherst and Maryland Institute College of Art in Baltimore.

**Zachary Lundgren** received his MFA in poetry from the University of South Florida and his BA from the University of Colorado at Boulder. He is currently pursuing a PhD in rhetoric and composition at East Carolina University. He is also a poetry editor for *Sweet: A Literary Confection* and a founding editor for *Blacktop Passages.*

**Dan Lundin**'s short stories have been be published in *Corium, H_NGM_N, decomP, Echo Ink Review, NANO Fiction, Everyday Genius,* and elsewhere. He smiths words and constructs things (as much as the law will allow, wink) in South Pasadena, California.

**Michael Malan** is editor of *Cloudbank,* a literary journal in Corvallis, Oregon (cloudbankbooks.com). He is the author of *Overland Park* (Blue Light Press, 2017), a collection of his poetry and flash fiction. His work has appeared in *Epoch, Cincinnati Review, Denver Quarterly, Poetry East, Hayden's Ferry Review, Potomac Review,* and other journals.

**Jane Medved** is the author of *Deep Calls To Deep* (winner of the Many Voices Project, New Rivers Press 2017) and the chapbook *Olam, Shana, Nefesh* (Finishing Line Press, 2014) Recent work has appeared or is forthcoming in *Juked, Gulf Coast On-Line, Queen Mob's Teahouse, The Cortland Review, 2River View, The Atticus Review,* and *Vinyl.* She is the poetry editor of the *Ilanot Review* and teaches at Bar Ilan University, in the Shaindy Rudolph Creative Writing Program. A native of Chicago, Illinois, she has lived for the last twenty-five years in Jerusalem, Israel.

**Heike Mueller** is a Swiss artist whoe studied art education and painting in Basel and Amsterdam. She contin-

ues to teach and maintain a rigorous studio and exhibition practice while building a family. Widely represented in Germany and Switzerland, Mueller has exhibited extensively in galleries and art fairs throughout Europe for the last twenty years. She now lives and works in Basel with her husband and three sons.

**Bonnie Naradzay** leads poetry workshops at a day shelter for homeless people and at a retirement center, both in Washington DC. Her poems have appeared in *New Letters, RHINO, Tar River Poetry, Poet Lore, JAMA, Anglican Theological Review, Seminary Ridge Review, Split This Rock, The Ekphrastic Review* (www.ekphrastic.net), *The Northern Virginia Review, Delmarva Review, Pinch,* and others. In 2010, she was awarded the New Orleans MFA Program's Poetry Prize: a month's stay in Ezra Pound's daughter's castle in Dorf Tyrol (northern Italy). She completed a master's degree in liberal arts at St. John's College in Annapolis in 2017.

**Calvin Olsen**'s poetry and translations have appeared in *AGNI, The Missouri Review Online, The London Magazine,* and many others. A former Robert Pinsky Global Fellow and recent Pushcart Prize nominee, Calvin now lives in Chapel Hill, N.C., where he is poetry editor for *The Carolina Quarterly.*

**Tom Paine**'s poetry is upcoming or published in *Tinderbox, The Nation, Fence, Green Mountain Review, Hunger Mountain, Forklift, Hotel Amerika, Epiphany* and elsewhere.

**Christine Poreba**'s poems have appeared in numerous journals, including *Subtropics, The Southern Review,* and *The Sun Magazine,* and various anthologies. Her book, *Rough Knowledge,* was awarded the Philip Levine Prize. She lives in Tallahassee, Florida, with her husband and their young son.

**Alex Quinlan** lives in Tallahassee where he is pursuing a PhD in poetry at Florida State University. His poems and nonfiction have appeared in journals including *Bat City Review, Beloit Poetry Journal, OH NO!, Pebble Lake Review,* and *Tusculum Review.* He first appeared in *Tampa Review* in 2007 as an AWP Intro Journals Prize winner.

**Molly Rideout** is a recent fellow with Antenna Spillways. Select previous publications include the *Mississippi Review, Front Porch Journal, Bluestem* and *Flyway Journal,* with interdisciplinary text installations at four Iowa public libraries and around rural Wisconsin. Her interdisciplinary work has received a Pushcart nomination and has been featured in Poets & Writers, on Iowa Public Radio and by the American Library Association. She currently lives in Columbus, Ohio, where she is about to complete her MFA at The Ohio State University. Research for "The Metairie Loop" was funded by Antenna Spillways. Learn more at mollyrideout.com.

**Robert Ross**'s paintings have been exhibited in a growing number of venues throughout Central Florida, including Anita Wooten Gallery at Valencia State College, Winter Park City Hall, Orlando City Hall, Maitland City Hall, Orange County Chambers, Gallery at Avalon Island, and Casselberry Art House. He has been in the Winter Park Paint Out sponsored by the Albin Polasek Museum, and he has won several awards for his paintings in the Winter Park Autumn Art Festival. He received his art education at Oakland University, Crealdé School of Art in Winter Park, and in master workshops taught by Stuart Shils. He is represented by Arts on Douglas Gallery in New Smyrna Beach, Florida.

**Mark Rubin** has published one book of poems, *The Beginning of Responsibility* (Owl Creek Press). His work has appeared in *The Gettysburg Review, The Ohio Review, Prairie Schooner, The Virginia Quarterly Review,* and elsewhere. A past recipient of the Discovery/*The Nation* Award and a National Endowment for the Arts Fellowship, he lives in Burlington, Vermont, where he is a psychotherapist in private practice.

**Peter Schireson**'s writing has appeared in *Quiddity, Hotel Amerika, Painted Bride Quarterly, Pleiades,* among others. His chapbook, *The Welter of Me & You,* won the Coal Hill 2013 Chapbook Prize. He holds an MFA from the Program for Writers at Warren Wilson College.

**John Schneider** was born and raised in Wisconsin and has lived and worked in Berkeley, California, for most of his adult life where he has studied poetry with Robert Hass. Recent poems have appeared in *Glassworks Magazine; fort da; Wilderness House Literary Review; Anak Sastra; Edge Literary Journal; West Trade Review; The Literary Nest; The Mayo Review; 2 Bridges Review; The Bookends Review; California Quarterly; Sliver of Stone Magazine; Worcester Review; Potomac Review; Slipstream Poetry Magazine;* and *Tampa Review.*

**Sabatino Smith** is a poet and industrial designer from Boston, Massachusetts. He began writing during his early college years under the mentorship of Gloria Monaghan at Wentworth Institute of Technology. His interest in the Boston/Cambridge poetry scene introduced him to local poets such as Ted Richer, William J. Barnum, Chad Parenteau, and the community at one of the longest running poetry readings in the Boston area, Jack Powers's "Stone Soup."

**Pennell Somsen** graduated magna cum laude from City University of New York Baccalaureate for Unique and Interdisciplinary Studies with a major in "The Study and Translation of Latin American Women Writers." Her translations of stories by Nadia Villafuerte and Roberto Azcorra Camara have appeared in the *Rio Grande Review, Latin American Literature Today, Delos Journal, Midway Journal, Reunion: The Dallas Review,* and *InTranslation* (*Brooklyn Rail*).

**Rob Stephens** is an Adjunct Professor at Malone University in Canton, Ohio, where he lives with his wife Jaclyn and three children. His poems have previously appeared in *Copper Nickel, Rattle, Epoch,* and other magazines. He was selected by Billy Collins to win the 2015 Scotti Merrill Award to attend the Key West Literary Festival.

**Zack Strait** is pursuing his PhD at Florida State University. His work is forthcoming in *Poetry.*

**Adam Tavel** won the 2017 Richard Wilbur Award for his third collection of poetry, *Catafalque* (University of Evansville Press, 2018). His earlier books are *The Fawn Abyss* (Salmon Poetry, 2017) and *Plash & Levitation* (University of Alaska, 2015). You can find him online at adamtavel.com.

**Cammy Thomas** has published two collections of poems with Four Way Books: *Inscriptions* (2014) and *Cathedral of Wish,* which received the 2006 Norma Farber First Book Award from the Poetry Society of America. Her poems have recently appeared in *The Maine Review, The Missouri Review, Salamander, WomenArts Quarterly,* and elsewhere. A fellowship from the Ragdale Foundation helped her complete *Inscriptions.* She lives in Lexington, Massachusetts.

**Gordon Thompson** earned an MFA from the University of Florida, and teaches now at the Cranbrook Schools in metro Detroit. His poems and essays have appeared in

*North American Poetry Review, Southern Humanities Review, Medium,* and elsewhere. He has worked, studied, and traveled in more than fifty countries.

**Nadia Villafuerte**'s works include two books of short stories—*Barcos en Houston* (2005) and *?Te gusta el latex, cielo?* (2008)—and the novel *Por el lado salvaje* (2011). She is included in the anthologies *México 20, New Voices, Old Traditions* (Pushkin Press, 2015), *Palabras mayores, nueva narrativa mexicana* (Malpaso Ediciones, 2015), *Ruta 70* (Selector, 2017), among others. Her translations into English have been published in *Mexico20, Rio Grande Review, World Literature Today, Latin American Literature Today, Delos Journal Reunion: The Dallas Review* and *InTranslation,* among others.

**William Walker** delivered boxes in Manhattan highrises long enough to qualify for a pension from FedEx. His work has recently appeared in *Subtropics, The Southampton Review* and *FRiGG Magazine.*

**Randall Watson** is the author of *The Sleep Accusations,* which received the Blue Lynx Prize for Poetry (currently available through Carnegie Melon Press), *Las Delaciones del Sueno,* (published in a bilingual edition by the Universidad Veracruzana in Xalapa, Mexico), *The Geometry of Wishes* (published by Texas Review Press), and *No Evil Is Wide* (a revised version of "Petals," winner of the Quarterly West Prize for the Novella, by Madville Publishing). He is also the editor of *The Weight of Addition,* an anthology of Texas poetry published by Mutabilis Press.

**Hannah Weyer** is an American filmmaker and writer living in New York, who has written, directed, and produced narrative and documentary films. Her films have screened at the Human Rights Watch, Sundance, and the New York Film Festivals and won recognitions, including awards from LoCarno, Sundance, Doubletake Documentary, and South by Southwest Film Festivals. Her documentaries, *La Boda* and *La Escuela* aired on PBS as part of the POV-American Documentary series. Screenwriting credits include work that premiered on HBO, including *Life Support* (2007), directed by Nelson George, and which earned a Golden Globe award for its lead actress, Queen Latifah. Other writing credits include a novel set in Far Rockaway, Queens, entitled, *On The Come Up,* which was published by Nan Talese/Knopf in 2013. It received a 2013 Barnes and Noble Discover Great New Writers award and Weyer was an NAACP Image Award Nominee for Debut Author.

**John Sibley Williams** is the author of nine poetry collections, most recently *Disinheritance.* An eleven-time Pushcart nominee and winner of various awards, John serves as editor of *The Inflectionist Review.* His work has appeared in journals including *Yale Review, Atlanta Review, Prairie Schooner, Midwest Quarterly, Sycamore Review, Massachusetts Review, Columbia, Third Coast,* and *Poetry Northwest.*

**Michele Wolf** is the author of the books *Immersion* and *Conversations During Sleep,* winner of the Anhinga Prize for Poetry, and the chapbook *The Keeper of Light.* Her poems have appeared in *Poetry, The Southern Review, The North American Review, The Hudson Review,* and many other journals and anthologies, as well as on *Poetry Daily, Verse Daily,* and *Poets.org.* Raised in Florida, she now lives in Maryland, where she is a contributing editor for *Poet Lore* and teaches at The Writer's Center in Bethesda. Her website is michelewolf.com.

❖  ❖  ❖